OUTDOOR RECREATION MANAGEMENT:

Theory and Application

Revised and Enlarged

Venture Publishing Inc.

Cover Design by Sandra Sikorski
Design and Copy Editing by Susan Lewis
Production Supervision by Bonnie Godbey
Library of Congress Catalogue Card Number 87-82085
ISBN 0-910251-20-7

OUTDOOR RECREATION MANAGEMENT:
Theory and Application
Revised and Enlarged

by Alan Jubenville
University of Alaska, Fairbanks

Ben W. Twight
The Pennsylvania State University

Robert H. Becker
Clemson University

1987

THE AUTHORS

ALAN JUBENVILLE

Dr. Jubenville has had many professional experiences dealing with recreational use of natural resources. Originally from Virginia, he had much early education and experience in the coastal plains of the Southeast. Since that time, he has worked for several state and federal agencies and a private consulting firm. He received a BS degree in forest management in 1962 from North Carolina State University, an MS degree in silviculture/ecology in 1964 from West Virginia University, and a PhD degree in wildland recreation management in 1970 from the University of Montana. After receiving his doctoral degree, he became the state outdoor recreation extension specialist at The University of Illinois. From there, he moved to the University of Wyoming, where he helped develop the outdoor recreation curriculum and conduct research on river recreation.

In 1979, Dr. Jubenville joined the faculty of the School of Agriculture and Land Resources Management at the University of Alaska-Fairbanks. Here, his research interest has shifted more to recreation management theory. He has authored three books, four contributions to anthologies, fifteen journal articles, and many user-oriented publications. His most recent field studies have focused on trail erosion in the White Mountains Natural Recreation Area and the management of of the Kenai River, a world renowned sport fishery.

BEN W. TWIGHT

Dr. Twight was raised in the California State Park System, was employed seasonally by the US Forest Service, studied Wildlife Conservation and Forestry at the University of California at Berkeley, and then became a permanent employee of the US Forest Service.

Later transferring to the National Park Service, Twight was a ranger and law enforcement specialist at Yosemite National Park for five years, and manager of the Ohanapecosh District at Mt. Rainier National Park for three years. He returned to graduate school at the University of Washington for his MS and PhD degrees in sociology and public administration.

He has taught at West Virginia University and is currently Associate Professor of Forest Resources at Penn State, where he also authored *Organizational Values and Political Power,* a book on the political battle between the Forest Service and the Park Service for Olympic National Park.

ROBERT H. BECKER

Dr. Becker is Director of the Regional Resources Development Institute (RRDI) and Professor of Parks, Recreation & Tourism Management at Clemson University. He earned his MA and PhD degrees from the University of Maryland and his BS from The Pennsylvania State University. Prior to his work at Clemson, he was associate director of the Wisconsin Water Resources Center at the University of Wisconsin (Madison).

Dr. Becker has been involved in resource management and impact assessment issues through projects on dredge spoil assessment research with the GREAT I, II, & III programs on the Upper Mississippi River, social and community impact assessment with the Lock and Dam #26 evaluation, Lower St. Croix River Management, and marina development projections for the Iowa Conservation Commission. He is currently involved in assessing the impact from dredging activities on the Chattahoochee River and Cumberland Island area for the National Park Service. He has also served as a consultant for conflict management needs of resource management agencies and has studied fees, charges and subsidies on the public lands.

In addition to his research involvement, Dr. Becker has served on the research advisory committee to the Upper Mississippi River Basin Commission and provided expert testimony on resource-management issues for the Office of the Attorney General, State of Wisconsin.

PREFACE

More people are participating in various outdoor recreation activities than ever before. Because of changing lifestyles, new recreational technology, and improved economic conditions, both the activities themselves and the patterns of participation are more diverse. These have created a need for more new recreational opportunities and changes in many of the existing ones. Management is finding it more difficult to maintain existing opportunities, try to improve the quality of those, and still respond to the demand for new ones. It is a seemingly thankless job, particularly in the face of shrinking government budgets.

This book offers no instant solutions to the plethora of problems facing the outdoor recreation manager. In fact, we think the worst thing we could do is to offer such (even if they are good ones) because the problem set is constantly changing due to changing social and environmental conditions. The more effective manager, over the long run, is not the one who is solution-oriented, but process-oriented. The process-oriented manager sees the "big picture," understands how the total system works, has knowledge of the causal links within the system, and creates a process by which solutions are carefully developed, analyzed, and implemented.

If one scrutinizes the situational variables in most problems, the major cause is often some current or past management action, or a change in the external social environment. An open-systems approach to management helps to better identify those causal relationships and to isolate the critical variables, including previous management actions. From a more positive perspective, one can better predict the impact of resource allocation decisions and adjust strategies to minimize impact prior to implementation. Also, a systems model applied to a given area should help to identify the potentially important social changes (populations, family makeup, participation patterns, etc.) that may affect the area and its management programs. By anticipating change, we can be more active in adjusting the management programs to meet the changes in the social environment, rather than waiting and then reacting after the impact.

In sum, the one thing this text stresses is the open systems model. As with any system, when the input is constant, it is said to be in a dynamic equilibrium. Alter any input and you alter the equilibrium. In recreation management, the primary output is the recreational opportunity. If the system is in equilibrium, then we are providing stable opportunities to the using public. Alter the inputs and you alter outputs. The ultimate measures of success in such an open model are satisfied clientele groups. Stability is critical to keeping this clientele satisfied over time. In turn, these groups provide the support for the agency in the political/budgeting process so necessary to maintaining that stability.

All of this points to the significance of Part I, Management Framework, where the recreation management system and the equilibrium theory are fully explained, along with the interaction of the agency with the public in a decision-making mode. The remaining three sections focus on subsystems — the visitor, the resource, and the service — discussing the specific programs under each subsystem. No attempt is made to stereotype management prescriptions for various clusters of similar recreational opportunities. It cannot be done. Ideally the systems approach should provide you and the process by which problems and the critical links can be identified and legitimate prescriptions developed that overcome obstacles with minimum secondary effects.

Contents

THE AUTHORS   V

PREFACE   VI

PART I. MANAGEMENT FRAMEWORK   1

    CHAPTER ONE. HISTORICAL ROOTS   3
        FOR FRAMING THE FUTURE

    CHAPTER TWO. THE OUTDOOR   11
        RECREATION MANAGEMENT MODEL

    CHAPTER THREE. THEORETICAL   23
        FOUNDATIONS

    CHAPTER FOUR. THE PROBLEM-   35
        SOLVING PROCESS

    CHAPTER FIVE. INVOLVEMENT OF   45
        THE PUBLIC IN DECISION-MAKING

    CHAPTER SIX. ASSESSING IMPACTS   57
        IN THE REAL WORLD

PART II. RECREATIONAL RESOURCE   67
MANAGEMENT

    CHAPTER SEVEN. SITE MANAGEMENT   69

    CHAPTER EIGHT. TURF MANAGEMENT   77

    CHAPTER NINE. MANAGEMENT OF   87
        OVERSTORY VEGETATION

    CHAPTER TEN. MANAGEMENT OF   101
        NATURAL ECOSYSTEMS

    CHAPTER ELEVEN. VISUAL   117
        RESOURCE MANAGEMENT

PART III. VISITOR MANAGEMENT   139

    CHAPTER TWELVE. DISTRIBUTION   141
        OF VISITOR USE

    CHAPTER THIRTEEN. INFORMATION   151
        SERVICES

    CHAPTER FOURTEEN. INTERPRETIVE   163
        SERVICES

    CHAPTER FIFTEEN. PUBLIC SAFETY   173

PART IV. SERVICE MANAGEMENT   187

    CHAPTER SIXTEEN. HAZARD   189
        MANAGEMENT

    CHAPTER SEVENTEEN. MAINTENANCE   199
        MANAGEMENT

    CHAPTER EIGHTEEN. CONCESSION   209
        MANAGEMENT

PART I.
MANAGEMENT FRAMEWORK

As suggested by W.H. Newman, management is a social resource that offers great potential for helping modern man to effectively and efficiently achieve stated goals. However, this requires great skill in integrating social and biophysical factors into a total human design that also accounts for specific situational conditions. This section of the book is aimed primarily at providing an overview of management as it pertains to recreation areas and clientele — regardless of particular circumstances. It is intended to provide the conceptual framework for succeeding sections, showing readers how the recreation manager, the organization, the resource, and the visitor can be integrated into a systems management approach. Such a holistic systems theory is appropriate for recreation area management in today's complex society. Also, systems models can help us to readily see all the basic elements involved in management and how they relate to one another. In other words, we must first understand the management system on a conceptual level in order to better appreciate what effect our decisions about a single element of a specific subsystem will have on the entire system. In later sections, we will dissect the system into subsystems and then identify specific management programs.

This section does not focus specifically on administrative or organizational management matters such as budgeting, and personnel. That is not the intent of the book. Instead it focuses on resource, visitor, and service management in a conceptual framework in order to provide a better understanding of succeeding sections.

Obviously many management concepts might help in understanding the visitor and thus improve the delivery of public recreation services. Social psychology has contributed much to our understanding of recreationists — their motivations, perceptions, and behavior. This rich body of literature has provided insights into why people do what they do. However, to be meaningful to management, user response (and that is what we are trying to accomplish when we implement a particular program) must be cast in a managerial context. That is what this section attempts to do — to develop the managerial framework. Thus, contrary to social psychological concepts that other authors have emphasized, we have chosen to emphasize managerial concepts — *outdoor recreation* managerial concepts.

CHAPTER ONE

HISTORICAL ROOTS...FOR FRAMING THE FUTURE

Figure 1-1. Active Participation in Outdoor Recreation Activities (Photo by B.W. Twight)

Before jumping into a synopsis of the history of outdoor recreation management, we would like to establish a mood or concern for appropriate management of recreational opportunities on public lands. Hopefully this quick digression will firmly establish in your mind a need for both management in general and *appropriate* management specifically.

THE NEED FOR MANAGEMENT

Probably most of us can painfully reflect on some situation which adversely affected our own recreation participation. The situation cried out for appropriate action by the recreation manager, yet there was no relief in sight. Some of these problems are obvious; others are more subtle. Let's look at some hypothetical situations so that we all have a common

understanding of the need for appropriate management strategies.

Developed Sites. A 100-unit forest campground is located in the heavy clay soils of the Piedmont region of North Carolina. The season of use is generally from April 15 to September 15. Your first visit to the site shows almost all the ground vegetation is gone. There has been no effort to harden the heavily used portion of the site, and even the sparsely used portion is showing extreme wear.

Sheet erosion is occurring and almost all of the A_1 soil horizon has been lost. No organic matter can be seen in the upper soil horizons. Siltation is evident in the nearby stream. Some stagheading (dieback) is taking place in the mixed hardwood stand, even though it is only sixty years old.

You show up for a weekend of camping and fishing with the family. It rains. The fishing is non-existent and the whole site turns to mud. The problems may appear to be obvious, but based on our knowledge of the user/resource interaction, they were highly predictable. Why, then, has this situation been allowed to occur?

A small oval lake is used heavily by water skiers, fishermen, and swimmers from a local resort. The fishermen usually use the lake early in the morning and late in the afternoon. The water skiers and swimmers use the lake during the middle of the day. However, conflict often exists between the three groups. Fishermen do not like the water skiers because they disturb the water and swamp fishing boats. The water skiers do not like the other user groups on the lake because they limit the good skiing and create safety problems. The fishermen, with the support of the statewide Izaak Walton League, have even introduced a bill into the legislature that would ban waterskiing.

There has never been a serious accident on the lake, but several incidents have occurred in which minor injuries were reported. One swimmer was bruised by a skier as he swung wide of the boat on a turn. Some minor vandalism of boat trailers has occurred, and exaggerated rumors of other conflicts have circulated. Perhaps you have already formulated some simple solutions while reading about this situation. But, more importantly, you should recognize that it is not going to resolve itself.

Your opening discussion might focus on "appropriate" management actions. Is there such a thing as too much management, overmanagement to the point of detracting from the experience people derive from the particular opportunity? Suppose that to solve the lake problem, you develop a daily schedule of exclusive time periods for each user group. In other words, a certain number of limited entry permits are established for each group according to time period. In order to be fair, you establish a random-drawing process twenty-four hours in advance of participation. This action may eliminate the original conflicts between user groups and increase safety, but we might question the wisdom of such a program. Are there other alternatives that would accomplish the same goals, yet allow

maximum participation? Would we in effect be creating an undesirable situation for many of the users? Would the involvement of representatives from each user group provide a more acceptable solution? Might the result be underutilization of a valued natural resource? Finally, in terms of management efficiency, have we artificially inflated management costs because we did not seek the least costly solution?

Dispersed-Use Areas. Too often we hear that dispersed-use areas, including wilderness, should not be managed; however, situations do exist that require management action. To procrastinate in implementing this action is really self-defeating — the situation merely gets worse.

For example, much of the traffic in the backcountry of the Evergreen Scenic Area, which is a 17,000-acre roadless area, enters through a common point at Sugar Mountain Campground. People travel that trail for a mile or so and then fan out to camp, fish, and relax around the many mountain lakes. As a result, shorelines around the more accessible lakes are showing severe deterioration, litter is strewn everywhere, and horse users and backpackers are even conflicting over the better camping and fishing spots. This may be an unusual type of situation, but even to the casual observer this is an unmanaged situation that must be controlled.

Smith Wilderness, a 240,000 acre wilderness in Western Montana, has high concentrations of hiking in one major drainage area. This trail winds its way through several wet meadows, and as trail use creates a rut through the wet meadows, water is funneled onto the trail, causing muddy conditions and then even greater rutting due to compaction and erosion. People fan out to avoid the problem, creating multiple trails. These same problems could have just as easily resulted from motorized, dispersed use. The point is that dispersed recreation, even in designated wilderness areas, is not immune to problems requiring management. However, solutions may be more limited.

In that regard, is there such a thing as

overmanagement of dispersed recreation? Assume in the Smith Wilderness problem that the manager responded with some site rehabilitation and limited the number of people using the trail, explaining these actions through an information program. Again, are we underutilizing a resource because we have aimed our management program at maintaining the weakest link in the chain — the trail segments that go through the wet meadows? Have we inflated the cost of management because we did not relocate the trail away from the meadow?

Much has changed in the delivery of public outdoor recreation opportunities, yet change has often come slowly. Perhaps that is the way it should be. Our future, while not a mirror image of the past, certainly reflects our previous managerial experiences. Thus it is important for future management to reflect not only on where we are in state-of-the-art practices, but also how we got there.

A BRIEF HISTORY

Outdoor recreation management has evolved over about a hundred years, but we have only been faced with spiraling recreational use in the face of dwindling resources during the last thirty-five to forty. The following discussion is simply an effort to capsulize this brief history.

Although there are earlier instances of outdoor recreation management to focus on, the one significant event that drastically changed the course of the parks and conservation movement was the establishment of Yellowstone National Park. It was the embryo stage of outdoor recreation management in a public-land context, the ushering in of the "Custodial Era."

Custodial Era. The Yellowstone National Park Act of 1872 opened the door for the establishment of large areas of land for public purposes, including recreation. Several additional national parks were created during the late 1800s. The western national forest lands were established under the Forest Reserve Act of 1891, and other lands were added later. The important management strategy that evolved during this early period was that the lands were to be held in reserve — to be protected but not necessarily utilized. Thus most public lands were held in a custodial state with little access, no recreational facility development, and no sense of urgency for outdoor recreation management.

Even with the establishment of the National Park Service in 1916, there was very little change in public use of public lands and in the need for outdoor recreation management. The Industrial Revolution had brought people to the cities, some of which had expanded to large urban spaces; however, long hours of work in the factories, lack of transportation, and low incomes severely limited participation in outdoor recreation.

Some increased interest in outdoor recreation became apparent in the late 1920s, but even this waned at the onset of the Great Depression. Thus, once again there was no urgent need for even the most rudimentary management program. That period did bring transition, and ultimately the end of the Custodial Era, however, in the form of intensive recreation development and the construction of access roads and trails by the Civilian Conservation Corps and the Work Projects Administration.

Now all that was needed to usher in the management era was an upgrade in the economy. World War II did just that — casting the country into a period of economic prosperity. People had more money and time than ever before, and they began to seek pleasurable leisure experiences, particularly in outdoor settings. This new interest in the out-of-doors caused little concern among the land managers (land custodians), since most of them found it difficult to interpret the real significance of increased recreational participation. Nevertheless, the end of World War II marked the end of the Custodial Era and the beginning of the "Extensive Management Era."

Extensive Management Era. Although many people were reluctant to recognize the rise of the new era, its impact did become evident to some concerned observers. During the 1950s and 1960s, public land use expanded greatly, and many agencies attempted to increase facilities and access in order to accommodate more people. Examples of these programs were Mission 66 (National Park Service) and Operation Outdoors (U.S. Forest Service). In addition, increased logging on the national forests provided thousands of miles of coincidental access to formerly isolated areas.

The main emphasis of the Extensive Management Era was on increasing the supply of recreational opportunities. Although most of the management programs were extensive in nature, certain fundamental outdoor recreation management programs did evolve:

1. Resource management
   a. Site protection and maintenance
   b. Silvicultural treatment of overstory vegetation
   c. Integration with other resource management programs
   d. Recreation road construction and improvement
2. Visitor management
   a. Informational services
   b. Concession services
   c. Expansion of interpretive programs
   d. Public safety

During the late 1960s, some managers saw a need not only for expanding both resource and visitor management programs but also for opening up new areas to users. By this time, many new kinds of recreational equipment was becoming available on the market, such as snowmobiles, trail bikes, and ATV's (all-terrain vehicles). Thus there was a need not merely to provide new opportunities and services, but also to integrate these on a sytems basis for more efficient management. It was insufficient to provide a few varied opportunities and attempt to reduce possible conflict between visitors. The visitor and his equipment had become sophisticated technologically, which required changes in existing management strategy. There was a need to update the programs — to provide for

resource management in order to protect the resource base, and to provide for *visitor management* in order to maintain opportunities for the various user groups. These two broad programs needed to be integrated to insure congruent decision-making that provided sustained-yield public recreation of benefit to all users.

Intensive Management Era. The beginning of the Intensive Management Era is difficult to isolate. Some people feel that we have not yet reached that level; others feel that we may never reach it. Many agencies are trying to coordinate the capability of the resource with the perceived the needs of visitors. In this era, the emphasis appears to be on the need for developing and updating baseline data on both the effect of visitor use on the resource and styles of visitor participation in a particular area, including the visitor's perceptions of quality recreation experiences.

One prominent strategy that has risen during this era is management by objectives. With this strategy, the recreation manager is forced to evaluate baseline data and develop specific management objectives for each newly planned area. The problem is that we have often couched our objectives in vague generalized terms, sought oversimplified models to achieve those objectives, and measured our output in visitor days.

We need new ideas, and recreation managers with increased personal vitality, to search for new ways of conducting old business. Research was never designed to solve all problems; its purpose is to improve the existing body of knowledge in order to lessen the uncertainty of managerial decision-making. Yet there will always be uncertainty to deal with. What is needed are both a framework within which management objectives are developed and a bureaucratic decision-maker who is willing to deal with uncertainty in developing programs to meet those objectives.

The Role of the Manager. Historically, the manager has assumed the above role much like the *in loco parentis* of the college set in the 1950s. He or she has simply decided what is in the best interests of visitors and set about achieving that outcome. The underlying assumption here is that the manager preserves the outdoor experience for visitors, and that the ends (whatever the manager has decided on as the desired experience) justify the means. Under this paradigm, the manager ignores the role of the individual in producing the recreational experience, and assumes that all desired outcomes can be ultimately achieved through direct manipulation of visitor behavior.

Wilderness epitomizes this situation. Managers have waved the banner, "search for solitude," as the justification for limiting the numbers of people going into Lake Isolated (a hypothetical area). After all, those poor wretched recreationists could not possibly be have a good experience if they had to share that lake with twenty other people. But the records speaks for itself. How many studies have you read where people were *en masse* dissatisfied with the experiences they had, or were having, in a given environmental setting? We have not located one.

There is good reason for that. People do not choose a particular recreational opportunity, understanding that there is always some uncertainty in any choice, to produce dissatisfaction. *Au contraire*, they make such choices with every intention of being satisfied. That is the role of the user or visitor (Figure 1-2). The user takes charge of his/her recreational experience by first evaluating an array of potential recreational opportunities within their social, economic, and psychological constraints, then choosing the one that appears to offer the greatest utility, then actually participating. Even after this process, something can go wrong which neither the manager nor the user can control. Maybe you had a fight with your girl- or boyfriend before you left; maybe you and your tent-mate did not get along; maybe it rained all week, everything got soaked, and you became hypothermic; or maybe...

Without getting mired down in details (hopefully they will come later), the point is that the users are in charge of their recreational experiences and that they exercise that authority by choosing their own opportunities and preparing for them prior to actual participation. What does that leave the manager in charge of? The recreational opportunity, of course!

In the Lake Isolated example, the manager has ignored opportunities created by past management such as the realigned trail that reduces the gradient, the widened and surfaced trail, foot bridges across intervening creeks, a paved parking lot at the access point, and, oh yes, the sign — WELCOME TO LAKE ISOLATED. Potentially, each one of these actions create a new recreational opportunity for some users. Collectively they would spell D-I-S-A-S-T-E-R if the intent was to provide a low-density opportunity at Lake Isolated, an Alpine lake setting that was carved out by the

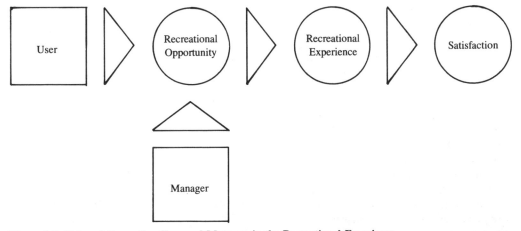

Figure 1-2. Roles of Recreation User and Manager in the Recreational Experience

last glacial period. Not understanding that past management actions have molded present use patterns, the manager now introduces one more element of change, a limited-entry permit system, which in turn may change users' perception of the opportunity even more.

Again, do not get bogged down in details. This is not an attempt to vilify the manager. What we are trying to say is that he or she is not in charge of the experience of every individual. The job is producing the opportunity — the generic experience associated with the particular environmental setting — by developing and mixing a particular set of management programs. That generic experience places the sideboards or constraints on possible experience outcomes.

MANAGEMENT WITHIN AN ORGANIZATIONAL FRAMEWORK

Even if you are comfortable with the idea that the manager provides the recreational opportunity, how efficiently you can perform that role depends much on how you are organized to manage. If decision-making power is held by some central authority, divorced from the resource conditions, management decision-making often becomes routinized or stereotyped. Under that type of regime, the benefit of the knowledge of the on-the-ground manager is lost. Unfortunately his or her motivation to implement even the simplest programs is often also lost.

On the other hand, if you were to organize the agency under a completely decentralized authority, each manager might develop his or her own program independently. This may create inconsistencies in program policies, resulting in a total lack of coordination and cooperation — almost organzational anarchy. Obviously there must be some balance to foster decision-making at the lowest possible level of the organization and yet maintain some reasonable consistency in those decisions across the organization. While much of this is often determined by the style of management, how you organize to actually accomplish your

mission will determine your theoretical efficiency. We say theoretical efficiency because you must also realize that each "pigeonhole" on the organizational chart is filled with a less-than-perfect human being just like most of us.

Rather than lead you through some circuitous discussion about something with which we are totally unfamiliar, let us make our point with an example about efficiently performing your role as an outdoor recreation manager. A State's Department of Natural Resources was so hampered by its organization framework that it had lost much of its effectiveness and efficiency. Each major division had separate regional boundaries, yet the agency was expected to operate as a totally integrated, well-coordinated organization. If a park manager wanted to improve the fishery habitat in a lake, which included removing the existing fishery and draining the lake, he or she may have had to contact the engineer for one district, the fishery biologist for another district, and so on — a complete lack of organizational integrity. The same park manager might have had to go to two different districts to obtain the services of a forest pathologist for a tree disease problem, depending on whether the problem was in the northern or southern portion of the state park. There has since been a reorganization of this agency into an effective operating organization.

The point is that in order to be effective in your management programs, you must first properly organize to be efficient and effective. Otherwise, subsequent management decisions will also be inefficient and ineffective. There is no magic solution; in fact, an effective organization is probably one that continually reevaluates its organization framework in light of the constantly changing society around it.

SELECTED READINGS

1. Batten, J.D. 1966. *Beyond Management by Objectives.* New York: American Management Association.

2. Beck, A.C., Jr., and E.D. Hillmar (eds.) 1972. *A Practical Approach to Organizational Development through MBO-Selected Readings.* Reading, Mass: Addison-Wesley Publishing Co., Inc.

3. Bittel, L.R. 1972. *The Nine Master Keys of Management.* New York: McGraw-Hill Book Co.

4. Cheek, N.H., Jr. 1976. "The Case for the Increased Regulation of Human Access to Parklands: Established Fact or Organizational Myth?" Proceedings of Recreation Management Institute, College Station, TX: Texas A & M University.

5. Clark, R.N. 1979. "The Recreation Opportunity Spectrum: A Framework for Planning, Management, and Research," USDA-Forest Service Gen. Tech. Report PNW-98.

6. Clawson, M. 1963. *Land and Water for Recreation.* Chicago: Rand McNally & Co.

7. Clawson, M., and J.L. Knetsch. 1966. *Economics of Outdoor Recreation.* Baltimore: The Johns Hopkins Press.

8. Cox, R.H., and L.R. Askham. 1984. "Implications of Interforest Management Organization." *Journal Park and Recreation Administration* 2(2):46-53.

9. Doell, C.E., and L.F. Twardzik. 1973. *Elements of Park and Recreation Administration.* Minneapolis: Burgess Publishing Co.

10. Edginton, C.R., and J.G. Williams. 1978. *Productive Management of Leisure Service Organizations: A Behavorial Approach.* New York: John Wiley and Sons.

11. Gray, D.E. 1983. "American Management Lessons from Japan." *Journal of Park and Recreation Administration* 1(1):1-6.

12. Harris, C.C., B.L. Driver, E.P. Bergerson. 1984. "Do Choices of Sport Fisheries Reflect Angler Preferences for Site Attributes?[14]" *Proceedings — Symposium on Recreation Choices Behavior.* USDA-Forest Service General Technical Report INT 184.

13. Jubenville, A. 1986. "Recreational Use of Public Lands: The Role of the Manager." *Journal of Park and Recreational Administration,* 3(4):

14. Koontz, H. (ed). 1964. *Toward a Unified Theory of Management.* New York: McGraw-Hill Book Co.

15. Newman, W.H. 1972. *The Process of Management: Concept, Behavior, and Practice.* Englewood Cliffs, NJ: Prentice-Hall, Inc.

16. Schreyer, R. 1984. "Social Dimensions of Carrying Capacity: An Overview." *Leisure Sciences* 6(4):387-394.

17. Scott, W.R. 1981. *Organizations: Rational, Natural and Open Systems.* Englewood Cliffs, N.J.: Prentice Hall.

18. Seidman, H. 1980. *Politics, Position, and Power: The Dynamics of Federal Organization, 3rd Edition.* New York: Oxford University Press.

19. Simmons, R.H., and E.P. Dvorin. 1977. *Public Administration, Values, Policy and Change.* Port Washington, NY: Alfred Publishing Co.

CHAPTER TWO

THE OUTDOOR RECREATION MANAGEMENT MODEL

Before we begin a discussion specifically on the outdoor recreation management model, we first need to define what a model is, why a model is needed in outdoor recreation, and why a holistic, or systems, approach is necessary to develop an outdoor recreation management model. *Webster's New World Dictionary* states that a paradigm is a model or pattern, a copy made to represent a real object or situation. This representation can come in many forms. It may be a physical model, such as a statue. It can also be a situational model that depicts events or situations in terms of critical factors and the interrelationships of those factors.

Obviously the static, physical model can be beneficial to the manager in displaying the existing static resource situation, such as a terrain model. However, a situational model, where critical variables are identified and interrelationships established, lends itself more to the dynamic situations with which most managers are faced. The manager can ask the "what if..." questions and have a better understanding of the probable outcomes, even if he or she does not know the exact probabilities. For example, if we know that trail use and trail erosion are a function of trail gradient, then we can ask what happens if we increase the gradient and remove the surfacing material on the trail to Lake Isolated (the example in Chapter One. We can predict that use will probably decrease, and that erosion will increase, even though we cannot predict the exact amount of increase/decrease. The emphasis in the program to maintain low density use in Lake Solitude, however, shifts from a limited-entry permit system to control use to increasing gradient with associated erosion-control measures. Thus, for recreation management, the situational model is the more appropriate of the two models.

The intent of this chapter is to show the recreational opportunity as a situation within a managerial context, i.e., as elements, functions, and variables that make up the managerial environment and facilitate the movement of the recreationist from motivation to the recreation experience, and ultimately to a level of personal satisfaction within that experience. The first step is to describe the elements in the system.

A system is a set of interrelated and interdependent parts, or subsystems, which can react as a total organism under given situations. Each subsystem may have several phases that are also interrelated and interdependent. If one subsystem or phase of a subsystem is altered, then the whole system is affected; therefore the boundary of a system is flexible to meet both external and internal changes. As a model of a system grows and changes, it also develops a history that will have some predictive value. For example, for a given input we may reasonably forecast its effects over the entire system.

A system can be either open or closed. A closed system is theoretically self-contained. An open system recognizes that certain input from the external environment is vital to its existence and in return it produces certain output. By external environment, we mean the social environment which lies outside the system's boundary, but may directly affect any subsystem within the boundary.

The typical outdoor recreation management organization is an open system, directly affected by changes outside its physical, organizational, and legal boundaries such as by degraded water quality due to upstream land-use changes or new legal requirements such as the redesignation of a stream to wild-river status through the political process. Because of the interrelationships within that open model, we must consider the effect of any decision on the total organizational system — not just in solving a particular problem in a given subsystem. Thus a holistic approach is essential to good management.

After we get a picture of the total system in our organization, we can dissect it into subsystems and then relate each management program back to the recreational opportunity to be provided. Many detailed, complex subsystems can be reintegrated to form a single highly complex, fully integrated management system. A complex systems model should enable us to understand the interrelationship between subsystems internally and the social environment externally. Theoretically, we could predict the effects of manipulating a given variable in a subsystem on other variables within that subsystem or on the total system; however, we must also keep in mind that this is an open system where external factors are continually affecting the internal operations and changing the program composition of the system. For example, a highly publicized injury in one park or zone can affect how the total system responds to hazard management in the future.

Many of the important problems facing the manager are very complex and affected by various social and political external influences. Thus a model helps us to acquire an understanding of those complexities. Even with the limited information we have about certain environmental and organizational variables a system model can not only benefit the outdoor recreation manager, but point out the need for baseline information in areas where voids now exist. It may also suggest priorities for future research.

THE PRIMARY INPUT OF THE SYSTEM

Input are the basic descriptors of any system. They place boundaries on what is to be included in the system's management model. In outdoor recreation management, there are really three primary input — the visitor, the natural

resource base, and the management organization. We will focus on the nature of each input, the general relationships of these input, and the overall concept of the system.

The first and probably most important element in the system to be considered is the visitor or recreationist, since he or she creates the demand for the recreational experiences that require the other two elements. It is for visitors that recreational opportunities are planned and managed in our modern society. They generally have special recreational interests and expect the system, which is designed to provide recreational opportunities, to meet their needs. The organizational system usually responds to interests at the user group level — for example, to wilderness hikers and auto campers — rather than to individual interests. This has concerned some managers because they feel they should provide for *all* diverse recreational interests. However, as pointed by A. Jubenville, S.C. Matulich, and W.G. Workman:

> Clark and Stanley (1979) recognized that quality is a relevant notion across the entire spectrum but argued, along with much of the profession, than an objective of diversity assures quality. This ill-founded notion is rooted in the belief that recreational quality is so highly personal that management should not be dominated by mass or average tastes. As noted by Davis (1963), it is one of those conceptual weeds that have grown up (and gone to seed) in the outdoor recreation movement.[11]

Often when we try to manage for everyone's interest, we end up satisfying no one. The natural resource base (environmental setting) is the medium in which the activity takes place. This element can be conducive or disruptive in the movement toward satisfying visitors with a single recreational opportunity. It is important to realize that it is absolutely necessary to provide a physical environment that is conducive to pleasant experiences; however, because of the professional value systems of many recreation managers, we have often misjudged what really are the environmental needs of recreationists. It is not necessarily the physical characteristics of the recreational site that are important, but, rather, how they are perceived by the user. Perhaps we have placed too much emphasis on the resource itself, without regard to how it affects the visitor. We have postulated a need for certain types of environmental settings, such as a pristine environment for the hiker, or maximum privacy for the auto camper, when in fact other environmental settings may be sometimes more satisfying. A pristine environment may be satisfying to an experienced hiker group, but appear hostile to a less experienced one. A modern trailer campground may be very attractive to one camping group, but very unattractive to another.

In many instances, however, the physical characteristics of the resource are a direct indicator of potential recreational pursuits. Given the opportunity, the skier will seek environs that offer good skiing conditions over a lengthy season; the sightseer will seek those landscapes that offer maximum aesthetic diversity and unique types of viewing opportunities; and so on.

Management is the third of the three system elements. Again its ultimate goal is to enable various user groups to have satisfying recreational experiences. It coordinates the activities and services on the available resource base with the needs of visitors. It is the element that protects the integrity of the recreational opportunity and the resource base — the essence of the opportunity.

The interrelationships of all three elements are as follows:

1. The resource affects the visitor.
2. The visitor affects the resource.
3. The resource situation affects management programs.
4. The management programs affect the resource situation.
5. The visitor affects management programs.
6. The management programs affect the disposition of the visitor.

Specific interrelationships are meaningful only in the context of the type of recreational opportunity we are trying to offer in a given situation.

PRIMARY FUNCTIONS

The functions of the system describe the subsystems — visitor management, resource management, and service management. Visitor management is manipulating the visitor (either voluntarily or otherwise) in order to create a pleasing social environment for the activity. Resource management refers to manipulating the resource in order to enhance the recreational opportunity or protect the site from deterioration. Service management refers to provisioning for certain visitor services within a given recreational opportunity while minimizing the queuing associated with that opportunity. The three subsystems, or primary functions, must be integrated to produce a given recreational opportunity.

Resource Management. The resource management subsystem consists of two phases — resource input and the resource management programs aimed at managing those input (See Figure 2-1). Maintaining resource values is important and is accomplished through monitoring the effects of current custodial programs on the resource base at some prescribed level. It is not a matter of eliminating the impact of use on the resource. Instead it is aimed at keeping impact within some acceptable level or improving the resource's ability to sustain a higher level of use within acceptable limits. Monitoring, then, is carried out at the interface of the resource with human use. It tells us how well we are doing and indicates what direction we should shift the program to move it within acceptable limits.

Resource management programs vary from the very site-specific, such as the introduction of a hardy ground cover to stabilize a site under intensive use, to the environmentally protective, like maintaining secondary vegetation through the introduction of fire. In all programs, the emphasis is not on maintaining the resource as an end in itself, but

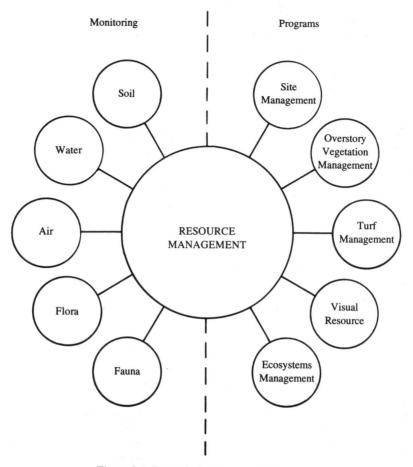

Figure 2-1. Resource Management Subsystem

on achieving some desired outcome — a specified recreational opportunity.

Resource management programs include:

1. *Site Management.* This is the manipulation of the developed site to maintain the quality of the resource setting and to rehabilitate it where necessary. Site management is an intensive program whose functions are to protect the site from overuse by recreationists and to maintain a desirable, aesthetic environment in which the activity is to take place.

2. *Overstory Vegetation Management.* This primarily includes silvicultural practices related to the management of intensive use areas, such as developed sites along roads and trails and around bodies of waters. Many of these practices are initiated prior to any recreational development in order to prepare the site, and they may continue throughout the life of the development.

3. *Ecosystems Management.* Here we focus on specific controversial areas of management concern as they relate to the fragments of ecosytems that remain. The most controversial management strategy concerning ecosystems has been the suppression of fire in the large public areas dedicated to dynamic natural ecosystems. Thus our specific discussion will deal primarily with fire-management programs.

4. *Visual Resource Management.* This is a

program designed to assess the visual impact of any manmade activity or development, and, where appropriate, to enhance the appeal of the landscape. It is a process in which the characteristics of the landscapes are inventoried, analyzed, and classified based on their ability to absorb development with minimum visual impact. This process incorporates the perceptions of visitors.

We often do not give enough consideration to the visual effects of a development, even a recreational development. The public that uses these resources demands that we retain the aesthetic appeal that attracted them there in the first place.

Visitor Management. The function of visitor management is described in Figure 2-2. The manager has many visitor information and education programs at his or her disposal in order to help visitors choose various opportunities or to manipulate visitor use. Information systems are marvelous management tools; they can help inform users so that they can choose rationally between environmental settings and management-influenced sites that best suit their interests. Such information has been successful in influencing the choices of ''new'' visitors to an area, but the ''old hands'' typically ignore it.

Public safety is a concern of management regardless of the type of recreational opportunity being provided. However, the

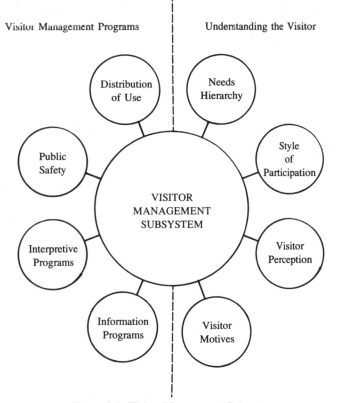

Visitor Management Programs

Understanding the Visitor

Distribution of Use

Needs Hierarchy

Style of Participation

Public Safety

VISITOR MANAGEMENT SUBSYSTEM

Visitor Perception

Interpretive Programs

Information Programs

Visitor Motives

Figure 2-2. Visitor Management Subsystem

specific public safety program, as will be shown later, must be consistent with the requirements of the opportunity. In some instances, a simple sign or brochure may be sufficient; others may require strict regulatory enforcement. Educational programs are also important, and should be used to improve both the users' understanding of the landscape and their use of that landscape. Many of the negative effects for which users are blamed are often done out of ignorance rather than willful intent. Good educational programs can help to alleviate some of these problems.

You can then direct specific *visitor management* programs toward specific user groups, creating a dialogue in which the user and manager attempt to understand each other. The manager should also try to consider visitor input in developing management programs. These are the visitors' needs hierarchy, style of participation, and perception.

1. *Needs Hierarchy*. The needs of the individual in terms of what he wants from the recreational experience are important. These needs have been summarized by Maslow in a hierarchial structure.[13] Maslow theorized that needs are the primary influences on an individual's behavior. When a particular need emerges, it shapes the individual's behavior in terms of motivation, priorities, and action taken. Motivated behavior is the result of the tension — either pleasant or unpleasant — experienced when a need presents itself. The goal of this behavior is the reduction of the tension or discomfort, and enables the individual to satisfy his or her need. Only unsatisfied needs are prime sources of motivation, though A.S. Mills suggests this theory may not hold for leisure time.[14]

2. *Style of Participation*. Style of participation is important to the proper management of the recreational opportunity. There can be great differences in the way people participate in a given activity. For example, one study found differences in styles of elk hunting (trophy hunter, meat hunter, and equipment hunter). These are called the macrocharacteristics, or macrobehavioral

patterns or participation. J.A. Wagar[18] separated camping into seven styles: transient, central, long-term, forest, peak-load, backcountry, and wilderness. All activities can be divided into distinct styles of participation that would help the manager to better structure management strategies for enhancing macrobehavioral patterns.

The microbehavior is also important, but unfortunately we do not have many studies that focus on participant microbehavior. Such conduct in hikers would include, for example, how they travel a wilderness trail, interact with one another, and respond to various environmental stimuli. This information could help managers maintain or enhance normal visitor reactions. If it becomes necessary to alter use patterns, a knowledge of the microbehavior can also help managers understand the potential effects of specific management strategies.

3. *Visitor Perception*. Ultimately, how people participate is based on their perception of the recreational opportunity provided by management. That perception includes not only the resource such as a lake and surrounding shoreline, but also manmade provisions such as roads, boating facilities, services, etc. Even in the absence of empirical data, we should be able to predict general user response to obvious program changes. Others may be more subtle and less predictable. The point is that managers must be able to link management action to visitor perception.

Service Management. Service management refers to the provisioning of facilities, services, and related ancillary programs to accommodate the user (See Figure 2-3). This provisioning must fit within some appropriate criteria. The basic framework for judging appropriateness is the Recreational Opportunity Spectrum, which will be discussed in more detail in Chapter Three. Its logic dictates that toward the more primitive portion of the outdoor recreation spectrum there should be fewer facilities and that these should be more rustic in character, requiring less service and more self reliance.

Constraints | Programs

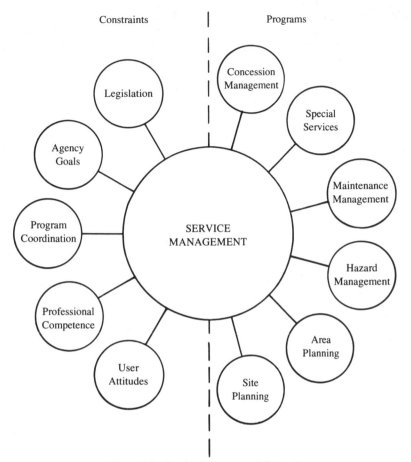

Figure 2-3. Service Management Subsystem

Service management can be separated into several programs:

1. *Area planning* is a resource allocation process where natural and fiscal resources are allocated to provide specified recreational opportunities. As part of that process, managers provide access and facilities for visitors. These are the manmade attributes that visitors initially respond to in choosing a particular site to recreate. Thus the area planning process is very important to service management, but it also creates the need for ancillary programs such as concessions, maintenance, and hazard management.

2. *Concession management* is directed toward providing specialized facilities/services in order for the visitor to enjoy a particular environmental setting. What kind of accommodations are needed? What services should be provided? Who will provide them? And how will they be regulated? The using public is generally charged directly for the specialized facilities/services. The question, then, is, what is the better vehicle for doing this? Typically this has been a concession lease where the entrepreneur pays a fee to the public agency for the right to provide the facility/service.

3. *Maintenance programs* are aimed at protecting public investment in the facilities

and maintaining acceptable accommodations for the using public. It is the first level of management, whether it is done on trails or modern buildings. Other services may enhance the use of the site, but maintenance is absolutely essential.

4. *Hazard management* is a program directed at reducing the risk of natural or man-made hazards to visitors. It is not risk management, a business-management term which means to minimize the risk of losses to the firm. Here, in a broader sense, it mean that the recreation user acts as the firm to minimize his/her personal risk involved in a given recreational opportunity. The recreation manager provides specific programs to "accommodate" or assist the user in minimizing risk, but the user is still the actual decision maker — still in charge of his/her own behavior.

INTEGRATION OF THE FUNCTIONS

The integration of functions is a difficult process because of the number of possible interactions between all the programs in each subsystem. A diagram of this would create such a maze of lines that we would have difficulty in tracing interrelationships. We must realize, however, that there is an interdependence within the system; that is, a decision made in one program area can have a drastic effect on the other programs (See Figure 2-4). Therefore the manager must consider all the ramifications of a particular decision since you can, with an understanding of these interactions, manipulate one program to produce a desired outcome in another. For example, suppose you need to improve site conditions in a wilderness area where outfitters (a service management function) have tended to camp near a lake, causing the resource to deteriorate — a resource management problem. Since we are not allowed to manipulate the resource directly (in terms of management), we can either redistribute use voluntarily, or, through an outfitter permit, limit his/her use to allow the site to recover naturally.

In a more complex interaction example, let's look at a segment of a major river system that is managed as a wild river for which the primary activities are scenic floating and fishing. There are only three access points along that portion of the river. Now let's suppose that the visitor (visitor subsystem) is a novice floater who has depended primarily on the commercial outfitters with concession leases for floating the river. He is attracted to the area by the outstanding scenery, and regards floating only as a secondary activity. He enjoys the experience and does not perceive any problems (such as crowding, noise, and so on) that would affect the quality of his experience.

Information on floating is available through the agency and through advertisements by the commercial outfitters. A recent study showed that most people found out about floating trips through contact with friends. Education is primarily through natural history interpretation during the float trips, but other subtle kinds of education can take place because of the surroundings. Each outfitter, as a condition of his permit, is required to present a minimal interpretative talk. A self-guiding brochure of the area is being developed by the agency for the private floater.

Use has increased rapidly, especially on the commercial float trips. At certain times of the day, several boating parties must wait their turns to launch. The policy on launching is that the previous boat must be out of sight before the next one can be launched; this is done to reduce congestion in the water.

Public safety has not been a problem since most people go out on a commercial raft under the guidance of a skilled boatman. All craft must meet minimum safety standards, and no one is allowed to launch his/her craft, except at the designated access points. The few safety problems have been caused by several unskilled private floaters who did not appreciate their own limitations in craft maneuvering. No serious accidents have occurred.

Resources management problems are minimal since people are not allowed to stop and get out of their craft. This eliminates environmental impact except at access points, where some site deterioration is taking place.

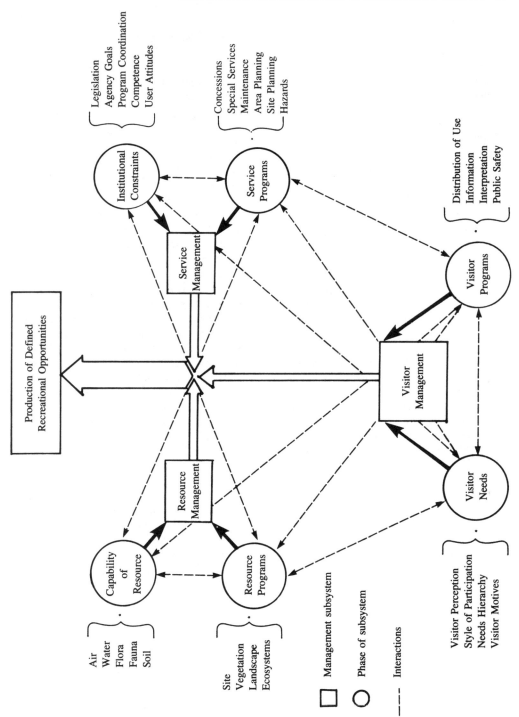

Figure 2-4. The Outdoor Recreation Systems Model. This model shows the integration and interaction of the subsystems. An asterisk (*) indicates areas where the external environment may affect the operation of the system.

No overnight use is allowed.

Service management has probably the greatest effect on the entire system. Several concessionaires operate on the river who encourage participation by advertising float trips. Most outfitters offer a good service that is well-received by the commercial floater. No complaints of any substance have been received.

Access to the area is limited to gravel roads leading to the three access points. These roads, in effect, restrict the total amount of use that the river can receive. Total commercial use is also limited, in a more formal manner, through a quota system of 75,000 visitor-days per year. Psychological barriers to river use have been overcome by the presence of a qualified boat operator to handle the trip. Also, the agency uses a river patrol to enforce policies and ensure visitors' safety on the water.

Obviously, other factors could be mentioned. The purpose here is to delineate a management system and indicate how it operates without passing judgment on any phase of it. Now, with our knowledge of the system and how it works, we can better understand the effects that a given decision may have on the various subsystems. Each phase may have an effect on every other phase.

SUMMARY

The visitor is the main beneficiary of an outdoor recreation systems management model. There is a need for service and resource management in recreation only if there is a demand and support for the agency's programs. Agencies develop specific visitor management programs to direct users toward satisfying experiences. By so doing, they gain the user support.

The service management subsystem offers basic features, including access, facilities, and other accommodations, which are commensurate with institutional constraints, resource limitations, and visitor needs. Resource management programs attempt to maintain the existing resource base within acceptance limits of change (based on either agency goals, visitor perceptions, or both). When use exceeds these limits, feedback through the system may indicate a need to reduce the impact by means of a visitor redistribution program (visitor management), which in turn should signal a need to adjust area or site planning, number of accommodations, and services. Another possibility is to manipulate the overused site by using cultural site treatments to increase its durability — as long as this manipulation is acceptable to the user (and the agency) and does not disrupt the activity or the services provided. Even temporary disruption is permissible if the majority of the people support the temporary inconvenience in order to have a better-managed site in the long run.

A systems model is the only logical approach to managing the natural resource base for recreational use because it simply depicts the highly complex interaction of visitor, resource, and the manager. While all possible interactions may not be fully appreciated, we understand enough to know that the three subsystems are linked together and that any change in one can affect the others. Without that knowledge, we could continually solve problems in one area and possibly cause catastrophies in others.

One final suggestion is that you use an open model. As pointed out in Figure 2-4, external factors influence and/or govern a given subsystem, which in turn affects the entire system. Since a closed, static model cannot realistically describe the dynamic changes that occur in a recreation system or society, the open model is invaluable for its great emphasis on monitoring external factors. When management does not adapt quickly to changes in external forces, public support wanes for *all* their programs.

SELECTED READINGS

1. Alden, H.R. 1973. "Systems for Analyzing Impacts of Outdoor Recreation Programs on Environmental Quality," *Outdoor Recreation and Environmental Quality.* Foss, P.O. (ed.). Ft. Collins, CO: Colorado State University.

2. Boulding, K.E. 1956. "General Systems Theory: The Skeleton of Science" *Management Science* 2(3):198.

3. Brown, F.R. (ed.) 1977. *Management: Concepts and Practices*. Mt. Airy, MD: Lomond Publications.

4. Cox, R.H., and L.R. Askham. 1984. "Implications of Interforest Management Organizations," *Journal of Park and Recreation Administration* 2(2):46-53.

5. Davis, R.K. 1963. "Recreation Planning as an Economic Problem," *Natural Resources Journal* 3(10):329-349.

6. Deutsch, K. 1949. "Some Notes on the Roles of Models in the Natural and Social Sciences," *Synthese* 7:506.

7. Frissell, S., and G.H. Stankey, 1972. "Wilderness Environmental Quality: Search for Social and Ecological Harmony," *Proceedings of Society of American Foresters*.

8. Hellriegel, D., and J.W. Slocum, Jr. 1982. *Management: A Contingency Approach*. Reading, MA: Addison-Wesley Publishing, Co.

9. Johnson, R.A., F. Kast, and J.E. Rosenzweig. 1967. *The Theory and Management of Systems*. New York: McGraw-Hill Book Co.

10. Jubenville, A. 1986. "Recreational Use of Public Lands: The Role of the Manager," *Journal of Park and Recreation Administration* 4(1):53-60.

11. Jubenville, A., S.C. Matulich and W.G. Workman. 1986. *Toward the Integration of Economics and Outdoor Recreation Management*. Bulletin 68, Agricultural and Forestry Experiment Station, Fairbanks, AL.

12. Lange, O. 1965. *Wholes and Parts: A General Theory of System Behavior*. Oxford: Pergamon Press.

13. Maslow, A.H. 1970. *Motivation and Personality,* Second Edition. New York: Harper & Row Publications, Inc.

14. Mills, A.S. 1985. "Participation Motivations for Outdoor Recreation: A Test of Maslow's Theory," *Journal of Leisure Research* 17(3):184-199.

15. Pezoldt, C. 1985. "Park Management in the year 2001," *Journal of Park and Recreation Administration* 3(4):Viii-X.

16. Stankey, G.H. 1972. "A Strategy for the Definition and Management of Wilderness Quality," *Natural Environments: Studies in Theoretical and Applied Analysis*. Baltimore: The Johns Hopkins Press.

17. Webber, R.A. 1979. *Management Pragmatics*. Homewood, Ill.: Richard D. Irwin, Inc.

18. Wagar, J.A. 1966. *Campgrounds for Many Tastes*. USDA-Forest Service Research Paper INT-6.

CHAPTER THREE
THEORETICAL FOUNDATIONS

Recreation management is a relatively new professional field with roots in social psychology. Many theories have been advanced to explain user behavior; most of which has been drawn from motivational literature. Thus much of "our" theory reflects the demand, or user side, of the recreation equation. On the other hand, there appears to be a renewed interest in the study of the "supply side," what the manager provides.

In any new profession, there is always an internal struggle in searching for the truth. Of course we all understand that this struggle never ceases; but at least searching for the truth usually adds other peices to the total puzzle. And we all gain a little bit professionally and personally because of the effort. Rather than try to cover the waterfront of all possible theories and concepts dealing with recreation mangement, we confess to being mere mortals and thus will simply limit dicussion to the interface of demand and supply. While this interface has many paradigms, two primary patterns filter out of the literature — recreational carrying capacity (RCC) and recreational opportunity spectrum (ROS). Many of us have at times felt that we had arrived at the truth, that the struggle was over. We felt comfortable with one of the paradigms. If you feel this way, don't proceed, clinging tightly to your own biases, looking for a slip, a mistake, or a fault in logic. You will certainly find them. Instead, relax and enjoy the discussion. view it with an open but critical eye.

Actually we find both paradigms — RCC and ROS — to be conceptually sound in the abstract. The problem has been that, in the rush to solve management problems, we operationalize the paradigm without first fully exploring the concept and then seeing if it applies to how the world (the interface between user and manager) really works. Fittingly, then, this chapter steers away from operational aspects and looks at both RCC and ROS in the abstract. Not only are they sound concepts, they are not competing models and actually complement one another. Together they form the theoretical foundation of outdoor recreation management.

RECREATIONAL OPPORTUNITY SPECTRUM

While many authors have suggested a recreation-management continuum, J.A. Wagar was probably the first to advance the idea from a purely managerial perspective.[31] However, the first definitive publications were probably the ones published by P. Brown, *et al* and B.L. Driver and P. Brown.[10] These later publications concerned themselves with the theoretical production of distinctive recreational experiences or psychological outcomes. R.N. Clark and G.H. Stankey described the continuum as a spectrum of recreational opportunities and the role of the manager as a provider of those opportunities.[9]

The Operationalized Theory. Clark and Stankey define the setting for a recreational opportunity as *the combination of physical, biological, social, and managerial conditions that give value to a place.*[9] An opportunity involves qualities provided by nature (vegetation, landscape, topography, scenery), qualities associated with recreational use (levels and types of use), and conditions provided by management (development, roads, regulations). By combining variations of these qualities and conditions, management can provide a variety of opportunities for recreationists.

Figure 3-1. The Recreational Opportunity Spectrum

This variety can be expressed in a continuum called the Recreational Opportunity Spectrum (See Figure 3-1). Such a framework recognizes the link between the environmental setting and the psychological outcome, the recreational experience itself. It is based on the assumption that recreationists choose to participate in those activities that are consistent with a particular environmental setting and that the setting may be managerially influenced to provide different types of recreation opportunities. Thus ROS was intended as a "fundamental [aid] to multiple use natural resource planning and management decisions."[5]

Clark and Stankey go on to suggest that it is not necessary to understand the exact linkage between recreational opportunities and psychological outcomes in order to be an effective manager.[9] In fact, although some studies have shown such a linkage, most indicate that the motives that direct recreational experiences vary considerably even within a given activity, environmental setting, or individuals.[11] The literature is in agreement that people are driven by their motives but that those at specific sites do not necessarily share common motives. In other words, we may do the same thing at the same site, but for different reasons that produce different outcomes. Or we may do different things.

Unfortunately, the remaining factors offered by Clark and Stankey — social, managerial, biological, and physical — are not evaluated in terms of their own inter-relationships and their effects on the user's perception of the opportunity. They are simply dropped into the management blender, mixed,

and then poured out, as suggested in Figure 3-1, in neatly packaged, equal-interval classes of opportunities. While this treatment may be sufficient for conceptual discussions, the obvious next step is also taken — to operationalize the equal-interval continuum. Clark and Stankey's model is purely a schematic example for discussion purposes,[9] but the US Forest Service and the Bureau of Land Management actually adopted a cookbook version of ROS. Because the concept was never fully developed, there are four major problems with the operationalized version:

1. *It fails to recognize the importance of the specific biophysical attributes of the site.* Based on the present process, we could inventory our lands into various ROS classes. If sufficient acreage were placed into a particular class, we could assume that we are providing a sufficient supply for that opportunity. In order for that to be true, we would also have to assume that biophysical attributes are *not* central to recreationist's choices. Yet we know that use is not evenly distributed; it tends to be concentrated at the various natural attractors in the landscape and absent in areas having little attraction. Obviously, managerial actions may determine the general types and levels of use at these concentration points, but as suggested in the preface by Clark and Stankey, biophysical attractors are generally the focal points of recreational use in the landscape, regardless of managerial action.

2. *It fails to recognize cause-effect relationships.* ROS literature indicates that

physical setting, managerial setting, and social setting combine to produce the recreational opportunity. Social setting is described as density, or use per amount of area per unit of time, and ignores causal relationships in producing that density. However, the social parameters of a site are not something that can be determined by the direct intervention of management. Rather the generalized density of a site is an indirect function of management provisions such as increased access, increased visitor facilities associated with access, change in services, etc. Densities are always going to be higher at specific local natural attractors — a mountain lake, a unique geological feature, prime elk habitat, and so on — even in low density areas. Thus there appear to be important linkages that have been overlooked. The core of the opportunity are the specific biological and physical attributes of the site. These are what attract people. The social factor (primarily density in the literature) is considered a function of management actions in a particular environmental setting. Who is actually attracted is determined by these actions.

As you increase access, recreational use increases. Hold access constant and increase services, and the clientele will probably increase. In both cases, the aggregate makeup of the user group will likely shift to those preferring more access and/or services. The only situation in which this would not be true is where you would have a reasonably strong attractor and no physiographic constraints — as the case of the Southern California desert, where use has to be artificially constrained through regulation.

Without the understanding of cause-effect relationships, managers have often attempted to directly intervene to "create" the desired opportunity with limited-entry permit systems. The problem is that it becomes economically inefficient to provide increased access, facilities, and/or services that encourage a general density level and then spend additional operating dollars to limit use to some lower level.

3. *It fails to recognize that indirect managerial input such as permit systems have an effect on the opportunity produced.* Yet for many users, indirect input may have a dramatic effect on the user's perception of the site, even if all else is satisfactory. For some users, the imposition of direct behavioral restrictions may not only discourage a recreational or social opportunity, it may in fact cause them to move to another site where there are no restrictions.[25] As early as 1972, Knopf suggests that the aggregate attributes of the site, including management programs, influence the user choice.

4. *It assumes that a maximum variety of opportunities are offered through direct management action.* The operationalized model does not guarantee that a variety of opportunities will be offered on a large area or regional basis, even though it is often touted as ensuring such variety. Even if you were to institute a regional oversight committee or super agency to direct subordinate agencies in such a manner that a variety of management actions were assured, there would still be no guarantee of variety because such a method ignores biophysical input.

As suggested in item 1, biophysical input is central to the individual's choice of recreational opportunities; thus it would seem that a variety of opportunities is linked to a variety of biophysical attributes. Assuming, then, that maximizing recreational opportunities is a goal of the planner, the first step in achieving that goal would be proper resource management to ensure natural variation in the biophysical makeup of the landscape — protection, enhancement or rehabilitation.

With all its suggestions that help managers allocate and plan recreational resources, inventory recreational opportunities, do impact analyses, and match desired experiences with available opportunities, ROS appears to be nothing more than an inventory classification scheme in which the most important single ingredient is left out — the specific biophysical attractors.

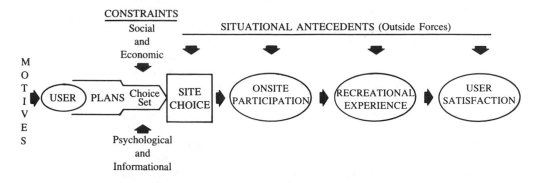

Figure 3-2. Flow Diagram of the Recreationists' Decision Process

The Conceptual Theory. The Conceptual Theory developed by Driver and Brown, and Clark and Stankey recognized separate and distinct roles for the manager and user. The manager provided the opportunity and the user created his/her own unique experience within that opportunity.

1. *The Role of the User.* As shown in Figure 3-2, the user is driven by motives to participate; however, because of personal constraints such as lack of time or money or personal commitment to others, the actual choice is typically more constrained than the set of opportunities that is theoretically available. Within that constrained choice, a user then chooses a site and pursues a recreational experience, that leads to personal satisfaction. This is very similar to models by R. Schreyer, R.C. Knopf, and D.R. Williams[26] and C.C. Harris, B.L. Driver, and E.P. Bergerson.[14]

   Satisfaction means how well the experience meets the expectations of the user.[28] Most studies that have measured satisfaction have found the users satisfied. After all, the site is deliberately chosen, within limits the user has set, to produce satisfaction. People make such choices to maximize their satisfaction according to a recent article by R. Schreyer, D.W. Lime and D.R. Williams.[27] These authors discovered that participants on eleven wild rivers rated the rivers between 2.9 and 3.2 on a five-point scale; yet their levels of satisfaction, using the same scale, varied between 4.6 and 4.8. While the rivers were not rated very high, people were well-satisfied with their choices.

   R. A. Holmes[16] measured a similar choice/response pattern for anglers on the upper Chena River, where enjoyment was rated good to excellent (1.92 on a 4-point scale where 1 equals excellent, 2 good, 3 fair and 4 poor). Yet they rated their perception of the fishing only fair to good (2.81 on the same scale). He found the two most important constraints on choice to be lack of leisure time (41.8%) and costs (15.3%).

   Choice of site, on-site participation, and the experience derived may also be influenced by external factors beyond the control of the manager or the user such as weather, spontaneous actions of others, etc.[17] These external factors, or exogenous input into the recreational experience, are beyond the control of the user or the manager, yet can exert tremendous influence over the quantity and quality of the recreational experience. A week of rain on your wilderness vacation in the Bridger Mountains would most likely produce a dissatisfying experience, yet may not negatively affect your perception of the recreational opportunity at all — particularly if you are convinced that the rainstorm was an atypical occurrence.

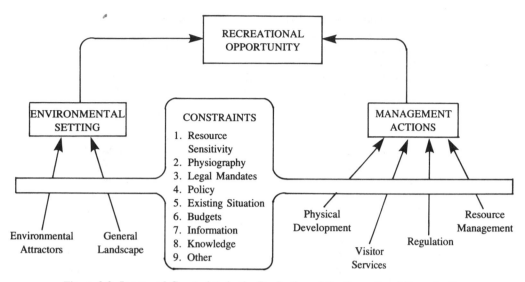

Figure 3-3. Input and Constraints in the Production of the Recreational Opportunity

2. *The Role of the Manager.* Figure 3-3 shows all the input into a recreational opportunity. The environmental setting and managerial actions reflect the supply-related function of the manager. While he or she does not create the environmental setting, it is the manager's responsibility to evaluate, dedicate, and manage sites for specific uses. Where he/she chooses to operate on the ROS is known as the ''anchor point'' on the recreational opportunity. All programmatic decisions must conform to the requirements of this anchor point.

From a recreational perspective, every acre is not of equal value; specific environmental attractors tend to be of greater value than the generalized landscape within which they occur. For example, bodies of water, prime wildlife habitat, and natural movement in the landscape such as waterfalls are more attractive to the user than the surrounding generalized landscape. The generalized landscape is important for visual continuity[22]. A waterfall would lose its attractiveness if the surrounding landscape were denuded; a rustic visitor center may be perceived as aesthetically pleasing and appropriate to a setting accessed by road, but inappropriate in a roadless area with primitive trail access.

Managerial actions are specific and may be applied to a site to attract certain user types, to protect or enhance resource attributes, or to maintain opportunities for specific experiences. These are the management devices that can be used to alter the value of the site to the user.[21]

If you are to manage for particular opportunities, it is important to understand what people are responding to and how you can managerially influence choice. Yet little is known about how people respond to the various attributes of a site. For discussion purposes, we have divided the attributes of a recreational opportunity into direct and indirect. Direct attributes are the obvious, tangible ones — environmental setting and physical developments (shown under Management Actions in Figure 3-3).

According to Jubenville and Becker, recreationists respond initially to the direct attributes that connote the essence of the site. More specifically, use tends to concentrate at the natural attractors, the more valued portions of the site. The type of user and level of use at these locations also generally reflect the type and level of access and associated facilities.[19] Thus, from a perceptual perspective, physical developments become as much an inherent quality of the site as the environmental attributes.

Indirect attributes such as visitor services, resource management programs, and regulations tend to be perceived as less tangible unless the environmental setting is enhanced or there is direct link between a physical development and a given service. Managers often ignore the effects of indirect attributes, or treat them as insignificant. Yet recent studies have shown them to have a significant impact on the users' perception of the site. For instance, users were displaced due to increased information services,[2] and wilderness hikers showed strong behavioral modification in response to the impact of a permit system on their recreational experiences.[30] Thus, while direct attributes represent the essence of the opportunity, indirect ones may ultimately affect choice.

Furthermore, that choice appears to be a multiplicative model rather than an additive one.[21] In the additive model, several factors contribute or add to overall user satisfaction. The environmental setting contributes so much, physical developments add so much, and, so on. Management has dealt with each input on an individual basis, with the assumption that each adds or detracts from overall visitor satisfaction. In multiplicative models users' perception of the site is based on an interaction of input. You could test for multiplicity if there was an interaction of input which was valued by some clientele group at zero. This follows the basic mathematical theorem that anything multiplied by zero is zero. It would be very rare in an additive model to have all attributes go to zero value. R. Gum, S. Garifo, and J. Loomis[13] found demand for steelhead fishing dropped to zero when water quality was perceived as poor, regardless of the level of access to the fishing streams. A. Jubenville and J.K. Feyhl[20] found a similar choice pattern for recreational development of a proposed hydroelectric project reservoir once people were made aware of the cold, silt-laden glacial water feeding the system. Birch Creek, a designated national wild river in Alaska, is no longer attractive to the canoeist, even though access has been improved greatly, because of the heavy siltation of the water from upstream placer mining.

Rarely would the package of management actions be valued at zero by all potential user groups. However, those who do value an entire package at zero would obviously not choose the opportunity or be displaced. You can also assume that displacement would occur at a much earlier stage, unless the environmental setting was extremely attractive or there were no available substitutes.

What does this mean to the manager? The value to be captured stems directly from the environmental setting. The package of management actions determine who is attracted to the environmental setting and enjoys those values. If an area is naturally unattractive (like the extensive black spruce bogs in Alaska) or is allowed to deteriorate beyond some acceptable level, any mangement program is not likely to capture much public value, unless such action is aimed at rehabilitating the site. You must recognize, of course, that with a changing set of management actions, a new aggregate user population will be attracted. This implies social succession — one social group succeeding another within a particular environmental setting — which will be discussed as distinct phenomena.

Social Succession. Social succession is simply a user response to a given recreational opportunity based on some change in the total system. People adjust to that change to maintain or enhance their own satisfaction, and the actual impact of change, although usually considered to be negative, can be positive. As pointed out by Jubenville:

> In terms of negative impact, the user can still create a desired experiential outcome through *amelioration* of the impact by changing behavioral patterns (e.g. one now fishes during the week instead of the weekend to avoid the crowds); *adaptation* to the change by lowering expectations for the site (e.g. because of fishing pressure one would expect to catch 10-inch trout instead of 14-inch ones); or *displacement* by voluntarily displacing oneself to a new site in order to be able to produce the desired recreational experience (e.g., switching to a new trout stream). The positive impact will come in the form of

enhancement of the site in the perception of the existing user (e.g., the access road to the stream has been improved to increase safety and reduce damage to the automobile); and *attraction* where non-users are now attracted to the site by the introduced change.[18]

The change-response pattern is dynamic, and that change is introduced not only by the manager but also the user and the exogenous input. Refer to Figure 3-2 and note that if you change any of the social and economic constraints, the choice set changes which in turn alters the individuals' decision. As suggested by Jubenville:

> The question, then, from a public land manager perspective, is not one of how to stabilize the change-response pattern, but what will be the effects of particular managerial input on the perception of the user, and thus, the change-response pattern? The accountability of management must be inextricably confined to the role of the manager, not that of the user.[17]

RECREATIONAL CARRYING CAPACITY

Carrying capacity has been an important theoretical management model since Wagar's monograph in 1964.[31] A lot of rhetoric on carrying capacity has inked the pages of literature. Our intent here is not to review this literature, but to give a brief overview of the basic theoretical model and offer a critique. More definite descriptions and critiques of the model can be found in *Leisure Sciences* 6(4)[24] and J.C. Hendee, G.H. Stankey, and R.C. Lucas.[15]

There are at least four described recreational carrying capacities: ecological (the impact of recreational use on the ecology), physical (the number of people an area can handle without queuing), facility (the number of people a facility can accommodate) and social (the number of people an area can sustain and still maintain a quality recreational experience).[4] F.E. Boteler goes on to say that, while each sounds good in theory, they offer

little utility to the manager looking for some *rational reason for limiting use.* The manager has sought some magical cutoff limit that is inherent in the area, but there isn't any. A.R. Graefe, *et al*[11] after an exhaustive review, conclude there is no inherent limit and that the concept is an elusive one. R. Becker, *et al*[24] prefer the term "illusive"[24] W.R. Burch, Jr. suggests that... "the universal use of recreation carrying capacity standards may have more to do with coinciding lines of ideology held by the manager and researcher than by the empirical data."[8] Unfortunately the researcher seems undaunted by it all, and continues to push back frontiers that don't really exist, or don't exist in the form that we envision. Rather than belabor the point that there is no carrying capacity, we are going to offer you an alternative that is real and potentially measureable, but not as exacting as measuring stumpage to the nearest cubic foot.

Carrying Capacity — A Dynamic Equilibrium. We will digress a little in order to lay the groundwork for the equilibrium idea. As reported by G. Bultena, *et al* (1981), the backcountry of Mt. McKinley National Park is partitioned into thirty-four management zones, ranging from 2,000 to 430,000 acres. Most of the zones radiate from the linear road corridor within the park. Based on some earlier studies of wilderness users in the "Lower forty-eight" that indicated most people preferred to see no more than two parties per day, use was restricted in the zones to six persons, or three parties of two people each. This represented a hundred percent probability that no parties would see more than two other parties. Four zones were selected as experimental and capacity limits were increased up to thirty persons. Daily, the average number of hikers in each of the experimental zones was 14.6 as compared to 2.7 in the thirty control zones (maximum of six people). The average number of daily interparty contacts was 0.9 parties per day in the experimental zones and 0.7 parties per day in the control zones.[7] These numbers do not represent a significant difference, and neither approach the original upper limit of no more than two parties per day. Furthermore, the data indicate that if the capacity limits are raised dramatically or removed, interparty contacts would not exceed the original standard. The Mt. McKinley zones are trailess and brushy, and you would not expect much interparty contact. However, wilderness statistics in the Lower forty-eight indicate that ninety-nine percent of the use is via trail and that trail systems typically occupy less than one percent of the total physical area. Obviously there is much more interparty contact under these circumstances. Maintain and upgrade the trails and the numbers of users increases. Put in foot bridges across creeks, and the trail system becomes even more attractive.

The point is that general patterns of use — total area, total number of users, and even activities — are primarily a function of the management actions applied to the particular environmental setting or the recreational opportunity itself. You manipulate some management program such as trail maintenance and you create a new opportunity and attract a new aggregate clientele group. In other words, introduced change creates a new equilibrium.

Some people are not bothered by changes. Some ameliorate the impact of more weekend trail users on the improved and maintained trail by visiting during the week or camping well away from the trail. Some adapt by assuming they'll see more people than they did in the past, but are still attracted by the good fishing in Heart Lake or the beautiful falls on Johnson Creek. Some are actually displaced because of the increased number of people on the trail. Others find the opportunity enhanced because they no longer have to fight the downfall across the trail or wade the streams. Still others are now attracted (another way of saying displaced from somewhere else) because of the improved trail conditions.

As suggested in Chapters Two and Three, if the inputs are relatively constant, there is equilibrium in any system. In the case of recreational use of public resources, there is an equilibrium between the recreational opportunity that the manager provides and the recreational experience that the user has. This might be represented as:

RO ⇄ RUP

where RO is the *recreational opportunity* and RUP is the resulting *recreational use pattern*. It is this equilibrium that represents the carrying capacity of an area — the dynamic equilibrium between use and recreational opportunity.[19] Introduce managerial change and you alter the equilibrium. That balance can also be affected by exogenous inputs like weather, wildfire, flood, and changes in potential user population. A new coal mine opens nearby and the aforementioned wilderness area becomes the playground for the hunter, fisherman, hiker, and horseman. Or some local residents take a wilderness orientation course and overcome their fears of visiting such an area. However, even if change is introduced that is beyond the control of the manger, the relative impact and direction of that impact are often predictable and mitigable through management actions. This places great emphasis not only on monitoring patterns of use and associated endogenous variables, but also the exogenous effects on those patterns.

In sum, managers are prime influencers or determiners of equilibrium by the way they manipulate opportunities. They must have some understanding of the effect on the recreational use pattern when they tweak some particular managerially determined attribute within the system. Without that type of conceptual understanding, even social, managerial or ecological baseline data are not useful for decision making. And no research provides the exacting kinds of answers to specific problems that many managers seem to look for from the scientific community. Professional judgements still have to be made, but in a logical framework with predictable results — at least predictable in terms of their general effects on patterns of use.

Carrying Capacity — A Resource Allocation Process. From the manager's perspective, carrying capacity is a resource allocation process where a predetermined recreational opportunity is achieved through the allocation of natural resources (land and water for recreation) and fiscal resources (physical developments, services, resource management programs, and regulations). Economic efficiency is assumed in achieving this equilibrium.

The idea behind resource allocation is the establishment or maintenance of a particular equilibrium. Typically we think of resource allocation as designating the land (resource) for particular uses. But when we do that we are also committing ourselves to certain management programs that are thought to best maintain desired use patterns. Thus, in the original planning stage, all of this should be spelled out. Having to implement a new program later on means that:

1. The original allocation decisions are not achieving the desired equilibrium.
2. The external influences have changed sufficiently to alter the equilibrium in order to maintain the desired RUP.
3. The original equilibrium is no longer desired and new goals have been established that require a reallocation of resources.

Let's look at an example to understand the linkage between the recreational opportunity and user response. The Jones River is recently designated a national wild river. There is very primitive trail access into its headwaters and it is difficult to portage a canoe two miles over a ridge to get to floatable water. To solve this problem, mangement pushes a road over the ridge to within one quarter mile of Jones River and constructs a new wide trail from the modern parking lot to the river's edge. A canoe rack is also situated halfway so people can rest along the one quarter mile portage.

As a result of these improvements, use doubles the first year and nearly triples the second year. Manager yells, "Too many people on the river. We have to institute a limited entry system to achieve the 'old' equilibrium." Translated, this means, "We don't like the mess we have created." Fifty thousand dollars have been spent on capital improvements to get more people into Jones Wild River and now management is willing to spend twenty thousand more a year on a limited-entry permit system to keep them from using it.

Worse yet, they will never achieve the previous equilibrium with an artificial rationing system. Assume that one hundred type-A users frequented the upper Jones River when it was a type A opportunity. Now, with the introduced change and social succession, there are 950 type B users and fifty type A users. If you attempt to achieve the previous equilibrium with a limited-entry system, the response might be something like this: The permit system was the last straw for the type-A users and they were displaced. So you hand out one hundred permits to type B users. Not necessarily. Now type C users show up because they can be guaranteed a low density experience with easy access — ninety days in advance. The permit system is still another change introduced into the system which causes a new equilibrium with a new aggregate population of one hundred type B and C users. Through regulation you can achieve former levels of use but you cannot achieve the former equilibrium. To do that on the Jones River would require a rollback of the new access to its former level, while maintaining other input at a status quo.

In the above resource allocation process, it is also important to recognize that what has been produced is a particular recreational opportunity. All subsequent programs must be aligned with that opportunity. For example, while all of us recognize that you cannot have a primitive recreational opportunity in a given environmental setting and put in roads, what about cabins? Foot bridges? A map that locates and describes all the hazards? Rustic hand rails on steep trails? Beer delivered by mule train? Directional signs on trails? Mandatory two-way radios while hiking? Remember that equilibrium is not something that is achieved with a stroke of the pen. It is based on the perception of users in relation to the total natural and managerially influenced attributes of the site.

Perhaps as important a management question as spending the least amount of money to maintain a given equilibrium is how to determine an equilibrium point in the first place. An equilibrium point, or recreational opportunity, is also called the "anchor point" on the recreational opportunity spectrum. Economists would identify that point as having the greatest net benefits to society. With non-market valuation techniques we could estimate the benefits of all possible anchor points and their associated costs and thus determine which anchor point would give us the greatest net benefits.

Federal guidelines recommend *willingness to pay* as the appropriate economic measure of the benefits of using public resources for recreation. There are three ways of estimating these benefits: 1) *Unit day value*, which uses expert opinion on average willingness to pay; 2) *travel costs*, which use out-of-pocket expenses to indirectly measure consumer surplus; and 3) contingent valuation, which uses simulated markets in an interview process to estimate willingness to pay. In the contingent valuation method (CVM), a sample of the affected population are asked their maximum willingness to pay contingent on hypothetical change in existing recreational opportunities. R.G. Walsh describes each of these approaches in detail.[32]

Typically, at present, market values are measured directly and then compared to descriptions of recreational opportunities and public concerns. At best, this can only be described as a subjective decision making process which most managers give greater credence to than, say, the CVM estimate of those values.

One thing for certain is that the present practice of using participation levels as an estimate of the value of a given opportunity is a poor one because it assumes that all users value the resource equally. If that were the case, all one would have to do to capture more net benefits is somehow increase use. Sufficient case studies indicate that in various conditions a given resource may provide greater net benefits under low-density rather than high-density use. In that case, either the total benefits are high because users value the opportunity highly or costs soar under high-use conditions, or both.

The net benefits concept, however, is still a valuable one; Jubenville and Becker offer a simple constraints model that conceptually identifies the anchor having the greatest public benefits within a least-cost framework. Basically it is a filtering process where the most limiting constraints (Figure 3-3) are identified that delimit the segment of ROS (Figure 3-1) within which the resource allocation decision is made.

Limits of Acceptable Change (LAC). LAC, although not a new concept, is a maturing one that focuses on management prescriptions to achieve and maintain a given recreational opportunity. Earlier versions were spawned out of frustation with the carrying-capacity model where some magic number was sought as the cutoff limit for use of a given area. Unfortunately the early version of LAC seemed to focus on arbitrary standards to achieve an arbitrarily defined magic number — a backdoor approach to the "determination" of a carrying capacity.

The more mature version focuses on prescriptive rather than technical decision-making. That is, the manager decides what kind of general recreational use patterns are desired and then develops a set of prescriptions for the site that can cause the desired equilibrium. As part of that process, the manager must describe local conditions, the potential effects of recreation use on those conditions, the acceptable limits of change due to use, and then management prescriptions to achieve a given opportunity within LAC. In other words, the manager must describe in detail the equilibrium to be achieved and the factors which may limit that achievement (See Figure 3-3). Then he or she must specify those programs that will ensure, within these limiting factors, the achievement of equilibrium.

SUMMARY

The Recreational Opportunity Spectrum model, as presently operationalized by agencies, ignores input from the environmental setting. This chapter tries to incorporate that input into a holistic view of the recreational opportunity. It is the role of the manager to provide the recreational opportunity through the resource allocation process.

However, it is up to the user to respond to these opportunities, within his/her limitations of time and money, and experience a recreational activity that leads to personal satisfaction. The goal of the user is to maximize, within whatever personal constraints, his/her own utility function. This is the very reason, when we measure satisfaction at a given site, that we find satisfaction to be high with little dispersion around the mean.[4] It is also the very reason that researchers have not been able to establish a relationship between use density and satisfaction.[1,11,12] After all, if you are looking for a low-density opportunity, you don't select a high-density opportunity and expect to be satisfied.

If you try to achieve a given equilibrium on the ground and become frustrated because you always seem to overshoot or undershoot the target, don't give up. Management is not an exacting science. The answers cannot simply be cranked out of a microcomputer with mathematical precision. All decisions must be tempered with professional judgement, not personal value judgements. Even then the "right" answer must be continually refined and nurtured. We believe that what we said was, "All managers are human. They can't be replaced by the computer, so we must continually work hard to achieve any measure of success. And success is judged on how well we achieved the selected anchor point, or equilibrium, on the continuum of recreational opportunities."

SELECTED READINGS

1. Absher, J.D. and R.G. Lee. 1981. "Density As An Incomplete Cause of Crowding in Backcountry Settings." *Leisure Sciences* 4(3):231-247.

2. Becker, R., and A. Jubenville. 1981. "Displacement of Users Between the Lower St. Croix and Upper Mississippi Rivers." *Journal of Environment Management* 13(3):259-267.

3. Becker, R.H. 1983. "Forest-Recreation Management." *Forest Science*. R. Young (ed.). New York: John Wiley and Sons.

4. Boteler, F.E. 1984. "Carrying Capacity As a Framework for Managing White Water Use." *Journal of Park and Recreation Administration* 2(2):26-36.

5. Brown, P., B.L. Driver, and C. McConnell. 1978. "The Opportunity Spectrum Concept and Behavioral Information in Outdoor Recreation Resource Supply Inventories: Background and Application." *Integrated Inventories of Renewable Natural Resources: Proceedings of the Workshop.* USDA-Forest Service General Technical Report RM-55.

6. Buist, L.J., and T.A. Hoots. 1982. "The Recreational Opportunity Spectrum Approach to Resource Planning." *Journal of Forestry* 80:84-86.

7. Bultena, G., D. Field, P. Womble, and D. Albrecht. 1981. "Closing the Gates: A Study of Backcountry Use-Limitation at Mount McKinley National Park." *Leisure Sciences* 4(3):249-267.

8. Burch, W.R., Jr. 1981. "The Ecology of Metaphor — Spacing Regularities for Humans and Other Primates in Urban and Wildland Habitats," *Leisure Sciences* 4(3):213-230.

9. Clark, R.N., G.H. Stankey. 1979. *The Recreation Opportunity Spectrum: A Framework for Planning, Management, and Research.* USDA-Forest Service General Technical Report PNW-98.

10. Driver. B.L., and P.J. Brown. 1978. "The Opportunity Spectrum Concept in Outdoor Recreation Supply Inventories: An Overview," *Integrated Inventories of Renewable Resources: Proceedings of the Workshop.* USDA-Forest Service General Technical Report RM-55.

11. Graefe, A.R., J.J. Vaske, and F.R. Kuss. 1984. "Social Carrying Capacity: An Integration and Synthesis of Twenty Years of Research." *Leisure Sciences* 6(4):395-431.

12. Gramann, J.H. 1982. "Toward a Behavioral Theory of Crowding in Outdoor Recreation: An Evaluation and Synthesis of Research." *Leisure Sciences* 5(2):109-126.

13. Gum, R., S. Garifo, and J. Loomis. 1984. "Methodology and Activity Determinants of Recreational Values." Annual Meeting of the Regional Hatch Project, W-133, USDA, Las Vegas, NV.

14. Harris, C.C., B.L. Driver, and E.P. Bergersen. 1984. "Do Choices of Sport Fisheries Reflect Angler Preferences for Site Attributes." *Proceedings — Symposium on Recreation Choice Behavior,* p. 46-54.

15. Hendee, J.C., G.H. Stankey, and R.C. Lucas. 1978. *Wilderness Management.* USDA-Forest Service Miscellaneous Publication No. 1365, USGPO, Washington, DC.

16. Holmes, R.A. 1981. "Angler Effort, Exploitation and Values on the Upper Chena River, Alaska." MS Thesis (unpub.), University of Alaska, Fairbanks, Alaska.

17. Jubenville, A. 1986. "Recreational Use of Public Lands: The Role of the Manager." *Journal of Park and Recreation Administration* 3(4):53-60.

18. Jubenville, A. 1983. "Wilderness Recreation Management: A Conceptual Framework." *Alaska Science Conference Abstracts,* Whitehorse, Yukon Territory.

19. Jubenville, A., and R.H. Becker. 1983. "Outdoor Recreation Management Planning: Contemporary Schools of Thought (Chapter 4, Section 4)." *Recreation Planning and Management.* Lieber and Fesenmaier (eds.). State College, PA: Venture Publishing, Inc.

20. Jubenville, A., and J.K. Feyhl. 1986. "The Typical Recreation Planning Model Does Not Fit Large-Scale Alaskan Hydroelectric Projects." Unpublished manuscript. University of Alaska, Fairbanks, AK.

21. Jubenville, A., S.C. Matulich, and W.G. Workman. 1986. *Toward the Integration of Economics and Outdoor Recreation Management.* Bulletin 68, Agricultural and Forestry Experiment Station, University of Alaska, Fairbanks, AK.

22. Litton, R.B., Jr., and R.H. Twiss. 1967. "The Forest Landscapes: Some Elements of Visual Analysis." *Proceedings, Society of American Foresters,* pp. 212-214.

23. Nash, R. 1982. *Wilderness and the American Mind.* 3rd Edition. New Haven, CT: Yale University Press.

24. Schreyer, R. (ed.). 1984. "Theme Issue: Social Carrying Capacity." *Leisure Sciences* 6(4).

25. Schreyer, R., and R.C. Knopf. 1984. "The Dynamics of Change in Outdoor Recreation Environments — Some Equity Issues." *Journal of Park and Recreation Administration* 2:9-19.

26. Schreyer, R., R.C. Knopf, and D.R. Williams. 1984. "Reconceptualizing the Motive/Environment Link in Recreation Choice Behavior." *Proceedings — Symposium on Recreation Choice Behavior.* p. 9-18.

27. Schreyer, R., D.W. Lime, and D.R. Williams. 1984. "Characterizing the Influence of Past Experience on Recreation Behavior." *Journal of Leisure Research.* 16:34-50.

28. Schreyer, R., and J.W. Roggenbuck. 1978. "The Influence of Experience Expectations on Crowding Perceptions and Social Psychological Carrying Capacities." *Leisure Sciences* (4):373-394.

29. Stankey, G.H., S.D. McCool, and G.L. Stokes. 1984. "Limits of Acceptable Change: A New Framework for Managing the Bob Marshall Wilderness Complex." *Western Wildlands* 10(3):33-37.

30. Van Wagtendonk, J., and J.M. Benedict. 1980. "Wilderness Permit Compliance and Validity." *Journal of Forestry* 78(7):399-401.

31. Wagar, J.A. 1964. *The Carrying Capacity of Wild Lands for Recreation.* Forest Science Monograph 7, Society of American Foresters, Washington, D.C.

32. Walsh, R.G. 1986. *Recreation Economic Decisions: Comparing Benefits and Costs.* State College, PA: Venture Publishing, Inc.

CHAPTER FOUR

THE PROBLEM-SOLVING PROCESS

From our reading prior to this chapter, we know that an agency attempts to provide a given number of recreational opportunities. However, we also need to understand the process by which the system responds when something goes awry in creating those opportunities. The term "decision-making" suggests a rational process where you choose between conflicting courses of action to accomplish stated objectives based on some known input. Uncertainty, both in terms of input and probable outcome, is integral to the process.

In outdoor recreation, we often use limited biophysical and social baseline data in our decision-making. The uncertainty caused by the lack of information on a specific situation results in the possibility that a decision may not be the most desirable one. Decisions made with that type of uncertainty and risk — a situation that frequently arises in outdoor recreation — may ultimately lead to failure in accomplishing objectives.

S. Kassouf describes the decision-making process in terms of normative decision theory or the logic of deliberate choice under uncertainty.[12] These terms imply a formal and deliberate attempt to evaluate all circumstances, to formulate viable alternatives, and to choose a given alternative that will satisfy well-defined goals. For most day-to-day decisions, we do not use either a formal model or a formal process such as the normative decision theory, though we may follow a process subconsciously. In outdoor recreation, however, this process is useful. Problems arise when our orderly process of accomplishing objectives is disrupted.[3] This chapter focuses on the problem-solving process, which can be described as the process that is used to overcome disruptions and continue moving toward long-range goals. By understanding the problem-solving model, managers can better focus their efforts to achieve their goals, thus minimizing the effects of these problems.

THE PROCESS

Problem solving requires four elements: a model, concepts, an analytical process, and data. These need to be understood and then fused together in the problem-solving process.

Model. Before attemtping to solve a problem, we must understand the total system — subsystems consisting of program sites, specific programs, and interrelationships, as developed in Chapter Two. Usually a problem is isolated within one subsystem, but understanding the linkage between subsystems can help in identifying potential solutions and also minimize impact on other subsystems. In sum, a management model, if constructed properly, can give the manager a means of systematically and realistically viewing a decision in terms of its effects without using the "trial and error" process. No model is going to eliminate the uncertainty, but a systems approach should reduce it and thus improve decision-making.

Concepts. In Chapter Three we discuss a conceptual understanding of the manager's role in producing recreational opportunity. In summary, that opportunity is the anchor point along the recreational opportunity spectrum (ROS). You remember that the ROS is a continuum of management strategies as applied to a given *environmental setting*. That environmental setting is what attracts the visitor or clientele and gives value to the recreational opportunity. The package of management actions applied to the environmental setting determines the total number of people actually attracted; visitors respond to recreational opportunities in a multiplicative fashion (environmental setting x management action), and equilibrium is achieved between the general pattern of use and the recreational opportunity provided by management. Conceptually, a problem arises when we fail to achieve the desired equilibrium. Problem-solving must then be viewed as a new attempt to achieve a given equilibrium, or the predetermined anchor point on the ROS.

Analytical Process. When a manager is confronted with a problem, he or she needs not only a conceptual framework from which to approach the problem and a model to show relationships, but also an analytical process to organize the attack on the problem. The critical aspect is the proper identification of the problem. It can never be solved unless it can be identified, isolated, and articulated in terms that allow a meaningful response by the manager. Another critical necessity is a pool of competing alternative solutions.

Data. Ideally, baseline data collection should be part of the ongoing management program so we can more quickly recognize disruption in the recreation opportunity, or disequilibrium. We also have a better understanding of what conditions existed prior to disequilibrium, and what changes were introduced that may have caused the problem. But data are not always available and may not be worth the cost relative to a particular decision. Understanding the general systems model and the linkages within the system, along with some systematically collected observations over time, should allow you to mentally or graphically simulate the particular situation. Such a simulation may be sufficient for problem-solving in the absence of real data.

THE PROBLEM-SOLVING MODEL

The problem-solving model, a synthesis of

several potential models, shows the logical flow of events from the initial identification of a problem to the implementation of a course of action (See Figure 4-1). It is commonly called a sequential model because a sequence of events leads to a possible solution — not any single event. After determining that a problem exists, the next step is stating the exact nature of the problem. It needs to be described in a manner that the manager can respond to; the outcome of the whole process depends upon this. Developing a "pool" of alternative solutions is the next step. Various alternatives are examined and evaluated and the best solution chosen — one that reestablishes the desired equilibrium at the least cost in terms of both the particular course of action and support from the system's social environment.

You should consider three concepts in relation to the problem-solving model:

1. *Closed-system Versus Open-system Model* The open model varies in its degree of openness depending on demand and support for the final decision. In a closed model, there is a known set of alternatives, and the manager reaches a decision by a logical process. The closed model assumes the following:

   1. Objectives are predetermined.
   2. All alternatives are previously defined.
   3. Analyses of problems involve identifying and ranking the already-defined alternatives.
   4. Selected alternatives maximize objectives.

The closed model is typically used for solving routine problems. It helps the manager to handle these kinds of problems with a minimum input of time and effort. Many major management problems are often affected by external influences, but the closed model unfortunately treats them as if they did not exist.

An open model is a dynamic one that is influenced by external factors — including public opinion, as shown in Figure 2-4. This is the typical model for recreation

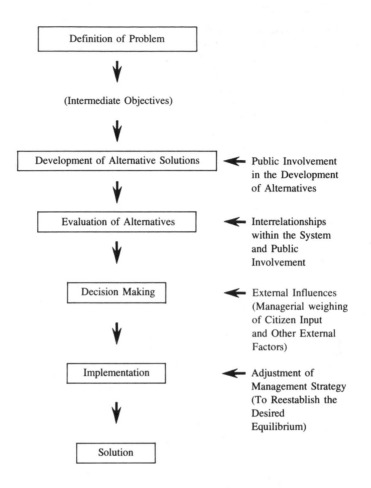

(Movement Back Toward Long-range Goals
and Agency Mission)

Figure 4-1. Open-system Problem-solving Model

management situations, one where the manager must deal with much uncertainty. By recognizing this, and monitoring external influences as well as internal ones, he or she can make better and more-informed decisions.

2. *Rationality of Choice*

A decision should be considered rational if it maximizes goal achievement within specified environmental constraints. Decisions have traditionally been viewed on a scale ranging from rational to irrational. The irrational ones are those that don't conform to constraints or maximize goal achievement.

D. Hellriegel and J.W. Slocum disagree with the traditional view; they consider a broader perspective of decision-making, especially that which involves value judgments — i.e., the conscious or subconscious choice of values by an individual or organization — to be *rational*.[11] Hellriegel and Slocum's model eliminates the problem of having to be either rational or irrational in decision-making. We may respond based on our personal value system, which they call being rational and which most of us are already guilty of doing. Irrationality is generally not accepted as a typical characteristic of decision-making; however, most people could not function in the role of decision maker if they were not allowed some freedom of choice or personal expression. In other words, complete rationality may not always be achievable. According to H.A. Simon, bounded rationality is what many people perceive as being the rational process. It is based on the following three elements:

1. Instead of seeking a single optimum solution to a problem, an individual might establish a very limited range of outcomes that would be satisfactory. He calls this *satisficing*.
2. An individual, to obtain the specified outcome, undertakes only a very limited search for possible alternatives.
3. Some factors outside the control of the decision-maker will ultimately affect the decisions. This further supports the precept that rationality is generally tied to a limited frame of reference from an individual perspective. Sometimes this frame of reference is the result of professional socialization.[18]

Decision-making, under bounded rationality, is portrayed as simplistic, pessimistic, and almost wholly rational. Thus bounded rationality affects the quality of decision-making in two ways: 1.) The scope of problem-solving process becomes very limited. All problems are treated as if you are dealing with a closed system. Solutions are often temporary, or worse, they cause problems rather than solving them. 2.) Management withholds or omits information from the public so as to minimize the influence of external factors — in essence trying to approximate a closed-system model.

In sum, all decisions are, to a certain degree, rational. In order to reduce irrationality and improve the level of decision-making, we must follow a logical, systematic process for arriving at a decision and realize that value judgments may ultimately have to be made. In that vein, it is probably a good idea for all of us to periodically take stock of our professional values and personality characteristics and appraise how they might influence our decisions, in spite of what might be called "the rational choice."

3. *Systems Effects*

For most problem-solving in outdoor recreation management, we must concern ourselves with the effects of our decisions on the total system — i.e., "systems effects." This is not necessarily a simple input/output relation; a decision that alters a given portion of the system may, in turn, have drastic effects on other portions of the system. For example, a manager may increase the service capacity of a large campground by adding more facilities. The increase in "head count" is based on an increase in demand and user perceptions which indicate that it would still be possible to provide an enjoyable camping opportunity — even with the addition of more people to the camping area.

But suppose the poorly designed new facilities disrupt the visual harmony of the entire site so that previous users rebel at the decision to expand service capacity and are displaced by a less-well-behaved class of users. Suppose the increase in service capacity at the campground causes overloading on the adjacent small lake, one of the primary attractors, which then causes increased user conflict and even safety hazards for certain users. Suppose the increased capacity results in an accelerated rate of deterioration for the vegetation on the adjacent sand dunes, which in turn causes the dunes to be closed to all recreationists. This then causes a decrease in attendance, since the dunes are one of the primary attractions for the camper.

This type of vicious circle is a potential consequence of a single decision; however, a knowledge of the systems model can help you to see the potential consequence before you implement the decision.

Definition of the Problem. Before we can solve a problem, we must first define it. According to J.J. Bannon[3] the simplest description is "something is wrong." In recreation, a problem is a deviation from the normal, expected, or desired outcome for a given situation; however, it only becomes meaningful when the manager recognizes it and takes corrective action to remedy it.

After identifying a flaw in the system, you should isolate the specific problem. To do this, you must gather as much information as possible, sort the data, eliminate the insignificant variables, and then try to fit the significant ones together to determine the problem. Isolating the specific problem can sometimes be so complicated that it requires a team of specialists. If it is not isolated, however, managers cannot take any specific actions and their best efforts become a trial-and-error process. The situation is analogous to changing parts on a car, hoping that something will work to make it run better.

To isolate a problem, you must identify all its effects. Individually or in clusters these effects point to a cause. Sorting and possibly eliminating some of the subproblems should also help to isolate the real problem. Remember that the real problem may continue or even get worse if we only attack the symptoms or subproblems.

In the example of the sand dunes, a problem occurred when the loss of stabilizing vegetation caused management to close them to public use. We are assuming that the dunes are unique; the long-range goal is to maximize the recreational and esthetic potential of the dunes while maintaining their fragile ecosystem. Loss of vegetation is symptomatic of an underlying problem. We can make our decision based only on symptoms and then attempt to re-establish vegetation, but this attempt is doomed to fail simply since the cause of the vegetation deterioration is not eliminated — i.e. overuse.

So we step back one level and look at the overuse problem. Overuse caused the vegetation loss; thus if we control overuse and reestablish vegetation, our problem should be solved. Right? Probably not! Overuse should realistically be viewed as a subproblem.

Remember that there was no deterioration of the vegetation until we expanded and changed the campground to meet the increased demand for camping. Perhaps the real problem is the expansion of the campground, which ultimately caused the overuse.

We could even suggest that the real problem is in the area plan, which allocates the resource for specific recreational opportunities. If there is a growing demand for both "duning" and camping, the manager may want to separate the two activities yet keep each of them reasonably available. In the long run, we may be causing or greatly contributing to the site deterioration of the magnificent dunes by allowing camping immediately adjacent to them.

We encourage much use by the casual camper merely through location, access, and attractiveness. This may reduce the availability of the dunes for those who are actually seeking a quality opportunity. If we do not recognize the link between management programs and user response, we may further complicate the malady by increasing the automobile camping opportunities adjacent to the dunes while trying to re-establish dune vegetation.

A third step in problem definition is articulating the symptoms, subproblems, and finally the real problem. We must be able not only to isolate the real problem but also to describe it in terms of present form, causes, and significant historical data. Without this articulation, managers and their staffs may not be able to reduce or eliminate the causes and will simply revert to the trial-and-error solution method.

We must establish some intermediate goals to resolve the problem once it has been isolated and articulated. We can then put the entire system back on course, moving toward our long-range goals. This could be compared to a sailor who sets off for a distant island. He is right on course when the rudder breaks. First he has to isolate the problem — the broken rudder. His intermediate objective is to fix the rudder (elminate the cause of the malfunction). Once the problem is solved, he regains his original course and continues toward his long-range objective. This example may seem oversimplified, but it does show the proper sequence.

Development of Alternative Solutions. There are many ways of developing a pool of potential solutions, including:

1. Scoping sessions with staff, based on their previous experiences,
2. Scoping sessions with the interested public,
3. Review of literature, particularly previous management plans, case studies, etc.,
4. Contractual studies, and
5. Expert testimony.

Probably as significant as any of the above are the scoping sessions with your staff. These are the people who are the most knowledgeable and intimately involved with your particular problem. In fact, you should discover the most solutions this way, with the remaining portion coming from the other four alternatives. In most cases, a well-informed public can also contribute greatly to the pool of potential solutions.

What will be emphasized here are not the traditional ways of developing an array of alternative solutions with your staff, but a way of expanding that ability to discover new, potential solutions to often nagging, chronic problems. The process is called *brainstorming*, a term often equated with creative thinking.[3] In this process, the staff is encouraged to offer unrestrained ideas about solving the problem, without regard to the appropriateness of any proposed solution. This is where the problem solver allows him or herself the freedom to conjure up new alternatives for solving a problem without social, legal, or organizational constraints. Brainstorming encourages new ideas without judgments as to quality. Too often, we mentally evaluate an alternative and summarily dismiss it because it is too "far out." Brainstorming encourages new ideas — the "farther-out," the better.

It works like this. The problem solver and his staff are seated around a conference table while the specific problem is presented to the team. Everyone is given an opportunity to respond and solutions are initially stated in general terms, though more specific details usually come to the forefront as the group process proceeds. No judgments are passed on the ideas. When a judgment is deferred, there tends to be a maximum output of ideas, both in number and quality. The process continues until a reasonable number of ideas are recorded.

Too often brainstorming is viewed as an undisciplined, disorganized rap session by a group of organizational misfits. It is not felt to be logical. This type of criticism arises from the bounded mechanism with which most problem solvers surround themselves. Without new ideas, we would stagnate, and brainstorming is one way of reaching out for new, creative approaches to problem-solving.

In reality, brainstorming is not something that can be done well without training and practice. It may seem simple on the surface, but it is difficult to actually do. Most people feel strange in their first session; they feel too inhibited to formulate far-out ideas because of their education, professional training, and associations. With time and effort, however, a problem-solver can discard bounded rationality and search for new ideas to solve the problems that plague us. If this type of approach to problem-solving can be developed through training and practice, there is hope that in the future we will be better able to face and actually solve difficult problems.

Evaluating Alternatives. Judging the alternatives developed during brainstorming has been relegated to a separate step. No alternative should be either dismissed summarily or evaluated superficially and your evaluation should be viewed as reduction or elimination of the worst and reexamination of the best. The process does not simply mean perusing a few alternatives and selecting the best one. It is a concentrated effort in which the problem solver seeks all available information about each alternative, attempts to sort the information based on pertinence to the problem, eliminates undesirable alternatives through a series of reviews, and then ranks the better ones. You should make no attempt, at this point, to reach a decision.

After evaluating, you should also set aside those solutions which do not fit the intermediate objectives. At this point in the problem-solving process, the old-fashioned problem-solver often dismisses new ideas or alternatives, claiming that they will not work, that they are too expensive, or that they do not meet objectives. But this is a "cop-out," a reversion to bounded mechanism and a "why bother?" attitude. We have to stay in tune with the whole process if we are really going to solve today's problems today.

Begin by screening and classifying the more viable alternatives. Then sort and classify ideas into groups for analysis. They should be critically evaluated in relation to the established long-range objectives, and this evaluation should be just as judicious and creative as the development phase has been up to this point. In all cases, the effort extended should be equal to the complexity of the problem. Problems having obvious solutions may not require many steps in the problem-solving process; this is the closed system model of problem solving. Thus you do not need to spend a great deal of time and effort to arrive at a solution. For more complex problems, you should employ the open system model. In this way, you can search for new ideas among the staff and the public, then spend an appropriate amount of time evaluating each idea. Where a problem does not rate full-scale public involvement, use key people such as an advisory board.

In the dune problem, interrelated factors would include the following: information about the resource system (the dune ecosystem and the effects of visitor use); the visitor subsystem, including types of behavior patterns, visitors' perceptions of the recreational opportunities, and social impact; and the service subsystem. Questions concerning how the entire area was planned, why that particular campground was expanded, and what effects different decisions have had on existing use patterns must be answered before we can determine, at least hypothetically, what will be the effects of a particular alternative. Remember the immediate

objective — to stabilize the dune system — and the long range objective — to offer a quality hiking experience in that unique dune formation. It is hoped that the final decision reflects a combination of alternatives that best satisfy the problem at hand and consider the interrelated factors of management system, agency constraints on fiscal resources, public interest, and available information. Perhaps in the future, this approach will provide more and better information for decision-making.

Decision-making. The problem solver and the decision-maker may be the same person, or the information, analysis, and alternatives (including a priority listing) may be turned over to the manager or decision-maker by a staff specialist who has handled the problem. How this is handled is determined by the size and organization of a particular agency and the extent of the problem itself. The decisions made to solve a problem at each step ultimately determine the outcome; thus every step leading to the decision must be given careful attention. The decision-maker must be made aware of the potential effects of all alternatives so that when the decision is made results can be reasonably well predicted.

The final decision is generally influenced by external factors, including interest-group concerns, legislative mandates, time constraints, budgeting processes, trade-offs in other areas of operation, and so forth. On the dune problem, external factors that affect the decision may include a conservation organization that uses newspapers and television to argue for handling the problem in a particular manner. Perhaps a special envoy is even sent from a conservation organization's national headquarters to persuade the managing agency to permanently close the dunes to recreational use. Or they complain to Congress or take you to court. To counteract this, a state businessmen's organization may claim that there is no problem and that all that the agency is trying to do is drive them out of business. Then Senator Smith calls on the phone and says that he wants to hold a special hearing. Existing laws do permit this type of hearing, but it is not mandatory.

After reflecting on the existing situation,

you may decide that an environmental assessment report is necessary before you can proceed with the decision. Has the situation gotten out of control? Has it been blown out of proportion? Probably not! There are other external factors to be considered — environmental effects beyond the immediate area, regional economies, national goals, legal requirements, and reductions in other programs to concentrate on this one. The list may be almost unlimited, but the interest group's criticisms and the Senator's interest might have been avoided if you systematically involved affected groups in the problem-solving process. Perhaps this is the justification for separating problem analysis from decision-making. The problem-solver should probably be two people, each with a distinct role. The problem analyzer (probably a staff person) who would bring the process up to the point of decision making and involve the public, and the decision-maker, who would weigh external factors and make a final decision.

As part of the problem-solving procedure, managers may choose to have alternatives and evaluations reviewed by each major staff person, called jurying. Jurying provides an opportunity for a specialist to weigh the information that is related to his/her own area of expertise and to make certain recommendations which are based on this knowledge. Theoretically, jurying serves two purposes. First, it can create a better, more widely accepted decision because of the quality of the individual input. Second, it can create a more congenial atmosphere for the final decision to be supported and implemented. Also, never forget the potentially interested public. Involve them early in the problem-solving process. They will better support the outcome if they have had part in the decision.

Implementation. A decision can only be as effective as its implementation. Thus you must develop detailed strategies to put a plan into action. These strategies should include how a plan will be accomplished, when it will be accomplished, who will be involved, and what will be needed. The implementation of sensitive decisions may also require additional public involvement because, while they may agree with the proposed course of action, they may not agree with the actual implementation vehicle.

Too often a bad decision is blamed on errors in the problem-solving phase. In fact, most problem-oriented decisions that have been well thought out fail in the implementation phase for reasons such as lack of staff support, the unwillingness of a manager to commit the necessary resources, an inadequate time framework, or an uninvolved public.

The success of problem solving depends upon both a decision which is well-conceived and relevant to the specific problem and an implementation plan which is given sufficient staff support, resources, time, and public involvement. Many problems have evolved over years of neglect; it may take many more years to solve them properly. In general, the interested public has to be made aware of the time limitation, and most people are receptive to that limitation. Often, certain phases of a plan must be accomplished before the other phases can be implemented. If we proceed too rapidly, we may skip a step and doom the decision to failure.

In the case of the dune ecosystem, it may take years to fully reestablish vegetation, even though use has been either eliminated or restricted to certain paths. If use is allowed to continue at low levels over the entire area with reasonable controls, it may still take ten to fifteen years to revegetate, or perhaps forever.

For a long implementation period, it is necessary to monitor the results of each phase, possibly changing strategy to better implement the decision. This final phase of problem-solving is one of developing strategies, making task-oriented decisions, adjusting strategy, and supervising work needed to fully implement the decision that was reached through problem analysis. We may wish to put the program back on course, proceeding ultimately toward long-range goals and maintaining public support. But problem-solving is not complete until we have fully implemented the decision and returned the errant program to the originally charted course.

SELECTED READINGS

1. Albrecht, K. 1984. *Brain Building: Easy Games to Develop Your Problem-Solving Skills.* Englewood Cliffs, NJ: Prentice-Hall, Inc.

2. Anderson, B.F. 1980. The *Complete Thinker: A Handbook for Creative and Critical Problem Solving.* Englewood Cliffs, NJ: Prentice-Hall, Inc.

3. Bannon, J.J. 1972. *Problem Solving in Recreation and Parks.* Englewood Cliffs, NJ: Prentice-Hall, Inc.

4. Blake, R.R., and J.S. Mouton, 1961. *Group Dynamics — Key to Decision Making.* Houston: Gulf Publishing Co.

5. Braybrooke, D., and C.E. Lindblom. 1963. *A Strategy of Decision.* New York: The Free Press.

6. Brinkers, H.S. 1972. *Decision-Making: Creativity, Judgement, and Systems.* Columbus, Ohio: Ohio State University Press.

7. Collins, B.E., and H. Guetzkow. 1964. *A Social Psychology of Group Processes for Decision-Making.* New York: John Wiley & Sons, Inc.

8. Festinger, L. 1964. *Conflict, Decision, and Dissonance.* Stanford, CA: Stanford University Press.

9. Fox, I.K. 1970. ''The Nature of Planning Decisions in a Democratic Society,'' *Elements of Outdoor Recreation Planning.* Driver, B.L. (ed.). Ann Arbor, MI: University of Michigan Press.

10. Gore, W.J. 1964. *Administrative Decision-Making: A Heuristic Model.* New York: John Wiley & Sons, Inc.

11. Hellriegel, D., and J.W. Slocum, Jr. 1982. *Management: A Contingency Approach.* 3rd edition. Reading, MA: Addison-Wesley Publishing Co.

12. Kassouf, S. 1970. *Normative Decision-Making.* Englewood Cliffs, NJ: Prentice-Hall, Inc.

13. Kaufman, H. 1967. *The Forest Ranger.* Baltimore: The John Hopkins Press.

14. Kepner, C.H., and B.B. Tregoe. 1976. *The New Rational Manager.* Princeton, NJ: Princeton Research Press.

15. Koontz, H. (ed.). 1964. *Toward A Unified Theory of Management.* New York: McGraw-Hill Book Co.

16. Pressman, J.L., and A. Wildavsky. 1984. *Implementation.* 2nd edition. Berkeley: University of California Press.

17. Schlaifer, R.O. 1969. *Analysis of Decisions Under Uncertainty.* New York: McGraw-Hill Book Co.

18. Simon, H.A. 1976. *Administrative Behavior,* 3rd edition, New York: The Free Press.

19. Stevens, L.A. 1984. *Thinking Tools.* Stockton, CA: Stevens and Shea Publishers.

20. Twight, B.W., and M.S. Carroll. 1983. ''Workshops in Public Involvement: Do They Help Find Common Ground? *Journal of Forestry* 81(11):732-734

21. Wickelgren, G. 1974. *How to Solve Problems.* San Francisco: W.H. Freeman & Co.

22. Van Grundy, A.B. 1981. *Techniques of Structured Problem Solving* New York: Van Norstrand Reinhold Co.

CHAPTER FIVE

INVOLVEMENT OF THE PUBLIC
IN DECISION-MAKING

In the last chapter, we identified several instances where public participation could or should be used in deciding what to do about a problem. In this chapter, we detail the specifics on obtaining participatory input from the social environment of our open system. Twenty years ago, public involvement was minimal and public apathy was great. Agencies seemed to prefer this arrangement because it meant little interference with management decisions. It certainly made decision-making much easier. Today, we seem now to want to go to the other extreme — to maximize user input. Yet we often seem to neither understand the limits of the system feedback we receive, nor have any good notion of how to incorporate it into decision-making.

Today's interest in involving the public in decision-making is an outgrowth of the environmental movement of the late 1960s and 1970s. People clamored to be heard on environmental issues, and interest groups pushed to institutionalize the process for public involvement, requiring agencies to air issues of resource use before the affected public. We now have laws and regulations in place to guarantee public involvement. However, there is no single guaranteed, foolproof technique for assessing public opinion and incorporating it into decision-making. We do know that public involvement strategy must be tailored to each particular situation. The overriding concern is the "reconciliation of conflicting minority interest groups, not the satisfaction of a silent majority."[5]

PUBLIC OPINION

In order to better understand how public input is related to decision-making, we must first understand public opinion in terms of how it is formed, why it is formed, and to what it responds. Public opinion has been summarized by H. Cantril into the following four principles:

1. *Identification Principle.* People ignore an idea, an opinion, or a point of view unless they can see clearly that it affects their personal fears, desires, hopes, or aspirations. Your message must be stated in terms of the interest of your audience.
2. *Action Principle.* People do not buy ideas that lack action. This may be either action taken (or about to be taken) by the sponsor of the idea or action that can be conveniently taken by the people to prove the merit of the idea. Unless a means of action is provided, people tend to shrug off appeals.
3. *Principle of Familiarity and Trust.* We buy ideas only from those we trust; we are influenced by or adopt only those opinions and points of view espoused by individuals, corporations, or institutions in whom we have confidence. A person is not likely to listen to or believe someone unless he or she has confidence in the speaker.
4. *Clarity Principle.* The situation must be clear to us — not confusing. Information we observe, read, see, or hear must also be clear — not subject to several interpretations. To communicate, you must employ words, symbols, or stereotypes that receivers can understand.[9]

These principles present some interesting characteristics of public opinion. If the public is to respond, information and ideas must affect his or her well-being or self-interest. Self-interest may be based on economic, aesthetic, or other concerns, so an issue, to have meaning for and cause the individual to actively respond, must be of personal importance. A person may feel he or she cannot tolerate the situation or contemplated action of the agency, or may feel compelled by the group norms of an organization. Despite involvement in organizational action, that person must still feel a personal commitment in relation to the issue.

None of this may actually take place unless the issue itself is clear. The public will then respond according to self-interest and the sense of urgency that stimulates a personal course of action. For any given issue, only a small portion of the population will become involved. The remainder simply do not feel the need or are already involved in more important activities. Today as never before, we lead socially complex lifestyles — at work, at home, and during leisure we have overcommitted our time and personal energy. If important social issues are to be faced, we must first reorient our priorities. At best, we can carefully select the issues we become involved with, and there are hundreds to choose from. While it may be easy to narrow down that list, we must still structure our priorities within that list.

Finally, the source of information drastically affects how people will respond. If we have confidence in the source and the political sytem, we may be more willing to respond in a positive, aggressive way. If we are alienated from the source, we may choose to ignore the issue or to respond in a strongly negative fashion.

In sum, influencing public opinion requires good communication; the message must be clear, identify the issue, give cause for action, and come from a reliable source. Nevertheless, only a limited number of people become involved at any one time. It is hoped that we can, in some way, dissect this problem to find out not only what sways public opinion but also how people arrive at their conclusions.

Based on a ten-year study, Cantril summarized public opinion in the following axioms:

1. *Opinion* is highly sensitive to *important events* (particularly mistakes).

2. *Events of unusual magnitude* are likely to *swing public opinion temporarily from one extreme to another.* Opinion does not become stabilized until the implications of events are seen with some perspective.

3. *Opinion* is generally *determined more by events than by words* — unless those words are themselves interpreted as an "event."

4. Verbal statements and outlined courses of actions have maximum importance when opinion is unstructured and people are seeking some intrepretation from a trusted source.

5. By and large, *public opinion does not anticipate emergencies;* it only reacts to them.

6. From the viewpoint of social psychology, *opinion* is basically *determined by perceived self-interest.* Events, words, and other stimuli affect opinion only insofar as they relate to this self-interest, and part of it is stimulated by the leadership in an individual's reference group.

7. Opinion does not remain aroused for any long period of time unless people feel the issue acutely involves their self-interest or unless the opinion aroused by group/community leaders is sustained by events.

8. *Once perceived self-interest is involved, opinions are not easily changed.*

9. *In a democracy, public opinion is likely to be ahead of official policy* when it involves self-interest.

10. When an *opinion is held by a slight majority* or not solidly structured, an *acknowledged fact tends* to *shift opinion* in the direction of acceptance.

11. At critical times, people become more sensitive to the *adequacy* of *their leadership*. If *they have confidence in it, they are willing to delegate greater responsibility;* if they lack confidence in it, they become less tolerant.

12. *People are less reluctant to have critical decisions made by their leaders if* they feel that somehow they, *the people, are taking some part in the decisions.*

13. *People have more opinions* and *are able to form opinions more easily about goals* than

about the methods necessary to reach those goals.

14. *Public opinion,* like individual opinion, *is colored by desire, and* when *opinion is based chiefly on desire rather than information,* it is *likely to fluctuate sharply with events.*

15. By and large, if people in a *democracy are provided educational opportunities* and ready access to information, *public opinion reveals a hardheaded common sense.* The *more enlightened people are about the implications of events* and proposals for their own self-interest, the *more likely they are to agree with the objective opinions of realistic experts.*[9]

The above statements summarize public opinion and how it is formed. The public reacts to identified issues, particularly perceived threats. These reactions are caused by events, rumors, prejudices, and stereotypes, and are generally correlated with level of education and perceived personal effects. If the public perceives itself as able to participate in decision-making, the intensity of their reaction will be based, to a certain degree, on their level of confidence in the leadership. It is the responsibility of the agency to develop and maintain the public trust. While people are better able to form decisions about goals than about methods of reaching these goals, they often have strong feelings on methods. Maintaining public trust often requires that the public be consulted on methods *as well as* goals, and the manager must be sensitive to public opinion. Finally, people should have access to information and be able to interpret it so that they can formulate a common-sense response to an issue, which is what Phase 1 is all about.

PUBLIC INVOLVEMENT AS A PROCESS

Today's public is better educated, interested in the management of public resources, and often well-versed on local management issues. More people and organizations are demanding the right to participate in decision-making. True feelings, however, are sometimes masked by the game-playing that occurs at public meetings. Organized groups may polarize the public in the hope that a compromise decision will be reached in their favor, or they may use the public meeting as an opportunity to deliberately create conflict. In such cases, input often is not very viable, and nothing is really accomplished except for the venting of feelings.

To make public involvement work satisfactorily requires commitment on the part of the manager. The manager's responsibility is to inform the user of the facts about a particular issue and to educate him as to how these facts fit together in the context of decision-making. Unfortunately, manager(s) often have only an intuitive feel for the significances of particular variables and how they might affect the outcome of the decision.

For example, a federal agency recently put out a draft resource management plan to which interested members of the public were supposed to respond with useful input that could be incorporated into the final plan. The plan included an inventory, four alternative plans, an environmental impact analysis, and applicable statutes. Detailed review showed that much of the data was not helpful in understanding or evaluating alternatives because of the way the agency had written them; only one of the four alternative plans could actually be implemented. Consequently public input on the document was worthless, except perhaps as a soothing ritual and a guarantee that only what the agency wanted to do in the first place would be selected. To legitimize the final recommended plan (which was alternative B — the only possible choice) pages of names of public participants were incorporated. A summary response stating that an additional 189 written comments had been received, reviewed and considered was also included. Serious input was obviously not encouraged in this case, nor were the comments apparently given more than a superficial review.

We seemingly solicit public comments because the law requires us to do so. Not much energy or imagination goes into the effort. Yet that is not the impression we get when we talk with managers. They want to improve public participation, but seem to have difficulty in breaking away from proven methods or methods required by law. In that context, this chapter is no revelation either. Hopefully the message that you do receive is that there is nothing wrong with the idea of public involvement but that some adjustments are needed. These include more critical links in the overall process, the applicability of particular ways of involving the public in particular situations, and the realization that the affected public should be involved in goal setting and establishing alternative ways of achieving such goals, as well as selecting the

Before examining this process, we should define "public opinion," the expected input. According to *Webster's New World Dictionary*, it is "the opinion of the people, generally as a force in determining social and political action." By definition, then, an anticipated result is some impact on decision-making. Yet many people are alienated because they feel a decision has already been made, and others enter a situation with an even more naive perspective — that they will have an impact on outcome. Tactics may vary from simple shows of power, to the power of logical thinking. But for the most part the public often becomes frustrated because they feel they have little impact. And the agency, as suggested in the above example, often spends much time and money for very little useful input while appearing to involve the public in decision making.

The following section attempts to address these concerns, from both the manager's and user's point of view. Rather than immediately assessing the potential of various methods, the discussion will focus on the total process, crticial links within it, and the roles/perspectives of the manager and user.

Figure 5-1 presents a flow model of the total involvement process. There are three phases to this process:

1. *Identification and enumeration of the issue.* The public issue is identified, investigated, and reported to the public through various media.
2. *Formulation of public opinion.* The individual, often via community or group leaders whom they respect, filters the information, integrates it with his or her own beliefs, and arrives at a conclusion.
3. *Integration of public input into decision-making.* The intent is to obtain feedback that can be used in decision-making.

Identification and Enumeration Phase. Identified issues for a particular area may include anticipating problems and needs by an agency, public response, or legal requirements. Some agencies use scoping techniques to identify issues involved with some proposed project, the revamping of a management plan, etc. Issues arise continuously. Some are important and some aren't, so management must determine relative significance in terms of public support of the agency. Usually issues arise because of change, or proposed change,

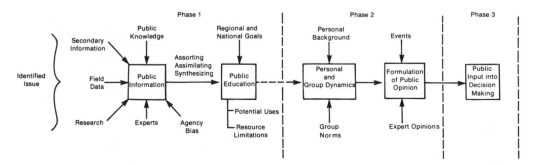

Figure 5-1. Model for Formulation and Integration of Public Opinion into Management Decision-making

in the agency programs. The question is how much change requires public involvement in decision-making. While there is no absolute answer, the best response is probably that signficant issues arise when the recreational opportunity is to be altered or when a well-known environmental feature is to be changed. The assumption is that social succession takes place, significantly altering the benefits to society. (See Chapter Three.)

While there are legal requirements for involving the public in decision-making in certain situations, these do no more than separate the significant from the insignificant issues. Beyond that, it is the responsibility of the manager to identify and prioritize issues where public consultation is important. Failure to do so may ultimately force dissatisfied parties into the political or judicial arena where results are often less than satisfactory. This means that the manager must monitor both the resource and the interested public through various media.

Once the issue has been isolated, the agency must then formally initiate an involvement process so that it can obtain the most useful input from the public. Information and education programs are the responsibility of the manager, and the rest of the process is dependent on the effort extended in the initial phase. In other words, if the manager does not do his job in Phase 1, the collective opinions formed in Phase 2 will probably not be very useful in decision-making. All available information should first be collected and then assimilated and verified before any additional field data collection is begun. In this way, field data can be used to verify existing data or to fill in any gaps in the available information. Too often, we duplicate our efforts by initiating field data collection before considering the information that is already available. In our haste, we may either collect too much data or require a greater degree of precision than is really necessary.

Data should be made available to the public in some useful form so that they also have the pertinent information on which to base their opinions. A majority of interested "publics" today are sophisticated enough to

understand the information if it is presented in a suitable manner, though they may need some assistance in interpreting data. This openness about the issue and related data can help in obtaining better public input and reducing public suspicion about "closed-shop" decision-making.

The manager must also educate the public, through interpretation of data, about the potential and limitations of an area for certain kinds of recreational opportunities. Potential rests with the attractiveness of the resource. It also depends on the ability of the resource to sustain recreational use; institutional constraints such as laws, policies, budget, and past land use; the existing situation; and the vision of management (See Figure 3-3). If the manager synthesizes this information and presents it in a straightforward manner to the public such that they know that the decision is to be made within a narrow segment of the Recreational Opportunity Spectrum, then feedback is more meaningful to the decision-maker. The example in the introductory section, where among Alternative Plans A, B, C, & D, only B can be implemented, is evidence that the process should have eliminated all *but* B. Public comments could then be sought on alternative ways of achieving B — B_1, B_2, . . . B_N. In this way, public input is based on knowledge and rational judgment and useful in the final decision. Furthermore, the public understands the trade-offs if such a course of action is implemented. Trade-offs are the recreational plans that are foregone in order to develop a particular recreation opportunity.

The need for education, as well as its potential effects, has been misunderstood. Some feel that public opinion should not be "manipulated" by information, that public sentiments should be unconstrained and or untainted by managers. Yet received input is often unusable because no reason is given for an opinion or it is based on misinformation. Educational sessions can help reduce misinformation, misunderstanding, and misjudgment. As a result, the quality of rational public input improves, and the quantity increases because of greater confidence in the agency. Even so, there are limitations. Each person has a unique personality and, in his or her own way, filters information in order to arrive at an opinion. Everyone also has biases related to specific situations or objects. We cannot eliminate these, nor should we try; but we can hope that each individual can become better prepared to make a rational, public-interest-oriented choice and can better understand his or her reasons for making that choice.

Formulation of Public Opinion Phase. The information and education process completes Phase 1. Phase 2 involved personal decision-making in which the individual, having a free choice to make, attempts to formulate his or her own opinions on an issue. There are actually two parts to this phase — personal and group dynamics. The personal involves unique background, beliefs, and biases that affect the information. The group involves responses as a member of a reference group — as a professional, as a conservation club member, as a snowmobiler, or as a businessman for example. The individual may also incorporate group norms and social expectations into his or her opinion. A decision may be further tempered by trends in events or the opinions of experts in whom the individual has confidence. This is why the television networks were requested to stop issuing election returns until the polls had closed. The networks were, in fact, influencing the final vote.

Phase 2 is the responsibility of the user. As mentioned earlier, on important issues the user forms an opinion based on available information. This does not mean that what is presented by the manager is received, accepted, and utilized by the individual. However, if done properly, through the proper media, the probability increases that the information affects public opinion. That probability is also influenced by other factors such as individual perception of the issue and individual trust or confidence in the agency.

Integration of Public Input Into the Decision Making Process. There is a need to effectively and objectively analyze public input on an issue so that managers can evaluate and

integrate it into the final decision, modifying the decision as necessary. This has been the greatest shortcoming to proper use of public input. The following four steps can help you integrate public input into a decision.

Analysis. According to R.N. Clark and G.H. Stankey, "the analysis process summarizes and displays the nature, content, and extent of input received."[10] A. Bleiker and H. Bleiker add that its objective should be to relay public messages to the decision-maker with minimal distortion and loss of detail.[7] No judgment should be made on its value or its applicability. Clark and Stankey recommend an applied content analysis approach to sort the information relayed in a manner useful to the manager. It is desirable to know not only what was said and who said it but also how it was said. As input, form letters and petitions are generally considered to be less important than personal letters.

Evaluation. Unlike analysis, evaluation is subjective in that the information is filtered and interpreted in relation to the issue; it should follow, however, a logical and objective process that relates information to the maintenance of system support (as shown in Chapter Four), in order to arrive at some conclusions about the input and incorporate these into the final decision. Considering the principles of public opinion, it seems desirable to interpret the input according to specific objectives. Sometimes these objectives can be compatible and accommodated within some overall goal for an area.

It is important in the analysis process to differentiate among local, regional, and national public input since the nature of the decision may merit weighing input in the evaluation step. Some issues may reflect broad national and regional concerns; others may more directly affect local conditions within minimal regional concerns.

In sum, evaluation is an interpretation of the validity and significance of public comments and an examination of these comments in relation to a particular issue. Knowing both the balance of opinion and the supporting rationale is critical; these elements define public values on any issue, and both are important to maintaining positive support from the social environment of the system.

Integration. Integrating requires consideration of public input, as evaluated by the manager, along with other factors such as legal responsibility, fiscal constraints, resource capability, environmental effects, and related social and economic conditions. It should be understood that the public input must be considered by the manager making a decision.

Implementation. Implementation requires program objectives which refine management goals in operational terms. Specific management prescriptions flow from these program objectives. For example, a goal might be to maintain ecological succession under "pre-Columbian conditions" in a particular wilderness. The focus would be on how to best accomplish this — let burn, control burn, or no burn — for each major management unit within the wilderness. Specific prescriptions would show exactly what needs to be done under particular conditions within a management unit, including the fact that public opinion is against the "let burn" policy. This would necessitate a greater interpretive effort, aimed at fire-ecology education.

The question is, How does public involvement fit into this problem-solving and decision process? On the surface, anyone who has ever actively participated as part of the public would give the obvious answer: "It doesn't fit." While this may be a legitimate condemnation of some management planning efforts, it should not arise if public involvement has been carried out earlier in the planning process, if *goals, objectives,* and *prescriptions* have been developed. Generally, management puts too much behind-the-scenes effort into forming goals and objectives, and then asks for and judges public input relative to those objectives only. The inordinate amount of staff time, data collection, and ego involved here are wasted because the agency predetermines the decision anyway.

What needs to be done, as suggested earlier in Chapter Two, is to use the public-involvement workshop to develop the set of objectives. Then groups with differing views can be sure their position is represented, and

their workshop representatives can come to grips with costs and trade-offs. In each succeeding level, they can acquire new data as needed and make refinements based on that data. These refinements can include not only strategy but also the goals and particularly the objectives.

If the public is involved at every level, they can help refine goals, objectives, and resulting management prescriptions, which is what T. Gallagher calls *cycle planning.*[17] The problem from a public involvement perspective, which cycle planning helps to overcome, is that with a static set of goals and objectives, the outcome (management prescription) may appear as essentially predetermined. Without being able to influence management objectives, the public understandably feels thwarted — no, frustrated — in its ability to influence the outcome. With cycle planning, they feel they have played a definite part.

APPLICATION

Media for Public Involvement. The following are the various media through which public involvement is encouraged. No one approach is completely satisfactory and each may be applicable for specific situations. Thus an agency may use all these media at any one time, even on a single issue.

Public Hearings. Public hearings are generally formal meetings in which testimony is given about a particular issue. Presentations must be prescheduled and are often recorded. While the potential is to reach large numbers of people at minimal cost, the actual number may be small and the costs very high. If many people *do* turn out for a meeting, feelings are probably very strong and the meeting may degenerate into polarized camps that play more to the audience than to management.[6] Because of this, group leaders often posture and exaggerate their views, hoping to mobilize additional public opinion in their direction. Thus issues are rarely discussed in a compromising fashion; that is, the focus is on points about which the various camps do not agree.

Public Workshops. Public workshops are designed to encourage discussion among participants. In order to direct that discussion, managers must establish an agenda. Then participants are presented with information about an issue and segregated into small informal groups for discussion and formulating a course of action. In the final step, the groups interact with one another so that each has the opportunity to hear the others' positions as well as to advocate its own. Ideally this format should allow participants the opportunity to search for those areas of interest that they have in common or can agree on; then negotiations focus on those items about which they do not agree.[6]

If the agency does its part in presenting all available information, defining the arena within which the decision will be made and sticking to the agenda, results should be beneficial to the decision-maker. However, members of organized groups often feel disadvantaged without their own information experts, particularly if they do not trust the agency or the opposition.

Solicitation. Solicitation of comments on public issues allows the individual to respond in writing to some prepared statement. Such general solicitation encourages feedback from the public, often in conjunction with a public hearing, public workshop, or prepared statement by the agency. While this may constitute a large percentage of the responses, often the information is not useful because people react to the wrong issue or area, or state their views in terms that are too general. Sometimes responses are even mass-produced, signed, and submitted by people who may have only peripheral interests.

Surveys. Surveys of public opinion on an issue, planning task, or management policy can give insight into visitor perceptions of both the problem and its possible solutions. These can help in making judgments about the effects of particular management strategies on the user or potential user. The potential user is important because often the most significant problems are those created by change. With change comes a new aggregate user population that may not recognize its self-interest until after the project/program is implemented. Thus surveying potential user populations can give better insight into total public opinion. The problem is that surveys are expensive, time-consuming, and often difficult to properly develop (questionnaire, sampling, and data analysis).

Advisory Committees. These committees may be formal or informal, but they all counsel the manager on general policy or specific issues. They should be aware that their role is only advisory. Each major administrative unit or program should probably have a formal committee that represents major segments of the public and that solicits public opinion. This opens a regular formal channel for public-management interactions but does not eliminate the need for general public input. Such formal interactions allow both committee members and agency people to explore a question more thoroughly, examine information more crticially, and arrive at a decision more deliberately. The informal committee can also give the manager a sounding board in lieu of general public input if it is composed of key individuals in dominant social positions. However, management must recognize that while the quality of the input can improve, all committees may not represent the public at large.

Continual Contacts. Continual contact with groups or associations of interested individuals can keep channels of communication open. A manager who is selective in his or her group contacts should also maximize the effectiveness of this technique, e.g., you can't just solicit input from the snowmobile club and ignore the cross-country club, unless the issue is the design and/or improvement of an already allocated snowmobile trail. Nevertheless, if you contact the group on their own turf without an adversary across the table, discussions should be less pretentious and more focused on issues of concern to both the club and management.

Expert Opinion. Expert opinion can be solicited on specific issues in relation to technical aspects — behavioral modeling, resource damage, and so forth — however, it is still up to the manager to make the decision by weighing the evidence and public opinion.

A Plausible Approach — The Workshop.
Soliciting and analyzing public opinion are
formidable tasks to which there are no easy
approaches. A complex approach may cause
people not to respond, but a simple one may
result in input that is not useful. The public
workshop can offer a balanced solution that
encourages maximum public input while
obtaining useful feedback. It also fits the basic
model (See Figure 5-1). To produce the
workshop model, one additional phase is
needed — the interphase, which is between
Phase 1, Identification and Enumeration of the
Issues, and Phase 2, Formulation of Public
Opinion.

Small-group communications characterize
the workshop model. People and agency
members are divided into small groups to
discuss the information they have received.
Each group, through discussion, should arrive
at a compromise solution about the issues.
Each member must listen to and assess the
discussion of others, express his/her own
feelings, and justify opinions to the other group
members. The summary of all the groups,
including justifications, should reflect the
sentiment of those people present. Under these
circumstances, pseudopolarization diminishes,
and real conflict is isolated. The issue is thus
reduced in scope, and specific details are
refined and re-formed into a more practical,
manageable problem. The input received thus
focuses on the real matter rather than a
collection of "problems" that are often alluded
to in typical public hearings.

Information and education are the two
basic management functions that must be
required for the workshop approach to work.
The information session should focus —
without highly technical language — on the
visitor, the resource, competing land uses, and
both national and regional public input. Experts
hired by non-agency interest groups must also
be allowed to present alternative technical
analyses for consideration.

The education session may be held directly
following the information session. For more
complex issues involving much information,
you may schedule it after some time delay so
that people can assimilate the material

presented and consult their own experts. The
three factors considered in interpreting
information are: potential of the resource for
certain uses, limitations of the resource for
desired activities, and associated trade-offs.
Expert views may differ on each of these.

The potential of the resource can be
evaluated in two ways: by what it can sustain
without suffering permanent physical
deterioration, and by what it can be used for.
Both factors should be discussed so that people
understand the available options, the potential
effects of a given option, and the assumptions
upon which these views are based.

Trade-offs are difficult to handle even if
you know the interrelationships between
various resource elements, and the difficulty
increases when we add the people-use factor.
Trade-offs, however, are essential in
understanding the potential effects of choosing
a given management option to meet a goal or
mixture of goals, and in intrepreting these
efforts for the public. Even if you cannot
attach an absolute value to a trade-off, you
should still be able to predict, with the
assistance of the technical staff, the relative
effects on different groups of a given option.

Small-group dynamics is accomplished by
dividing the larger body of people into groups
that are small enough for people to feel
comfortable in informal interactions. You must
consider six basic factors in order to ensure the
success of small-group dynamics:

1. *Size.* The size of the group may vary, but a
   maximum of eight to ten people is generally
   recommended. In a larger group, most
   people tend to have fewer interactions, and
   a few individuals dominate the discussion.
2. *Heterogeneity.* It is important that people
   with different views on the issue discuss
   these openly. If people with the same views
   make up the discussion group, they do very
   little critical analysis of the issue. They
   merely agree with one another without
   attempting to identify the real issues,
   formulate a logical response, or even
   understand their own stance. Heterogeneity
   does cause some personal tension; however,
   this is beneficial because it tends to cause

each individual to think about the issue, to examine their feelings about it, and to verbalize these feelings.

There are several ways to obtain heterogeneity. One of the more popular is to pass out color- or number- coded agenda sheets on a systematic basis as people enter the meeting room. Individuals can then be assigned to a certain group. You must have a similar technique for doing this; otherwise groups will be homogeneous.

3. *Leadership.* Leadership is difficult to handle because of the potential effect a leader can have on the group decision. Since the agency is often an interest group itself, agency leaders often tend to create more tension, reducing the effectiveness of the discussion and the final choice of options. Also, their presence apparently sometimes casts suspicion on the whole process.

There are two other possibilities — hire professional leaders or "brokers" who are not agency people but who have the ability to get people involved and negotiating, or allow the leadership to evolve or be selected from each group. The latter method sometimes works well, since in such a small group most participants do not allow the informal leadership to dominate their conclusions. Some theoreticians feel that one way to eliminate the air of dominance is to omit a table where people can establish positions of power, and to arrange chairs in a small circle. The former approach may also work well where there has been conflict and suspicion between interest groups.

4. *Deciding on Goals.* Participants should understand that they are to focus on those goals which they feel are desirable and obtainable. As was shown earlier in this chapter, people are more able to decide on goals than on methods of obtaining them. Since the agency will be seeking specific kinds of input on the issue, it should develop a set of open-ended questions that people can respond to.

5. *Reporting.* Each small group should then report their findings and their reasons for these to the whole assembly. They should also report gaps in information or inaccurate data associated with their decisions. This may help the agency in its deliberations and preparations for future workshops. Offer opportunities for minority reports if people disagree with small-group conclusions or if they feel that a single individual dominated the discussion.

6. *Information and Education.* Desirable small-group dynamics are predicated on information and education sessions. These are not designed to eliminate personal bias, but may include professional experts hired by outside groups. It is hoped that more information will give everyone a better background and make them more aware of all the ramifications of the issue.

Transactive Planning Theory. J. Friedmann offers a new approach to involving the public in planning and transactive planning, where the public is the essential decision-maker.[15,16] He describes a process to decentralize, debureaucratize decisions, where the public is involved throughout the entire planning process, even the implementation. The key element, according to Friedmann, is action facilitated by the professional planner but determined by the involved public. This is similar to Gallagher's cycle planning and Bleiker and Bleiker's SEACA, Substantial Effective Agreement on a Course of Action. The difference is that Friedmann tries to develop an underlying theory.

In 1973, Friedmann identified three critical components: 1) dialogue, 2) mutual learning, 3) societal guidance. Dialogue refers to personal communications between the client-public and the planner. Mutual learning occurs where the processed knowledge of the planner and the personal knowledge of the client are shared in a mutual exploration of the problem and possible solutions. Societal guidance occurs when, based on the dialogue and mutual learning, a substantial, effective agreement on a course of action is reached. Each potentially affected party, though drawn by self-interest, ultimately tempers that motivation with social responsibility as long as there is mutual respect and acceptance. Once the decision is made and implemented, acceptance increases and challenge decrease, at least successful challenges. Ashor and Stokes present two excellent case studies on recreation management problems using the *transactive planning approach* for the reader who wishes to pursue this further.[4,34]

SELECTED READINGS

1. Alston, R.M. 1972. Goals and Decisionmaking in the Forest Service. US Forest Service Research Paper INT-128.

2. Alston, R.M., and D.M. Freeman. 1975. "The Natural Resource Decision-maker as a Political and Economic Man: Toward a Synthesis." *Journal of Environmental Management* 3:1.

3. Arrow, K. 1951. *Social Choice and Individual Values.* New York: John Wiley & Sons, Inc.

4. Ashor, J.L. 1985. "Recreation Management in the Bob Marshall Wilderness Complex: An Application of the Limits of Acceptable Change Concept and Transactive Planning Theory," master's thesis (unpublished). University of Montana, Missoula.

5. Behan, R.W. 1978. "Why the Majority is Silent: Some thoughts to Ponder about Public Involvement while Waiting for the Sierra Club to Arrive. *Proceedings, Society of American Foresters,* pp 168-173.

6. Bleiker, H. 1976. "The Role of Values in Environmental Decision-Making and in Environmental Education," Fifth Annual Conference, National for Environmental Education, Atlanta, GA.

7. Bleiker, A., and H. Bleiker. 1986. *Citizen Participation Handbook.* Larmaie, WY: Institute for Participatory Management and Planning.

8. Borton, T.E., and K.P. Warner, 1971. "Involving Citizens in Water Resource Planning: The Communication-Participation Experiment in the Susquehanna River Basin," *Environment and Behavior.* 3(9):284.

9. Cantril, H. 1972. *Gauging Public Opinion.* Princeton University Press, pp. 226-230.

10. Clark, R.N., and G.H. Stankey. 1976. "Analyzing Public Input to Resource Decisions: Criteria, Principles, and Case Examples of the Codinvolve System." *Natural Resources Journal.* 16(1):213.

11. Clark, R.N., G.H. Stankey, and J.C. Hendee. 1974. "An Introduction to CODINVOLVE: A System for Analyzing, Storing, and Retrieving Public Input to Resource Decisions." US Forest Service Research Note PNW-223.

12. Creighton, J.L. 1981. *The Public Involvement Manual.* Cambridge, MA:ABT Books.

13. Cutlip, S.M., and A.H. Center. 1971. *Effective Public Relations* (2nd ed.). Englewood Cliffs, NJ: Prentice-Hall, Inc.

14. Daneke, G.A., and M. Farcia, and J.D. Priscoli (eds.). 1983. *Public Involvement and Social Impact Assessment.* Boulder, CO: Westview Press.

15. Friedmann, J. 1969. "Notes on Societal Action." *Journal of the American Institute of Planners* 35(5):311-318.

16. Friedmann, J. 1973. "The Public Interest and Community Participation: Toward a Reconstruction of Public Philosophy." *Journal of the American Institute of Planners* 39(1):1-12.

17. Gallagher, T. 1986. *Cycle Planning.* University of Alaska-Fairbanks. (in press).

18. Giff, J.R., G.N. Platts, and L.F. Miller (eds.) 1951. *Dynamics of Participative Groups.* Chicago: John S. Swift Co.

19. Gilbert D.L. 1970. "Public Relations and Parks." *Proceedings of the Third Recreation Management Institute.* College Station, TX: Texas A&M University.

20. Hendee, J.C., R.N. Clark, and H. Stankey. 1974. "A Framework for Agency Use of Public Input in Resource Decision-Making." *Journal of Soil and Water Conservation* 29(2):60.

21. Hendee, J.C., R.C. Lucas, R.H. Tracy, Jr., Tony Staed, R.N. Clark, G.H. Stankey, and R.A. Yarnell. 1973. *Public involvement and the Forest Service: Experience, Effectiveness, and Suggested Direction.* Washington, DC: US Forest Service.

22. Hornback, K.E. 1975. "Overcoming Obstacles to Agency and Public Involvement." *Environmental Design Research Association Annual Proceedings*. Lawrence, Kansas.

23. Kedder, L.H., and V.M. Stewart. 1975. *The Psychology of Intergroup Relations: Conflict and Consciousness*. New York: McGraw-Hill Book Co.

24. Kulas, R.E. 1973. "Group Size: A Comparison of Decisions Made by Six and Twelve Member Problem Solving Groups." masters thesis (unpublished). University of Wyoming.

25. Lundblad, D. 1972. "Community Workshop — An Experiment in Public Involvement." *The Grass Roots and Water Resource Management*. McKenzie, L. (ed.). Pullman, WA: Washington State University Press.

26. Mills, T.M. 1973. *The Sociology of Small Groups*. Englewood Cliffs, NJ: Prentice-Hall, Inc.

27. Phillips, G.M. 1973. *Communication and the Small Groups*. Indianpolis: Bobbs-Merril Co., Inc.

28. Pressman, J.L. 1970. "Decision-Making and Public Policy: The Perils and Possibilities of Fragmentation." *Elements of Outdoor Recreation Planning*. Driver, B.L. (ed.). Ann Arbor, MI: University of Michigan Press.

29. Reinke, K.B., and B. Reinke. 1973. "Public Involvement in Resource Decisions: A National Forest Seeks Public Input for Recreation Development." *Journal of Forestry* 71(10):656.

30. Rosenfeld, L.B. 1973. *Human Interaction in the Small Group Setting*. Columbus, Ohio: Charles E. Merrill Publishing Co.

31. Shaw, M.E. 1976. *Group Dynamics: The Psychology of Small Group Behavior*. New York: McGraw-Hill Co.

32. Stankey, G.H. 1972. "The Use of Content Analysis in Resource Decision Making." *Journal of Forestry* 70(3):148.

33. Stankey, G.H., J.C. Hendee, and R.N. Clark. 1975. "Applied Social Research Can Improve Public Participation in Resource Decision-making." *Rural Sociology* 40:65.

34. Stokes, G.L. 1982. "Conservation of the Blackfoot River Corridor — An Application of Transactive Planning Theory." Ph.D. Dessertation (unpublished), Colorado State University, Ft. Collins.

35. Schweitzer, D.L., D.M. Freeman, and R.M. Alston. 1975. "Ensuring Viable Public Land-Use Decisions — Some Problems and Suggestions," *Journal of Forestry* 73(11):705.

36. Twight, B.W., and M. Carroll. 1983. "Workshops in Public Involvement: Do They Help Find Common Ground?" *Journal of Forestry* 81:732-735.

37. U.S. Forest Service. 1980. *Public Participation Handbook, Vol. 1 & 2. USDA-Forest Service*. Washington, DC

38. Wagar, J.A., and B.W. Twight. 1983. "Communication and Public Involvement." *Section 23, Forestry Handbook*. 2nd edition. Wenger, K.F. (ed.). New York: John Wiley and Sons.

39. Young, R.C. 1970. "Establishment of Goals and Definitions of Objectives," *Elements of Outdoor Recreation Planning*. Driver, B.L. (ed.). Ann Arbor, Michigan: University of Michigan Press.

CHAPTER SIX

ASSESSING IMPACTS IN THE REAL WORLD

The relationship between people and their environment is marked by a procession of benefits and costs associated with use of natural resources. These benefits and costs are rarely, if ever, evenly distributed; some claimant groups derive mostly benefits while costs are borne by other claimants, user groups, or society as a whole. While it is impossible in one brief chapter to cover all the impact associated with allocation of resources, we will introduce concepts that may be useful in understanding the consequences of resource allocation and management decisions.

Impact results from disparate views of benefits and differing interpretations of what constitutes a "resource". In 1951 E.W. Zimmerman coined the phrase "Resources Are Not, They Become."[18] This means that objects do not possess inherent value; they become resources when assigned importance or worth by a group of people. These people may claim the object as a resource for a particular value or set of values. Or different groups of claimants may seek legitimate but incompatible uses for the object. For example, a tree may be viewed as a source of fiber for paper or lumber by one group of claimants and valued for aesthetic appreciation and recreation by another group. Both resource definitions of that tree are legitimate and mutually exclusive. Under those circumstances, if one group of claimants wins, the other must lose.

Thus management of natural areas becomes control of access to and the balance of legitimate claims for resources. This balance of claims must involve an examination of trade-offs, which requires enumerating impacts and evaluating the consequences of an action. Therefore selecting options becomes a statement of values, an expression of the legal and administrative strictures by which resources are offered or withheld.

Because we live in a world of choice and possibility, no one can predict the future. Therefore projecting probable futures and the consequences of a proposed action is a function of assumptions and random scenarios based upon empirical data rather than prediction. However, the actions taken today form that future. To project some future, then, we should examine our current actions and decisions and see if the foundations upon which those actions are built give us comfort or concern.

As professionals we typically seek technical solutions to societal problems. This search for ways of assessing the impacts of specific situations is, however, rational. Management based upon science is on the surface more appealing than management based strictly upon judgement. The awe caused by an equation often overrides the conventional wisdom of practical application or understandable explanations. G.M. Weinberg,[17] suggests that "by using words, we shall sacrifice the appearance of elegance, but we shall stay closer to the things we want to think about." So why the drive for explanations of outcomes based upon a quantitative foundation rather than a qualitative approach? Perhaps we believe that "The stature of a science is commonly measured by the degree to which it makes use of mathematics."[15] Or perhaps we were, and possibly still are, obsessed with what F. Egler terms "physics envy."[8] So we push for the technical solution — the objective answers to the often subjective questions. To discover technical solutions, however, we need a high level of concurrence about social values and scientific facts, a condition rarely met.

Figure 6.1, suggested by J.D. Thompson, offers a paradigm for selecting decision strategies.[16] To understand this paradigm, let's track the issue of whether a tract of land should be used for dispersed recreation or

AGREEMENT ON FACTS

		HIGH	LOW
AGREEMENT	HIGH	TECHNICAL/ COMPUTATION	JUDGEMENT
ON			
VALUES	LOW	POLITICAL (compromise)	INSPIRATION

Figure 6-1. Paradigm of Decision-Making Strategies

mineral extraction. The initial decision is political and occurs in an arena of elected officials. These officials consider the arguments of various interest groups who claim the resource and the social benefits of competing claims. Once they have agreed on values — to recreate or to mine — they can begin to assess management options. A technical, computational solution is possible only if agreement is reached about management parameters. Impact asessment is therefore only possible when there is accord about these parameters. Reviewing them results in a solution upon which all parties agree or as an outcome that must be referred to judicial review. Also, while the identification of impacts associated with specific actions or policies is a sound management practice, it is also a requirement of law.

Assessing the consequences of an action involves identifying a variety of impacts. These can be grouped into two general categories: *environmental impacts* which focus on changes to the physical and biological community as the result of some action or management policy; and *social impacts* which focus on the way actions or mangement policies affect people (including quality of life).

LEGISLATION AND POLICY

Public involvement in issues of natural resource allocation and management crystallized during the 1960's. Concern over development actions such as the Glen Canyon Dam project on the Colorado River, timber cutting programs on eastern US Forest Service lands, and large-scale water projects such as the Tennessee-Tombigbee Waterway and the cross-Florida barge canal led to the passage of the National Environmental Policy Act (PL 91-190), commonly referred to as NEPA. The philosophy for NEPA is stated in Title I of the act:

It is the...policy of the Federal Government...to use all possible means and measures...to create and maintain conditions under which man and nature can exist in productive harmony, and fulfill the social, economic and other requirements of present and future generations of Americans.

NEPA requires a systematic, interdisciplinary approach to integrating the natural and social sciences, along with the environmental design arts, in planning and making decisions which might affect the environment. NEPA also requires that unquantified environmental amenities and values be weighed on balance with technical and economic considerations, and that a detailed statement report the impact of a proposed action along with possible alternatives. This report, known as an environmental impact statement (EIS), has a specific requirement for an environmental impact assessment (EIA) and a social impact assessment (SIA), and must be developed in a manner to assure public involvement.

Figure 6-2. The absence of impacts is *not* required for a project to be undertaken. NEPA requires that impacts be identified and considered, and public interests be accounted for. (Photo by R.H. Becker)

Additionally, NEPA requires that all associated impacts be identified and considered as part of the allocation and management decision-making process (See Figure 6-2).

NEPA tells the agency that it must be comprehensive and consider all factors, but gives no directives as to how this monumental task is to be accomplished. Additional legislation such as the Clean Air Act, the Clean Water Act, and the Mining Reclamation Act establish similar impact evaluation requirements and established parameters for defining resource quality, but offer little guidance for the affected agencies.

To assure compliance with the wishes of Congress, Title II of NEPA provides for the establishment of a Council on Environmental Quality in the executive branch of government. Regulations developed by the President's Council on Environmental Quality (CEQ) for implementing NEPA offer some procedural direction for conducting impact analysis and producing the necessary documentation.[11] The initial phase of an impact analysis is developing an environmental assessment (EA).

The EA briefly reports evidence based upon existing information about the severity and types of impacts, including areas where effects may be unknown. The EA is used to determine if the impacts are of a sufficient nature to merit a detailed analysis and the preparation of a complete environmental impact statement (EIS). If the EA determines that they are of a significant nature, the agency initiates a complete EIS.

In general, these procedures call for a process known as "scoping" in which interested parties, including affected agencies, are brought together to define the proposed actions and identify possible areas of impact. The scoping phase of impact assessment defines the kind, depth, and intensity of the environmental analysis required to address possible consequences (See Figure 6-3).

Few impact analyses proceed beyond the preparation of an EA. For example, in 1980 the US Forest Service prepared almost 13,000 EA's and only 111 EIS's.[7] Critics of the process have argued that EAs have been prepared without adequately addressing possible

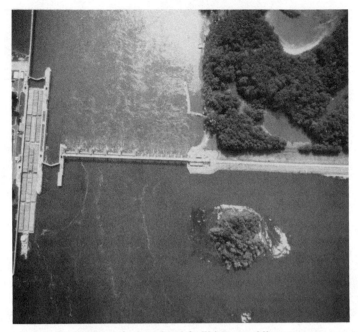

Figure 6-3. Expansion on development of recreational facilities on public waterways may require an EIS, even though the land is in private ownership. (Photo by R.H. Becker)

social and environmental consequences and further, that initial environmental assessments have been used to undermine the intent of NEPA by providing a thinly veiled rationale for proceeding with projects without adequately considering public interests.

Sometimes, however, agency decisions not to prepare a full EIS have been overturned in court, and the court has required the preparation of the statement. Criticism of this process usually centers on what constitutes "major" impacts, how well "reasonable" alternatives are developed, and the extent to which the public's interests are considered. But regardless of these criticisms, NEPA remains the most effective tool for ascertaining the desires of public and special-interest groups which, prior to NEPA, had difficulty voicing concern over public land-management programs.

NEPA continues to be defined through judicial review.* While a great deal of

variation exists in case findings, a few general themes have surfaced. First, the courts are reluctant to give broad interpretations of NEPA requirements. However, they have been willing to specify the roles of various agencies in oversight of granting permits. For example, a recent case involving modification to wetlands established that the US Army Corps of Engineers has permit review authority for modifications to wetlands with areas greater than one acre. In addition, the court clarified the definition of "wetlands" as lands with flora cover typically found on saturated soils. The presence of open water is not required.

The courts have also established the need to thoroughly consider all possible alternatives to proposed projects. This has been referred to as the "hard look" doctrine.[10] Other points of judicial review have centered upon whether public interests are adequately considered. This places considerable pressure upon managers to assure full public participation and increases the

*A summary of the pertinent case is presented in *The Law of Parks, Recreation Resources, and Leisure Services* by A.N. Frakt and J.S. Rankin. The text includes issues relating to NEPA, the Clean Air Act, and the Clean Water Act and the roles special-interest groups have played in promoting court actions.

importance of the manager as a mediator of competing claimant interest. Thus it becomes important for managers to involve the public in establishing the guidelines under which an area will be operated. For example, forest managers can involve the public in establishing ROS ''anchor points'', as discussed in Chapter Three, which are used to govern access and define appropriate activities in specific resource settings. Today public land managers are custodians of access.

A SYSTEMS APPROACH TO IMPACT ASSESSMENT

You should not undertake an environmental impact assessment without first defining a system of variables and associated relationships that are important to understanding the problem. Unfortunately you can usually identify hundreds of variables and thousands of relationships to describe even the most simple system. Reducing any system to a workable model is necessary before you undertake an assessment or environmental impact study. The difficulty in developing a workable model centers on sifting all possible variables to arrive at a parsimonious set that describes the problem and setting. Successful assessment of environmental and social impacts begins with a clear description of the resource setting to be affected and a clear description of the actions likely to cause the change.

Imagine assessing the impact of running a highway through a forest. We may be concerned with alterations to the physcial environment and have to assess variables along the route such as soil identification (fragility, productivity, depth to bedrock and type); slope and aspect; presence of water; amount of earth to be removed or relocated; presence of rare or endangered flora and fauna; amount of biomass removal; and habitat classification. (Your own list may be even more inclusive.)

Now consider the way the highway may affect the social qualities of the forest. We may speculate that the following variables are important here: noise, traffic levels, proximity to backcountry areas, number of existing trails, location of trails, numbers of visitors, type of visitors, attitudes of current visitors (here we could list many specific items), visibility from promontories, and breaks in the natural vista. (Again, your list may be different.)

Proponents of the highway project may also wish to include variables such as driving time between selected destination points, economic return to local communities, local land values, traffic levels on existing proximal highways, and cost of alternative routes. Various claimants will have their own way of describing the situation.

As the list of variables grows, the complexity of assessment grows. The number of potential relationships among variables is the number of variables squared. Thus a system with only fifteen may have as many as two hundred twenty-five relationships to be considered. And a system with twenty may have as many as four hundred! Our task of understanding even simple systems soon becomes enormous; consequently, it is not technically feasible to fully evaluate all of the interactions caused by proposed alterations to natural systems. Instead we must rely on procedures and models which systematically sift out a set of critically important variables and relationships which can be used to assess impacts. To work, this model must have the consensus of those natural resource claimants or users who are, or may be, affected by proposed actions. It must also have the rigor to withstand judicial review.

Intuitively, we may believe that decisions for allocating resources are human judgments. While we may use a technical solution to legitimize a specific conclusion, final decisions are based upon the wisdom of experience. Yet as G.A. Miller points out, the capacity of humans to process information is extremely limited.[12] Their limits in understanding interactions, according to Miller, are about seven relationships, plus or minus two. In other words, a brilliant manager can understand a system that has a maximum of nine possible interactions. Since the number of possible paired interactions in a system is the number of variables in the system squared, the brilliant manager can understand the relationships in a system with only three variables.

Thus, when faced with complex multidimensional choices, people naturally devise "simplifying strategies" and sacrifice a lot of information as they follow some easy road to a decision.[14] Most of these adaptations involve the creation of good/bad evaluation criteria and often result in suboptimal choices in difficult situations. The creation of such valuation scales often tend to characterize situations that are uncertain or that introduce change as "bad." Yet change and uncertainty are among the realities which managers are facing and will continue to face.

By definition, change means moving away from the status quo. Whether induced by socio-economic forces, shifting cultural mores, or legislative initiatives, change may cause the manager to focus on reactions to its effects and create conflicts. Often these conflicts put managers at odds with their public and support groups. Also, the anxiety created by change and conflict results in decreased agency morale — a loss of a sense of mission. Managers may feel they are perceived as part of an "us versus them" problem. This attitude further crystallizes the conflict, polarizes groups, and heightens anxiety.

The circular relationship of change and conflict is compounded by growing social complexity. Complexity is defined as the number of parts in a system. As systems become more intricate, simple truths and conventional wisdom become difficult to identify and enumerate. A feeling of isolation and a sense of "they don't understand" further separates resource managers from their public.[1]

The number of social groups focusing on special, narrow issues is growing. These groups place demands on resource agencies that are becoming more specific and less negotiable. Thus, as previously mentioned, managers may find themselves becoming mediators between special interests and gatekeepers of resources which are sought for often conflicting uses. Special interests often wax and wane with specific issues, so managers must also deal with groups and interests that seemingly appear without notice.

Having to anticipate probable conflicts that result further stresses resource managers.

Similarly, the explosive growth of knowledge and the increasing specificity of laws and regulations heighten complexity. Knowledge is cumulative — the more that is learned, the more elements have to be considered when resolving problems. Laws and regulations are likewise cumulative and further increase complexity. As T.M. Bonnicksen points out, all trends seem to indicate that growth in knowledge, growth in referenda and initiatives, and growth in special-interest groups will accelerate into the foreseeable future.[2] The result is increased complexity and greater uncertainty, so it is reasonable to ask if managers can keep pace with increased complexity and uncertainty.

Coping with complexity requires developing management techniques that are not paralyzed by uncertainty. New resource-management arrangements must build on the premise — indeed, the fact — that we live in a world of choice rather than determinism. They must provide frameworks for improving decision-making when decisions are ultimately based on judgment.

Assessing impact in resource recreation, park management, or environmental planning requires a systems approach which integrates the characteristics of the setting with the expectations and demands of the claimants. T.M. Bonnicksen and R.G. Lee present biosocial systems analysis as "an approach to organizing and tracking interactions between society and its physical environment."[3] The superiority of biosocial systems analysis is its capacity to require thoroughness from a manager and to explicitly state what a resource decision, policy or study emphasizes or ignores.

CROSS-IMPACTS ASSESSMENT PROCESS

T.M. Bonnicksen and R.H. Becker suggest a technique based on biosocial theory, the cross-impact assessment process (CAP), as an effective approach to integrate the interests of a wide array of groups and enhance the quality of management decisions.[4]

CAP was developed from a number of techniques that are collectively referred to as

Figure 6-4. The CAP process was developed to assess impact from increased barge traffic on the Upper Mississippi due to proposed expansion of Lock & Dam #26. (Photo by R.H. Becker)

cross-impact analysis. In general, these techniques estimate future changes in a set of variables based on certain hypothetical relationships among the variables. CAP uses a participatory approach and encourages consensus among claimants as to what variables and relationships are critical in assessing specific site impacts. CAP has proven to be a valuable tool for addressing problems for which no clear, indisputable solutions are apparent. By using a participatory approach in the early stages of impact assessment, the beliefs and claims of different interest groups are expressed and considered during policy formulation, thereby reducing subsequent conflicts (See Figure 6-4).

CAP relies on the judgment of an interdisciplinary group of well-informed individuals. The assumption is that a concise set of variables which adequately define a complex system is not available. Usually three to four independent and interdisciplinary panels of knowledgeable individuals assemble in face-to-face meetings to define the characteristics and the effects of a specific action. Panelists are selected according to their ability to

contribute specific knowledge and the breadth of view necessary to integrate that knowledge with the information provided by other panelists.

The first four panels used in the CAP assessment are called *foundation panels*. Each foundation panel should be limited in size to promote the exchange of ideas (about ten to fourteen people). Multiple foundation panels, as opposed to one, decrease the likelihood of excluding important variables. The final panel in this process is referred to as the *capstone panel* because it uses and refines variables identified by the foundation panels. To insure objectivity, you should select panelists to maintain a balance of expertise and public and private organizational affiliation. Examples of types of panel participants used in previous CAP programs include land developers, investment bankers, engineers, planners, ecologists, recreation specialists, biologists transportation planners, sociologists, area managers, foresters, water-resource specialists, landscape architects, private citizens, and local and state governmental officials.

The first stage in a foundation panel meeting is a brainstorming session to identify variables relevant to potential impact. Each variable added to the list is given a general name, such as land-use, and then made more specific by the assignment of a unit of measure, such as acres-by-type of use. After the variable identification list is completed, panelists are asked to individually select the twenty variables they believe are the most important. These selections are then tallied to provide a list of the top twenty variables which that collective panel believes are associated with a proposed action or program.

Next, the capstone panel uses the variables identified by the foundation panels to select the final set of twenty to thirty critically important ones which represent a core group. These variables define and assess impact on the park or forest area.

The capstone panel also identifies the relationships which link the final set of twenty to thirty variables together to form a system. This panel systematically decides whether or not a relationship exists between each pair of variables. A relationship is considered to exist when one variable is considered, in the judgement of the capstone panel, to have an impact or cause a change in a corresponding variable. In other words the capstone panel determines whether a change in variable X will cause a change in variable Z. After all possible relationships are identified, panelists rate the relative importance of each.

The cross-impact assessment process distills the conventional wisdom and collective judgements of a broad-based group of interested, knowledgeable individuals. Results allow the agency or area manager to analyze possible impacts and develop site-effect management programs. CAP assessment helps managers move from simply listing perceived impacts to their parks to analyzing why something is a threat or impact. Thus the cross-impact assessment process is a qualitative method which develops a consensus on values and facts needed for effective management.

Today's management environment requires a strong bond between those agencies charged with the stewardship of our public natural resources and those groups which claim resources for variety of uses. CAP provides a framework for improving decision-making and policy formulation when decisions and policies are ultimately based on political or judgemental strategies. (See Figure 6-1). CAP also recognizes the role of compromise in agreeing on the values and facts needed to implement an impact assessment or management plan.

As we look ahead to a future that is being shaped by decisions made today, we should insist that those decisions are based upon the collective judgements of all interested parties and explore ways to collect those qualitative judgements. As P.W. Bridgeman observes, "In my own case, pursuit of operational analysis has resulted in the conviction...that it is better to analyze in terms of doings and happenings than in terms of objects or static abstractions."[6]

Today, too many programs start with a "vaporous wish" phrased in eloquent but elusive language. This penchant for stating policies in vague terms leaves further definition and clarification to the implementation process. Yet as R.T. Nakamura states, conflicts erupt when the implementation process gets underway and policies are more clearly defined. Those charged with implementation disagree over what should be done and how; policy-makers intervene to reformulate priorities or to shift direction, and the program bogs down in conflict among various interest groups. The breakdown encountered during implementation is rooted in a lack of consensus and a lack of agreement.

Impact assessment and sound resource management are synonymous. The processes used to allocate resources mirror societal values. For land managers to maintain support and trust they must exercise their stewardship in a manner congruent with the expectations of society. Actions which appear capricious will be challenged. As much as any technical values derived from a systematic approach to resource management, consensus-building and constituent development must be part of strategic management. The techniques suggested in this chapter and throughout this text will help facilitate that goal.

SELECTED READINGS

1. Becker, R.H., F.D. Dottavio, and T.M. Bonnicksen. 1985. "Conventional Wisdom and Qualitative Assessment." In Wood (ed.) *Proceedings 1985 National Outdoor Recreation Trends Symposium II,* Vol. 1 pp. 80-88. USDI, National Park Service, Southeast Regional Office, Atlanta, GA.

2. Bonnicksen, T.M. 1985. "Initial Decision Analysis (IDA): A Participatory Approach for Developing Resource Policy." *Environmental Management* 9:379-392.

3. Bonnicksen, T.M., and R.G. Lee. 1982. "Biosocial Systems Analysis: An Approach for Assessing the Consequences of Resource Policies." *Journal of Environmental Management* 15:47-61.

4. Bonnicksen, T.M., and R.H. Becker. 1983. "Environmental Impact Studies: An Interdisciplinary Approach for Assigning Priorities." *Environmental Management* 7:109-117.

5. Boulding, K.E. 1961. *The Image.* 175 pp. Ann Arbor, MI: The University of Michigan Press.

6. Bridgeman, P.W. 1959. *The Way Things Are.* Cambridge, MA: Harvard University Press.

7. Bryan, H. and J.C. Hendee. 1981. "Social Impact Assessment in the United States Forest Service and Other Resource Management Agencies." Paper presented at the International Union of Forest Research Organizations (IUFRO) meeting, Kyoto, Japan, Sept.

8. Egler, F. 1983. Comments made at a wildlife ecology lecture, University of Wisconsin-Madison, Oct.

9. Everhardt, G., R.H. Becker, and F.D. Dottavio. 1983. "Assessing Encroachments: A Public Participation Approach." 39 P. Res. Report, USDI National Park Service, Atlanta, GA.

10. Frakt, A.N. and J.S. Rankin. 1982. *The Law of Parks, Recreation, and Leisure Services.* Salt Lake City, Utah: Brighton Publishing Co.

11. Jain, R.K., L.V. Urban, and G.S. Stacey. 1977. *Environmental Impact Analysis, A New Dimension in Decision Making.* NY: Van Nostrand Reinhold Co.

12. Miller, G.A. 1956. "The Magical Number Seven, Plus or Minus Two: Some Limits on Our Capacity for Processing Information." *The Psychological Review* 63:81-97.

13. Nakamura, R.T. 1981. "Strategies for Defining Policy During Implementation." pp. 113-134. In *Research in Public Policy Analysis and Management.* J.P. Crecine, Ed. Greenwich, CT: JAI Press, Inc.

14. Shepard, R.N. 1964. "On Subjectively Optimum Selection Among Multi-attribute Alternatives." pp. 257-281. In *Human Judgment and Optimality.* Shelly, & Bryan Eds. NY: John Wiley & Sons.

15. Stevens, S.S. 1962. "Mathematics, Measurement, and Psychophysics," in *Handbook of Experimental Psychology.* S.S. Stevens, Ed. NY: John Wiley & Sons.

16. Thompson, J.D. 1967. *Organizations in Action.* NY: McGraw-Hill.

17. Weinberg, G.M. 1975. *An Introduction to General Systems Thinking.* 279 pp. NY: John Wiley & Sons.

18. Zimmerman, E.W. 1951. *World Resources and Industries.* NY: Harper Bros.

PART II. RECREATIONAL RESOURCE MANAGEMENT

The management model (Chapter Two) and particularly the underlying theory (Chapter Three) emphasize the importance of the environmental setting — the prime attractors and the generalized landscape in which they occur. This section presents a series of resource management programs directed at maintaining or enhancing the environmental setting. Each chapter has a specific programmatic theme, going from the more intensively used sites, and thus more intensive resource management, to more dispersed-use areas and extensive programs.

Modern man has been caught in a philosophical debate of using versus preserving the ecological setting. The argument is often presented as an all-or-nothing choice. From a programmatic perspective, the argument deals with an illusion. Few if any areas exist that have not been influenced by modern man. Even the wildest have been penetrated, directly manipulated through specific activities, or indirectly influenced by external activities. And no one would suggest that these same areas should be cordoned off to prevent use, or that use, even in an unrestricted form, is going to cause wholesale destruction of the ecological webbing.

The debate from the manager's perspective, then, should not be one of use versus preservation, but *use versus use*. What type of use is appropriate for the area? And how can we best achieve that? How does that translate into specific resource management programs? Intensive versus extensive descriptors are not intended to reflect the relative value of the resource management program. On the contrary, each program is important and its relative worth must be judged in relation to the recreational opportunity to be provided. For a modern to semi-modern opportunity, intensive site management, such as introducing exotic vegetative ground cover and hardening the site, is just as inappropriate for a primitive recreational opportunity as introducing wild fires, and letting insect/diseases go unchecked.

CHAPTER SEVEN

SITE MANAGEMENT

Figure 7-1. The need for site protection and management is more obvious on the intensively used sites. (Photo by B.W. Twight)

Protection and renovation are necessary to maintain aesthetic and environmental values associated with developed sites. Trails, backcountry campsites, and other areas can potentially deteriorate if concentrations of recreationists gather there. Site protection means that positive management action reduces the effects of human use, or increases the site's resilience. It is important to correlate future management strategy with the site planning process so that you can protect site values through either proper design, or well-organized management strategies that work within the limits of the design.

Site renovation focuses on rehabilitating a deteriorated site. It can be a fallowing process which allows the site to recover naturally, or it can be an active process in which specific treatments speed up recovery.

$$\text{Site management is: } f \begin{cases} \text{Site location} \\ \text{Site design} \\ \text{Recreation use patterns} \\ \text{Environmental conditions} \\ \text{Management programs} \end{cases}$$

Figure 7-2. Concepts in Site Management

The well-managed site is one that is properly selected through the area planning process to provide a particular recreational opportunity and reduce possible environmental degradation. It is designed to fit the natural lay of the land, yet accommodate the normal behavioral patterns of visitors. Management strategies developed in accordance with the variables of site location, resource qualities, and expected use patterns protect the site after its development while complementing the normal use. They are also contingent on uncontrollable environmental conditions, which may cause the manager to periodically adjust his or her strategies according to seasonal conditions.

Program options available to the manager depend on where the particular site (anchor point) lies on the recreation opportunity spectrum. This is determined during the area planning (resource allocation) process. Actual site design also depends on the anchor point and the ability of a particular site to sustain the anticipated type and level of recreational use. The site absorbs recreational use in predictable ways, which you can plan for in initial management programs. However, aberrations can occur which are only detected through continuous monitoring. One significant kind of behavior is vandalism, which occurs out of ignorance or maliciousness. (See Chapter Fifteen.) Use patterns and impacts may also be different than originally predicted. Strategies to counteract these effects can range from deliberate non-action to stablization at present conditions, rejuvenation of degraded sites, and restoration to former conditions.

In sum, site management is first and foremost a function of proper site location. Without this, you can spend inordinate amounts of money to maintain acceptable conditions. Even then the results may be less than satisfactory to the clientele being served. Whatever programs are needed to maintain ground cover and aesthetics, minimizing abberrations should be a crucial part of your basic commitment to the site. Monitoring indicates the success of these programs and the need to adjust management strategies over time.

BASIC MANAGEMENT STRATEGIES

There are six possible basic strategies for managing recreational sites:

1. *Leave Open, Culturally Treat.* This is probably the most ideal situation — keeping the site open to public use while implementing some cultural program to maintain ground vegetation and soils. While this may be possible in cases of minimum deterioration, often symptoms of overuse are not evident until major deterioration has occurred. The site sustains heavy use with little external change in other than the species composition of its ground vegetation until it reaches a threshold at which rapid deterioration usually occurs. At that point, it is almost impossible to implement a "leave open and culturally treat" policy except on the most naturally productive, stable sites. It is simply not feasible to reclaim the site under those conditions.

The only effective way to implement this policy is on a regular basis, scheduled well before the threshold of site durability is reached. This means that each site should be thoroughly analyzed to determine the factors that may limit use, such as heavy soil, species composition, soil moisture, and soil nutrients, and that managers solve these problems through specific cultural treatment programs designed for each site. If soil moisture is a limiting factor in maintaining the vigor of vegetation during the heavy use season, it may be necessary to establish an irrigation program, perhaps during low-use periods early in the week. Under these arrangements light periodic applications are really preventive rather than remedial.

Ideally, we attempt to prevent the problems of overuse and then respond with remedial programs if preventive measures fail. The final decision is based on economics. Often it is more difficult to convince a superior that preventive programs are necessary when there are no external signs of deterioration than it is to justify higher expenditures later in order to reclaim a worn-out site. In the future emphasis may fall on preventive measures, which are probably the best choice in the long run, for maintaining recreational opportunities, least cost, environmental protection, and efficiency of management.

2. *Close, Natural Recovery.* If a site shows deterioration from recreational use, we can always consider closing the site and allowing the ground vegetation to rejuvenate itself. The recovery of most recreational sites is slow since recreational use is often relegated to areas that are poorer in terms of natural productivity. Thus, when these sites are in the earlier stages of deterioration, we should predict certain results and close the area at that point, allowing more rapid recovery.

This strategy is very appropriate for heavily used sites in wilderness areas, that must be allowed to recover naturally. You should also consider redesigning trail systems to encourage concentrations of use elsewhere. Heavily used developed sites, however, are generally auto-oriented and difficult to close without the loss of a significant recreational opportunity and a tremendous public outcry. Therefore merely closing a site — allowing it to recover naturally — is not an advisable alternative except under specific conditions.

3. *Close and Culturally Treat.* In this approach, the overused site is closed to public use and certain cultural treatments are introduced to speed recovery. These treatments may include the introduction of exotic species, soil aeration, and fertilization. Closing off the area is necessary if the treatment causes undue inconvenience to visitors, if visitors disrupt the treatment, or if the site does not fully recover while use continues.

Close-and-treat is an especially appropriate strategy for heavily deteriorated sites. It allows maximum recovery while minimizing recovery time and inconvenience to the visitor. Remember, however, to correlate appropriate information programs with any site closing so that people can understand what is being done. If at all possible, make alternate opportunities available to the public.

4. *Rest and Rotate.* In this program, additional sites are developed so that sufficient facilities are still available when other areas are closed for rejuvenation. This means that certain sites can be "rested" to encourage recovery and rotated on a regular schedule. Some managers are very receptive to this strategy and have tried to implement it in their own administrative units; however, most areas are not planned and developed in such a way as to allow rest and rotation. Often, what is described as a rest-and-rotation program is really a closure program, as described in strategies 2 and 3. This greatly reduces an area's capacity to handle normal visitor loads. Also, rest and rotation, particularly in more primitive portions of the recreational opportunity spectrum, often do not work because deterioration is typically more rapid than recovery. The exception would be where alternative sites are more environmentally stable than the original ones.

5. *Hardening the Site.* Hardening the site to sustain a higher-than-normal level of use is an option which can take two forms: the introduction of exotic plants (if permitted by policy) that can sustain themselves under particular heavy-use conditions, or surfacing high-use areas. Planting exotic ground vegetation is a viable choice where the site-specific effects of the particular species is known and no impact can be anticipated beyond the site. However, you must consider the economics of introducing and maintaining exotic species, the potential for spreading new diseases and noxious weeds, and the effects on the gene pool.

Surfacing, while it alters the environmental setting, can be made to blend with the requirements of the particular opportunity. On extremely heavy soils where use and precipitation levels are high, paving may be the only reasonable answer, particularly if other soil conditions are neither available nor suitable for development in the general area, or recreational use cannot be diverted to more suitable sites during high-moisture periods.

A more desirable solution may be to surface these high-use areas with other materials, such as gravel or coarse sand. This helps reduce compaction and retard erosion by encouraging water infiltration; it also tends to be more aesthetically pleasing. In moderate-use areas, you can use wood chips with a similar effect. In heavily used portions of a site — like around the picnic table — a reduced amount of erosion and dust is probably the best we can hope for. Plants simply do not survive in those conditions.

The implication here is that the problem should really be eliminated in initial site planning by properly surfacing known or suspected heavy-use areas. Certainly resurfacing on a periodic basis is necessary in order to check sheet erosion and dusty conditions and to maintain the tread surface; however, it is impossible to eliminate the dust problem that occurs with many medium-to fine-textured soils. Light watering and even some chemicals may help, but too much moisture while recreational use is high can cause severe compaction and surface erosion — the problem that surfacing was supposed to eliminate in the first place.

Remember, too, that some sites are supposed to be hard to accommodate an activity, a mode of travel, etc. Many different materials can be used for surfacing these areas — from wood chips to coarse sand to concrete. Your actual choice depends on use pattern and ROS restrictions. Site developments in the roaded portion of ROS typically feature heavily-used areas that are appropriately hardened to sustain rough treatment. In roadless portions, the decision is not so clear. In zones of easier access with prime attractors, hardening is probably the best answer. But what about the more primitive end of the ROS? While you can argue that surfacing high-use areas in the wilderness is not a viable option, the truth is that in many instances we already have — like the tread of a wilderness trail. Much of the new

wilderness in Alaska is suffering from these types of user-impact problems. Do you harden access points along lakeshores, gravel-bar landing strips, etc.? Or do you simply live with the consequences of the use patterns?

6. *Cut Out, Get Out.* In the past we have focused much of our attention in managing public lands on resource uses other than recreation. This has often created a *laissez-faire* approach to recreation management. We have allowed people to do almost anything, anywhere, and the results have often been less than satisfactory — conflict among user groups, resource deterioration, and a general decline in user satisfaction. This is similar to the "cut out, get out" policy of land management a century ago. At that time, the agency or enterprise merely harvested the renewable resource without any consideration for the future. Resources were inexhaustible — or at least we thought so.

In recreation management, some of these philosophies still exist. People seek outdoor recreation experiences on various sites. Yet sometimes, through abuse and overuse, they destroy the very site and opportunity that they so highly value. Their focus is seemingly on the present and not on the future as they destroy one oasis and then move on to another.

Can we afford a *laissez-faire* approach today? The answer has to be no. In view of spiraling demands and diminishing supply, we must protect our existing resources while trying to innovatively increase their use. This does not mean we must rigidly control access in order to maintain the resource; nevertheless, we must take an active role in managing the site to protect the resource and the opportunity now, ensuring that the site is maintained for future generations.

The "cut out, get out" philosophy will never be formally adopted as modern management policy, but it may become preeminent through benign neglect. The commitment at the time of development is to maintain the site at some acceptable level, yet use patterns and budgets change.

Technology can help maintain the site at reduced costs; however, at some point managers may simply have to let the quality of the site slip through benign neglect. Rather than allow a site to die a slow agonizing death so it no longer provides the desired, acceptable recreational opportunity, it should be dispatched. For example rather than neglecting a series of small family picnic areas because they are so small and scattered, wouldn't it be better to enlarge one or two to handle the load and close the others so you can still provide the opportunity and maintain it within budget limits? Under these circumstances, you must take care in site design so it offers the social intimacy of the smaller sites.

While all the classical strategies are presented and their limitations discussed here, there is another school of thought about site management: that deterioration is faster than recovery.[6,7] The contention is that except on better, more productive sites, recovery is much slower than deterioration, even when combined with specific cultural treatments. This casts doubt on the applicability of management strategies where recovery is extended over a period of time and/or when other sites are going to be affected by the closure of the treated site. While not conclusive, the above suggests that the original site selection process is a preeminent consideration in overall site management. The site should be designed to handle expected visitor loads and, where necessary, incorporate cultural treatment programs on a regularly scheduled basis from the beginning. All programs must be developed within ROS constraints.

POSSIBLE CULTURAL TREATMENTS

If cultural treatments are to be part of the site-management program, then the manager must choose the proper ones for particular circumstances. There are no universal recommendations because of the tremendous variation that occurs in local situations. Instead, a discussion of possible cultural treatments and their general application follows:

Soil Scarification. Soil scarification is the loosening of the topsoil in order to reduce compaction, which increases infiltration of water and exposes the maximum amount of mineral soil. This prepares a seedbed, improves soil-moisture conditions, increases soil aeration, and upgrades the physical properties of compacted soil. Scarification seems mandatory for renovating most overused sites in which soils have become compacted, vegetation has been lost, and sheet erosion has taken place. It should be one of the first treatments considered since the effectiveness of some other treatments are dependent upon soil scarification. There are no ROS restrictions on the use of scarification, only on the particular equipment involved.

Degree of scarification depends upon the problems associated with a particular site. To be encouraged, a plant species may not need extensive exposure to mineral soil for germination and survival. Therefore scarification may be light, done with hand tools such as rakes. On the other hand, the soil may be deeply compacted — with an almost total loss of pore space for air and moisture, particularly in the upper six to twelve inches where most root systems are located. This may require mechanical scarification with heavy equipment, such as a tractor disk, to reach the entire compacted area. Even if the deteriorated portion of the site is going to be planted or sodded, it is still advisable to improve the physcial properties of the soil by scarifying and leveling.

When you reduce soil clumping caused by compaction, pore space — and consequently, soil aeration — increases. Root respiration depends on the amount of oxygen (O_2) available in the soil. At low oxygen levels, root respiration is reduced. In turn, mineral absorption by roots is directly associated with the level of respiration. Fine-textured soils such as clays may have more pore space initially, but quickly become compacted under heavy recreational use, particularly during periods of extremely high moisture.

Irrigation. Water seems to be a major limiting factor in site renovation.[1] Regardless of other treatments used, irrigation seems mandatory for heavily deteriorated sites. Better results seem to come from watering, fertilization, and seeding, or from watering and seeding. No other treatment or combinations of treatments bring significant results in reestablishing ground vegetation without adequate water.

Two types of irrigation are possible, flood and aerial. In flood irrigation, portions of the site are surface-flooded by a ditch system that transports the water. However, the site must be closed during the irrigation period, and flood irrigation is difficult to design where there is much variation in topography. It is seldom used on recreation sites.

Aerial irrigation is used fairly extensively on medium- to high-density sites because of the ease of control, flexibility of application, and efficiency of water use. Aerial irrigation systems can be portable or permanently installed, as with an underground sprinkler system. It is easier to direct and control the volume of waterflow using the aerial system, and a portable system allows flexibility in handling local, isolated problems. For permanent sites in which irrigation is done on a continuous basis, an underground system is more efficient and can be regulated so that any portion of it works independently of the rest of the network. It can also be shut down and drained during cold-weather periods.

Some problems associated with irrigation are beyond the immediate concern of improving site conditions. W.G. Beardsley and R.B. Herrington[1] list these as site design, cost, engineering, and public relations. Site design is important so that irrigation can be done with minimum inconvenience to visitors. Unfortunately, long-term management programs are typically not addressed when most sites are planned.

If you decide to use irrigation as a means of site maintenance or site renovation, you must also face the problem of public relations. You should make people aware of any inconveniences and offer an explanation so that people understand the need for the irrigation program. If a site is closed, there should ideally be information available on an alternate site. Good public relations through a strong, positive, information program make people aware of the situation and of the action being taken.

Fertilization. Fertilization implies adding commercial fertilizers to the soil to improve plant growth. Too often, managers use some standard fertilizer mix (N-P-K, plus some micronutrients) without understanding the deficiencies of the soil. Proper fertilization requires some knowledge of soil chemistry. Most states have a soil-testing laboratory to examine specific nutrient deficiencies in local soil and to make recommendations about correcting them. These deficiencies must be related to the plant species that you wish to grow since each species may have different nutritional requirements and levels of tolerance for specific mineral elements.

Nitrogen, phosphorus, and potassium are the primary elements used in fertilizers; other macronutrients necessary for plant growth are calcium, magnesium, and sodium. Required micronutrients include sulfur, manganese, iron, boron, copper, zinc, and molybdenum. Symptoms of deficiencies in any of these elements may show up in the vegetation. However, the real problem may turn out to be the pH of the soil; at a given pH, some elements are not readily available in a usable form. For example, below a pH of 4.7, tree seedlings, particularly the more fastidious, deciduous species, suffer from a low availability of nitrogen, phosphorous, potassium, or other bases. An alkaline pH (above 7.0) may decrease the availability of phosphates, iron, boron, zinc, and manganese. If we consider both nutritional and biological needs, the desirable soil pH for coniferous species is around 5.0, although some healthy stands may have a somewhat lower pH. For deciduous species, the desirable range is nearer 5.7 to 6.5.[26]

Vegetation. Exotic vegetation can be used as a surfacing material, or to stabilize soil or improve aesthetics. Due to variations in climate and individual site conditions, there are no universally recommended species. State highway departments, agricultural experiment stations, and horticulture/gardening centers are usually good sources of information on local adaptability of species.

Thinning. This will be discussed in more detail in Chapter Nine. It is, however, important to recognize the potential for improving the growth and vigor of ground vegetation by removing shade and root competition. Usually this treatment, if needed, is done in conjunction with one or more of the above treatments.

MONITORING VISITOR EFFECTS ON THE SITE

You can use several techniques to monitor the effects of recreational use — line transects, milacre plots, and photo files. Always monitor from a permanent point so that you can obtain repeated measures over time. The line transect method is especially useful for measuring change not only in percentage of ground cover but also species composition. A more detailed discussion of this technique can be found in any applied ecology text.

The milacre plot method is commonly used to measure both the change in vigor and the percentage of ground cover. Permanent plots (6.6 feet square) are established in medium-to-heavy-use, light-use, and zero-use zones of sites and are measured at regular intervals. The zero-use zone is usually an isolated place located adjacent to the site and within the same vegetation type. This zone gives you an estimate of vegetative changes not directly influenced by recreational use — a form of ecological yardstick. In the medium-to-high-use zone (the primary recreational portion of the designed site), you can determine the extent of change in ground vegetation and thus plan needed management programs. Measuring the light-use zone should indicate overflow effects from the main portion of the site. Determine the number of sets of plots you need by the variability of site vegetation and use patterns. A set of plots is three — one for each zone.

The photo-file technique is merely photo recording vegetational changes from permanent photo points with a standard camera mount. The technique is extremely valuable in cases where you are primarily interested in changes in the percentage of ground cover at particular locations. With all of these techniques, exercise care to protect permanent points from careless destruction by users or there is no comparable data.

SELECTED READINGS

1. Beardsley, W.G., and R.B. Herrington. 1971. "Economics and Management Implications of Campground Irrigation — A Case Study." *US Forest Service Research Note INT-129.*

2. Beardsley, W.G., and J.A. Wagar. 1971. "Vegetation Management on a Forested Recreation Site." *Journal of Forestry* 69:728.

3. Burden, R.F., and P.F. Randerson. 1972. "Quantitative Studies on the Effects of Human Trampling on Vegetation as an Aid to the Management of Semi-Natural Areas." *Journal of Applied Ecology* 9(2):439.

4. Carey, J.B. 1965. "The Use of Soil Surveys in Making Engineering Studies in Recreation Areas." *Northeast Fish and Wildlife Conference.* Harrisburg, PA.

5. Cieslinski, T.J., and J.A. Wagar. 1970. "Predicting the Durability of Forest Recreation Sites in Northern Utah-Preliminary Results." *US Forest Service Research Note INT-117.*

6. Cole, D.N. 1981. "Managing Ecological Impacts at Wilderness Campsites: An Evaluation of Techniques." *Journal of Forestry* 79(2):86-89.

7. Cole, D.N., and B. Ranz. 1983. "Temporary Campsite Closures in the Selway-Bitterroot Wilderness." *Journal of Forestry* 81(11):729-732.

8. Cole, D.N., and E.G. Schreiner. 1981. "Impacts of Backcountry Recreation: Site Management and Rehabilitation — An Annotated Bibliography." *USDA-Forest Service General Technical Report INT-121.*

9. Echelberger, H.E. 1971. "Vegetative Changes at Adirondack Campgrounds 1964 to 1969." *US Forest Service Research Paper NE-142.*

10. Harper, J.C., II. 1963. "Growing Turf Under Shaded Conditions." *Pennsylvania State University, Agricultural Extension Special Circular 149.* State College, PA.

11. Helgath, S.F. 1975. "Trail Deterioration in the Selway-Bitterroot Wilderness." *US Forest Service Research Note INT-193.*

12. Herrington, R.B., and W.G. Beardsley. 1970. *Improvement and Maintenance of Campground Vegetation in Central Idaho.* US Forest Service Research paper INT-87.

13. Jemison, G.M. 1967. "Impacts of Recreation on the Ecology of Temperate North American Forests." *Proceedings, Tenth Technical Meeting, International Union for the Conservation of Nature* (Lucerne, 1966) 7(1):185.

14. Kuss, F.R., A.R. Graefe, and L. Loomis. 1985. "Plant and Soil Responses to Wilderness Recreation: A Synthesis of Previous Research." *Proceedings — National Wilderness Research Conference: Current Research* USDA-Forest Service General Technical Report INT:212.

15. Lapage, W.F. 1967. *Some Observations on Campground Trampling and Ground Cover Response.* US Forest Service Research Paper NE-68.

16. MacKie, D.K. 1966. "Site Planning to Reduce Deterioration." *Proceedings, Society of American Foresters,* p. 33.

17. Magill, A.W. 1970. *Five California Campgrounds...Conditions Improving After Five Years of Rercreational Use.* US Forest Service Research Paper PSW-62.

18. McEwen, D., and S.R. Tocher. 1976. "Zone Management: Key to Controlling Recreational Impact in Developed Campsites," *Journal of Forestry* 74(2):90.

19. Partain, L.E. 1966. "The Use of Soil Knowledge in Recreation Area Planning," Virginia Polytechnic Institute, Agricultural Extension Bulletin 301, p. 180.

20. Ranz, B. 1979. "Closing Wilderness Campsites: Visitor Use Problems and Ecological Recovery in the Selway-Bitterroot Wilderness, Montana." MS Thesis (unpublished). University of Montana, Missoula.

21. Reckman, R.W., J. Letey, and L.H. Stolzy. 1966. "Compact Subsoil Can Be Harmful to Plant Growth." *Parks and Recreation.* 43(2):334.

22. Ripley, T.H. 1962. "Tree and Shrub Response to Recreational Use." *US Forest Service Research Note SE-171.*

23. Rudolph, P.O. 1967. "Silviculture for Recreation Area Management," *Journal of Forestry* 65:385.

24. Stevens, M.E. 1966. "Soil Surveys as Applied to Recreation Site Planning." *Journal of Forestry* 64:314.

25. Tocher, S.R., J.A. Wagar, and J.D. Hunt. 1965. "Sound Management Prevents Worn Out Recreation Sites." *Journal of Forestry* 63(3):151.

26. Wilde, S.A 1958. *Forest Soils.* New York: Ronald Press Co.

CHAPTER EIGHT

TURF MANAGEMENT

Figure 8-1. The Development and Maintenance of Turf at High Elevation — Jackson Lake Lodge, Grand Teton National Park. (Photo by Alan Jubenville)

Too often we may overlook turf management because we feel it is applicable only in special situations, primarily in the modern portion of ROS. In reality, we all are involved in some form of turf management — whether stabilizing cut and fills, hardening a site for recreational use, or overseeing a special area such as a golf green. The objectives of a turf management program vary according to the needs of the particular recreational opportunity, but success depends on both analysis of local conditions and strategies that meet these conditions.

The basic systems that affect turf development are soil, climate, microclimate, and use. Soil is the medium in which grass seeds germinate, establish a root system, and

grow through absorption of water and minerals. The physical properties (depth, texture, structure, organic matter) and chemical properties (exchange capacity, available nutrients, pH) of the soil determine the natural productivity of the site and thus its potential and limitations. It may be possible to adjust some of these factors to increase productivity and sod maintenance on a particular site.

Climate also affects the potential for turf development. Temperature and precipitation directly influence level of turf maturation, adaptability of species to edaphic conditions, and relative hardiness of a site after recreation use. Thus management recommendations for specific regions should be based on species

Figure 8-2. Major Turf Grass Zones in the United States (From Sprague, H.B. 1982. *Turf Management Handbook*. 3rd Edition. Danville, IL: The Interstate p. 30)

adaptability and growth patterns. For example, if two grasses having different growth patterns are adaptable to a particular site, the one that ceases growth early might be more desirable in relation to a particular pattern of use.

You can alter soil conditions, species composition, and even cultural treatments to produce the desired turf. However, you must ask yourself the following: Is this what we really want to do in terms of particular recreational opportunity? Is it economically feasible? What are the probabilities that the program will succeed and how predictable is the outcome?

REGIONAL REQUIREMENTS

Turf grass species are generally adapted to particular climatic zones; but even within those zones, each species tends to adapt to specific microclimatic conditions. Recommended species and cultural treatments are based on zonal and microclimate variations. The different turf grass regions or zones are shown in Figure 8-2, and associated natural conditions are described in Table 8-1. General species recommendations for cool and warm regions are summarized in Table 8-2 and discussed in the following sections.

Cool Regions. The turf grasses best suited to cooler regions are the bluegrasses, bentgrasses, fescues, and ryegrasses. Each species has its own particular characteristics, which you should attempt to match to the needs of the site. The following discussion is limited to a few important species, since new varieties are constantly being developed that are superior for specific turf uses. For example, new turf grasses for golf courses require less watering; this conserves the limited amount of water available for that function.

Bluegrasses (Poa). The bluegrasses are the most widely used of the cool-season grasses. They are best adapted for moist, fertile, fine-textured soils within a pH range of 6.0 to 7.0, and respond well to fertilization and irrigation. Kentucky bluegrass *(Poa pratensis)* grows well during cool weather but becomes less vigorous during warm periods. Not shade tolerant, it requires a soil with medium to high fertility, nearly neutral pH, and good water-holding capacity. It is not hardy enough to sustain medium to heavy recreational use without deterioration. Roughstalk bluegrass *(Poa trivalis)* has characteristics similar to those of Kentucky bluegrass, but it is more adapted to moderate shade, particularly in warmer conditions.

Canada bluegrass *(Poa compressa)*, although not aesthetically pleasing because of its coarse appearance, is drought-resistant and therefore generally used where there are poor soil and low-moisture conditions.

Annual bluegrass *(Poa annua)*, an annual, is shade tolerant. Owing to its adaptation and profuse seed development, it can germinate and survive on compacted soils as long as the soil is not dry. However, since it tends to die-back during the summer, it is usually used only as a temporary site stabilizer or in a mixture of other grasses.

Fescues (Festuca). Chewing fescue *(Festuca rubra commutala)* is an improved strain of red fescue which adds bright green color to the turf grass mixture and improves wearability of the mixture in recreational areas. Also, it does well in a variety of environmental conditions.

Reed fescue (Festuca elatior arundinacea) is adaptable to a variety of soil-moisture and temperature conditions. It is suitable for sites maintained in a rough rather than manicured condition. Cuttings should be no less than four inches in height and then taken only at infrequent intervals. Fertilizing is necessary to maintain high productivity.

Meadow fescue *(Festuca elatior)* is a fast-growing yet persistent species that can be valuable in a turf mixture used to establish new sod.

Bentgrasses *(Agrostis).* Creeping bentgrass *(Agrostis palustris)* can grown in a variety of environmental conditions except shade. Suitable for golf greens and other closely manicured sites that have regular topdressings, it is not generally effective for lawns. Colonial bentgrass *(Agrostis tenuis),* on the other hand, makes a suitable lawn grass when mixed with bluegrass and fescue.

TABLE 8-1. NATURAL SOIL CONDITIONS IN THE PRINCIPAL TURF GRASS REGIONS*

Region	Average Rainfall (in. yearly)	Natural Vegetative Cover	Natural Soil Characteristics Topsoil (general conditions)	Subsoil (general conditions)
1. Cool Humid Region				
A. Cleared woodlands	30 to 50	Mostly forest	Thin, grayish-brown, acid	Yellowish or light gray, heavy textured, strongly acid
B. Corn Belt	30 to 40	Tall grasses	Dark brown, high in humus, slightly to strongly acid	Lighter brown, lower in humus, slightly to moderately acid
2. Warm Humid Region	30 to 50	Mostly forest	Thin grayish to yellow, strongly acid	Strongly red or yellow, heavier textured, strongly acid
3. Great Plains				
A. Northern	12 to 30	Short to tall grasses	Brown to dark brown, humus stronger near surface, neutral to alkaline	Brown or lighter colored, little humus, lime nodules present
B. Southern	15 to 30	Short to tall grasses	Reddish brown (except Texas Black-lands), neutral to alkaline	Light reddish brown, heavier textured, lime nodules present
4. Semi-arid and Arid				
A. Cool, northern	3 to 12	Sparse grass and shrubs	Light grayish, alkaline	Light grayish, hardpan common, calcarcous
B. Warm, southern	3 to 15	Sparse grass and shrubs	Light reddish brown, alkaline	Reddish brown, friable, highly calcareous
5. California Coast and Interior Valleys	10 to 20	Grass and shrubs	Dark reddish brown, neutral to alkaline	Reddish brown, some lime present
6. North Pacific Coastal Area	30 to 50	Mostly forest	Generally gray or grayish brown, thin, acid	Yellowish or light gray, heavier textured, strongly acid

Special soil conditions:

A. *Alluvial soils:* Found on the flood plains of rivers and lesser water courses. Formed from sediment deposited periodically by water. Often relatively rich in organic matter (if dark colored) and nutrients. Highly variable in texture.

B. *Excessively sandy soils:* Widely distributed. All sands are low in water-supplying power and subject to wind erosion. Generally low in nutrients, and easily leached by rainfall.

C. *Alkali and salty soils:* Occur locally throughout drier regions, wherever internal soil drainage is imperfect. Salty soils mostly occur on coastal plains, where sea or brackish water penetrates.

* From Sprague, H.B. 1982. *Turf Management Handbook.* 3rd Edition. Danville, IL: The Interstate, p. 15.

Table 8-2. Turf Grass Regions in the United States*

1. Cool Humid Region
   Suited to cool-season grasses such as bluegrass, fescue and bentgrasses. Soils generally acid, and often low in fertility. Sprinkler irrigation desired to supplement rainfall.
   1a. Transition Zone
       A difficult zone, where either cool-season or warm-season grasses may be grown. However, summers are too hot for desired growth of cool-season grasses, and winters are too long and cold for desired growth of warm-season grasses. Supplemental irrigation must be used carefully to encourage the type of grass desired. Soils are generally acid and low in native fertility.
2. Warm Humid Region
   Suited to warm-season grasses such as bermudagrass and St. Augustinegrass. Soils generally strongly acid, and may be relatively infertile. Sprinkler irrigation needed to supplement rainfall.
3. Plains Regions
   3a. Northern Plains
       Suited to cool-season grasses, but artificial watering is essential for good lawns. Soils are not naturally acid, and may be well supplied with mineral nutrients.
   3b. Southern Plains
       Suited to warm-season grasses, and sprinkler irrigation is indispensable for strong turf since it supplements uncertain rainfall. Soils are not naturally acid, but are less likely to be fertile than Northern Plains soils.
4. Arid and Semi-arid Regions
   Suited to cool-season grasses, but sprinkler irrigation must be provided throughout the growing season. Soils are not acid, and are generally well supplied with mineral nutrients.
   4b. Warm Arid and Semi-arid Regions
       Suited to warm-season grasses, but sprinkler irrigation is imperative throughout the growing season. Soils are not acid, but are somewhat less fertile than regions to the North.
5. California Coast and Interior Valleys
   Suited to warm-season grasses, but sprinkler irrigation is imperative during the warm, dry, growing season. Soils are generally not acid, and contain moderate amounts of mineral nutrients.
6. North Pacific Coastal Areas
   Suited to cool-season grasses. Rainfall generally adequate except in midsummer when sprinkler irrigation is required. Soils are usually acid, and have fair-to-low mineral nutrient content.

* From Sprague, H.B. 1982. *Turf Management Handbook,* 3rd Edition. Danville, IL: The Interstate, p. 4-5.

Velvet bentgrass *(Agrostis canina)* has important characteristics like shade tolerance, drought resistance, and ability to survive under varying temperature conditions. This makes it ideal for some specialized sites.

Ryegrass *(Lolium).* Perennial ryegrass *(Lolium perenne)* is probably the most widely used; in a seed mixture, it rapidly establishes a temporary sod until other grasses eventually take over and form the permanent sod.

Legumes. Although not classified as grasses, legumes are often used in conjunction with them for site stabilization and soil improvement. Herbaceous legumes have a taproot with nodules where bacteria fix free nitrogen from the air, enabling the legume and associated grasses to assimilate this nutrient.

Crownvetch (Coronilla varia L.). Crownvetch is a very competitive perennial, eighteen to twenty-four inches high but slow in initial establishment. Therefore it is usually mixed with grasses such as red fescue and ryegrass so that the grasses provide initial cover. Well-adapted to droughty, low-temperature sites, even in infertile, acidic areas such as road cuts (Beard, 1973), it is best suited for well-drained soils high in calcium, phosphorous, and potassium.

Lespedeza (Lespedeza spp.). Planted on roadsides and other low-use areas for erosion control, Lespedeza is a legume that is primarily effective in the transition between cold and warm-season zones. It is adapted to acidic, low-fertility soils, and is drought resistant.

True Clovers (Trifolium L.) Clovers, the most widely distributed legume, are suited to cool, humid areas on fairly fertile sites. They are sometimes used as a winter annual in warm humid climates. Drought tolerance is poor. Flowers are produced even at very low cutting heights.

Warm Regions. Most warm-region grasses are established by sprigging; only common bermudagrass and carpetgrass may be established with seeds. Consequently, although a monoculture may tend to be less attractive and less disease-resistant, a single species is generally preferable to a mixture of species. Since most warm-region species survive in any warm-zone area, it is imperative to select the one most suited to specific edaphic conditions and recreational use.

Common carpetgrass (Axonopus affinis). This is common turf grass restricted to the sandy, low-fertility soils and high-moisture conditions of the southeast coastal plains. Carpetgrass requires little care after initial establishment.

Common bermudagrass (Cynodon dactylon). This species grows well throughout warmer regions where moisture is not limited. It spreads quickly and lives long on any site with fertile, reasonably well-drained soil. As stated by H.B. Sprague,[11] common bermudagrass has four weaknesses: it is not shade tolerant; it turns brown with the first light frost; it has a high-fertility requirement and thus may be invaded by other species if not properly fertilzed; and it is not very green. Although it has only a moderate tolerance for drought, it is probably the most drought-resistant of all the warm-region grasses.

Hybrid bermudagrass. Several bermudagrass hybrids have been devleoped that are superior to the common species as turf grass. They are usually more vibrant in color and more vigorous in growth, have fewer fertility requirements, and are more disease resistant.

Zoysiagrasses (Zoysia). The zoysiagrasses are best suited to warm humid zones. They tolerate a wide range of soil conditions, except poorly drained areas. Slow to become established, zoysiagrasses can nevertheless survive high levels of use once they take root.

St. Augustinegrass (Stenotaphrum secundatum). This shade-tolerant grass is adaptable to a variety of soil conditions. It requires frequent fertilization and mowing to maintain vigorous growth. If soils are acidic, liming should be done to raise the pH closer to neutral.

Centipedegrass (Eremochloa ophiuroides). This has characteristics similar to those of carpetgrass. Centipedegrass responds well to fertilization, and can be used to regenerate worn-out sites.

DEVELOPMENT OF TURF

There are two ways of establishing turf — seeding and vegetative planting. Choice of method depends on grass selected for use, site conditions, and anticipated patterns of use.

Seeding. Seeding is usually done in early spring or early fall when temperature and moisture conditions are good. In cool regions, early fall seeding allows reasonable establishment before dormancy. In warm regions, you can usually seed in early spring. However, if moisture is not limited, you can seed at any time.

Seed mixtures are usually planted in cooler regions. The exact mix depends on site conditions and specific recreational use, but it usually includes perennial ryegrass, which quickly occupies a site until the permanent grasses establish a sod.

Seed quality is important and therefore ensured through federal and state laws. Species, purity, and percentage of germination must be shown on the label along with percentage of weed seeds.

After you have obtained the seed, you must prepare seedbed before planting begins. It is less expensive to install structures such as drain tiles or water bars at this time than after planting. If major reshaping is to be done to the landscape prior to planting, you should carefully remove the topsoil first and then replace it after the reshaping operation. You should also lime, fertilize, and add any organic matter to improve soil conditions prior to planting. Rotatill these additives into the soil to a depth of about six inches. The organic matter not only improves soil fertility but also increases its water-holding capacity. For example, if sandy soils are a problem, you can add organic matter and fines to improve water-holding and cation exchange capacity. Since lime and fertilizer are translocated downward, not laterally, surface application of these materials should be uniform prior to rotatilling.

Seed immediately after seedbed preparation. Seeding rates, expressed in pounds per acre or pounds per one thousand square feet, are based on species mixture, purity, and percent of germination, and seeds are broadcast evenly over the surface. The seeding technique recommended by Sprague is to divide the seeds into two equal portions.[11] One half is broadcast in one direction, the other half in a line perpendicular to the first half. Lightly rake the seeds into the seedbed, then roll the surface. Finally, lightly but evenly mulch the seedbed with straw.

Vegetative Plantings. You can plant vegetation by sprigging, spot sodding, or complete sodding. All these methods require the same ground preparation as seeding. Each has a preferred use, depending on circumstances, costs, and management objectives.

Complete sodding has often been overlooked because of the supposedly high cost of implementation. Yet cost analyses by a local park district indicate that on an area that is 2.5 acres or less, complete sodding is cheaper than other methods. This study takes into account the following local circumstances: high probability at high altitudes of at least partial failure of seeding; man-hours spent in maintaining constant attention prior to sod establishment; and short growing season.

Site stabilization on steeper slopes and the need to harden heavy-use portions dictate complete sodding. Management concerns should dictate the primary choice if there are sufficient monies to support the program.

In the sprigging method, separate the grass plant into sprigs or runners (pieces of stolons) that are planted to generate new sod. Spread the sprigs evenly over the area by means of a preplanned grid system; then push them into the soil until they approximately reach the root collar. You can use a notched dibble to push the sprigs into the soil. This minimizes damage to the sprig yet still maintains planting efficiency. Finally, press the soil down firmly with the heel of your boot.

You can also plant vegetation by the spot-sodding method, which involves planting small pieces of sod at regular intervals over an entire area. Lift the sod from the nursery and cut it into three-to four-inch squares, then lay them six to twelve inches apart. Make a hole for each piece of sod and plant them about one-half inch below surface level, securing them by stamping down with your shoe. As the plant takes hold, it sends out runners.

Usually, spot-sodding and sprigging take a considerable time to root a dense sod. You must water and possibly mow carefully in order to enhance turf growth and establishment, after which you must practice regular turf management.

MANAGEMENT OF TURF

Regular maintenance is essential for most grasses and particularly, for those located in areas of active recreational use. Here we will discuss two important aspects of turf maintenance: soil chemical treatments and cultural treatments of the sod.

Soil Chemical Treatments. Soil-acidity problems generally occur in areas of excessive precipitation or artificial watering. Although some grasses survive these conditions, all grasses grow better at a more neutral pH. One possible treatment to improve soil fertility is liming. For general recommendations on this method, consulting a person who is knowledgeable about local conditions, such as the county agent or soil conservationist, may suffice. In high precipitation areas, one to two tons of crushed limestone per acre should be sufficient to promote good sod development. However, soil analysis by a competent laboratory is the most accurate guideline since the relative acidity of soil can also vary according to texture.

After developing the sod, you should continue liming periodically to maintain a nearly neutral pH; this maximizes available plant nutrients. High soil acidity reduces decay of dead roots, thus decreasing humus breakdown. This in turn interferes with normal root development and percolation of water into the soil. Furthermore, highly acidic soils usually contain large amounts of certain elements such as soluble aluminum and manganese, which are toxic in large quantities, along with unusable forms of nitrogen. This is a result of acid-forming fertilizers that replace and leach calcium and magnesium from the upper soil layer. Correct this condition by applying crushed limestone.

Fertilizing is the other chemical treatment for improving soil fertility; however, it may create acidic soil conditions that must be corrected with lime if added nutrients are to be available for plant use. Again, you should fertilize only after a complete soil analysis has been made.

Fertilizers are usually labeled according to percentage by weight of available nitrogen (N_2), phosphate (P_2O_5), and potash (K_2O). These primary nutrients are necessary for vigorous plant growth. Thus one hundred pounds of a 10-5-5 fertilizer contains ten pounds of usable nitrogen, five pounds of phosphate, and five pounds of potash. As a general rule, an application of twenty-five to thirty pounds of a 10-5-5 fertilizer per one thousand square feet is advisable for seedbed preparation. Mix about two-thirds of the fertilizer throughout the soil and the remaining third into the upper inch. During the establishment of sod, you should also check the color of the young plants; for example, if the young leaves are pale green, additional nitrogen may be necessary.

Fertilize newly established sod with a 10-5-5 fertilizer applied at a rate of fifteen pounds per one hundred feet at least twice a year.[11] Watering aids in moving the fertilizer into the top inch of the soil, but sporodic light watering may also cause the germination of weed seed in the soil surface that competes with the grass seedlings.

In cool regions, apply fertilizer in the spring and fall. Fall applications accelerate the spring growth of the sod, particularly if the growing season is short. In warmer regions, applications are normally made in the spring and midsummer because of the lengthy growing season.

Cultural Treatments Of The Sod. Managers should be familiar with the following cultural treatments:
Cleaning. This is the removal of tree leaves to maximize the amount of light reaching the ground cover. Cleaning promotes healthy growth of sod from spring through the early fall. It also reduces undesirable surface moisture and heating; these can be detrimental to grass blades and promote conditions that lead to disease.
Topdressing. Topdressing — i.e., spreading a thin layer (one-fourth inch or so) of fertile topsoil over the sod and lightly working it in — can improve soil conditions on poor sites, level small areas, raise a surface, cover a vegetative planting, and protect from winter kill. You can modify soil texture through coring (removal of soil cores) and topdressing.

A specific application of topdressing is mandatory to maintain golf greens. Perform this procedures by first scarifying and/or thatching the area to remove matted bentgrass, then top-dressing it to improve the fertility of the site and the vigor of the grass.
Scarifying. this means mechanically disturbing the sod cover and soil surface to improve water percolation and aeration, allowing penetration of less mobile fertilizers. You scarify by slicing into the soil with v-shaped knife blades on a circular wheel. The slicing penetrates deep into the soil at some predetermined interval.
Aeration. This is the mechanical removal of sod-soil cores to improve soil aeration, increase water percolation and penetration of fertilizers,

Figure 8-3. Turf Management is Necessary to Eastern State Parks Where Summer Rains Generate Lush Growth (Photo by Gordon Wissinger)

and reduce root competition. You can obtain some of these additional benefits through other treatments, but improved soil aeration is best achieved by removing small cores. Slicing or similar scarification techniques that penetrate the sod do not remove any soil or sod; consequently, the point of penetration is closed more quickly.

Thatching. Thatch is the layer of dead and living stems between the green tops and the surface of the soil. Some thatch is desirable as a cushion to reduce soil compaction and to insulate the soil.[3] Excessive accumulation increases disease and insect problems and localized dry spots, and increases susceptibility to mechanical injury. You can control thatch build-up biologically through proper scheduling of the previously discussed cultural treatments. Also avoid excessive nitrogen fertilization and/or irrigation since they stimulate too much stem growth and a build-up of thatch. Control thatch growth mechanically with vertical mowing or power raking. Thatch buildup tends to be more of a problem on poorly drained, fine-textured soils.

Mowing. This procedure can cause great damage to mature grasses if not done properly. Where recreation use is anticipated or adverse environmental conditions already exist (such as shading), grass should be mowed at greater heights than normal, up to two inches, and possibly at less frequent intervals. Longer grass has a greater photosynthetic area and is consequently more hardy. Its "rougher" appearance may be a more desirable outcome than dead spots in the turf. Remember that the objective is to stimulate growth; if you mow at too short a height or too frequently, you may weaken rather than improve the vigor of the grass. Desired cutting height depends on the turf species; however, in recreation sites, other considerations such as aesthetics and playing conditions determine this. When those types of trade-offs are made, you must alter the cutting schedule and increase other treatments to compensate. On more intensively managed sites, remove clippings to increase aesthetic appeal and reduce possible diseases.

There is a growing use for chemical turf growth regulators. Chemicals decrease shoot growth rate, but do not completely retard growth, reducing mowing expenses. Completely retarding growth eliminates the recuperative capacity of turfgrass after recreational use, and weakens its ability to fend off possible diseases.

Watering. Water to supplement natural precipitation. In high-moisture areas, this may be necessary only during severe droughts. In dry areas, watering and irrigation systems can be very extensive. Water artificially to maintain turf growth for extended periods of time and at frequent intervals to get good penetration. Frequent intervals of light watering encourage weeds to germinate and grow in the sod.

Weeding. Weeding is important if you are to maintain a dense sod. This means you should perform all chemical and cultural treatments properly to foster good sod vigor after establishment. Any treatment not done properly can promote the growth of weeds, which should be checked. Once these weeds are established, you need selective herbicides to remove them. The use of the herbicides depends on local conditions and should be only undertaken by someone who is knowledgeable about the chemicals and their proper use.

If turf has not been maintained properly, you may have to renovate the sod. You must assess the problem and realign your maintenance program to improve the condition of the turf. You may even be faced with the decision to either revamp your program or start over with new turf! Such renovation should be carefully integrated with visitor control programs to protect the site during rejuvenation.

SEASONAL MANAGEMENT SCHEDULES

Some authors have offered specific schedules which they feel must be adhered to in order to properly maintain turf. We would suggest that there is sufficient variation in recreational use, environmental conditions, and species composition that local managers should develop their own seasonal schedules. This may mean separate schedules for each park or even for portions of a specific park that has different management programs.

This chapter only gives an overview of turf management and the main variables and management techniques used by outdoor recreation managers. More detailed information can be found in turf-management books or through local agencies such as the Agricultural Extension Service, the Soil Conservation Service, and other related state organizations.

SELECTED READINGS

1. Augustine, M.F. 1966. "Vegetation to Stabilize Areas in Building." *Soil Conservation* 32(4):78.

2. Barkley, D.B., R.R. Blaser, and R.E. Schmidt. 1965. "Effect of Mulches on Microclimate and Turf Establishment." *Agronomy Journal* 57:189.

3. Beard, J.B. 1973. *Turfgrass: Science and Culture*. Englewood Cliffs, NJ: Prentice-Hall, Inc.

4. Blaser, R.E. 1963. "Principles of Making Turf Mixtures for Roadside Seeding." Highway Research Records, No. 23. National Research Council. p. 79.

5. Curry, R.J., L.E. Foote, O.N. Andrews, Jr., and J.A. Jakobs. 1964. "Lime and Fertilizer Requirements as Related to Turf Establishment along the Roadside." Highway Research Records, No. 53. National Research Council. p. 26.

6. Hanson, A.A. 1965. *Grass Varieties in the United States*. Agricultural Handbook No. 170. Agricultural Research Service, US Department of Agriculture.

7. Hanson, A.A., and F.V. Juska (eds.). 1969. *Turfgrass Science*. Agronomy No. 14. Madison, WI: American Society of Agronomy, Inc.

8. Hood, R. 1964. "Turfgrass Management Stretches Dollars." *Ohio Public Works* 95(7):76.

9. Musser, H.B. 1962. *Turf Management*. US Gold Association.

10. Proceedings of Scotts Turfgrass Research Conferences.

11. Sprague. H.B. 1982. *Turf Management Handbook*. 3rd edition. Danville, IL: The Interstate.

12. Triplett, G.B., Jr., and R.R. Davis. 1966. "Spot Treatment for Perennial Grass Weeds." Research Summary, Ohio Agriculture Research and Development Center, p. 9.

13. Venegris, J. 1973. *Lawns: Basic Factors, Construction and Maintenance of Fine Turf Areas*. Indianapolis: Thomson Publications.

CHAPTER NINE

MANAGEMENT OF OVERSTORY VEGETATION

The primary emphasis of this chapter is silvicultural treatments of overstory vegetation before, during, and after site development. Specific kinds of vegetation management are discussed, as well as related visitor-management practices. The chapter also presents possibilities for site redevelopment, when vegetation reaches the point of biological maturity and you must decide to either abandon the site or regenerate the stand.

The timing of treatments can be extremely important. When done prior to development, they can reduce the shock of recreational use and increase the vigor of the trees, making them better able to sustain themselves. Successive treatments during and after development are based on need determined through monitoring.

SILVICULTURAL TREATMENTS PRIOR TO DEVELOPMENT

The three primary silvicultural treatments are thinning, sanitation cutting, and clear cutting.

Thinning. This practice requires coordination with long-range planning. Thinning prepares the site for development and improves the condition of vegetation prior to recreational use (See Figure 9-1). Site preparation may precede site development by two to ten years, depending on how the vegetation responds. It may be done at regular intervals until an area opens for visitors, particularly if the species is susceptible to windthrow.

Thinning opens up stands of trees in order to increase light and reduce root and crown competition, thereby strengthening the quantity and hardiness of both the ground cover and the remaining overstory vegetation. This also improves aesthetics, reduces dust, increases natural screening, and promotes desirable shading conditions. You should cut off trees at ground level, which may require you to dig a small trench around the base of the tree so that the chain-saw operator can manipulate the saw. In thinning, you remove some of the dominant and codominant trees, along with all intermediate and suppressed stands. This improves both crown size and general vigor of the remaining trees. In addition, it serves as an improvement cut that favors certain more durable species on the new site. In the process, the light reaching the ground should aid in species composition and add vigor to ground vegetation. Specific recommendations must be based on intended recreational use, the silvical characteristics of the tree species, and the requirements for improving ground cover.

For wind-firm, even-aged stands of trees, one thinning is usually needed three to five years prior to development and involves removing about one-third to one-half the crown density. For truly uneven-aged stands, which contain a mixture of size and age classes, do not thin prior to development since the desired conditions already exist in theory. However, you typically find only two or three size and age classes, which appear in clusters or multi-story canopies. If size classes occur in clusters, thin each of these carefully to improve conditions for that portion of the site.

Multi-story stands are generally in some stage of successional change — i.e., the less competitive (intolerant) species has been invaded by the more competitive (shade tolerant) species. You can handle this in several ways, depending on species and type of recreational use. If the understory species is more desirable in terms of aesthetics and durability, you can remove the overstory

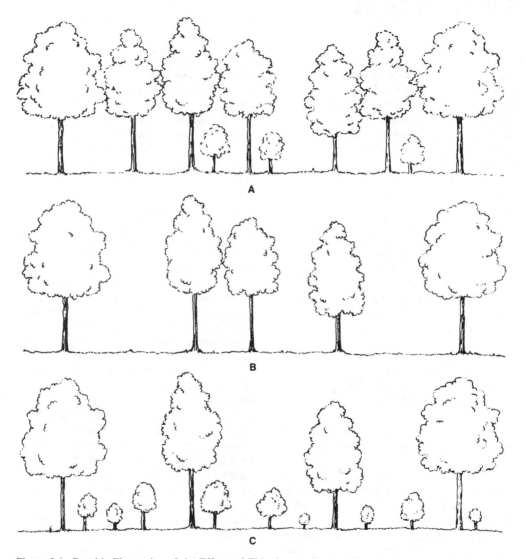

Figure 9-1. Graphic Illustration of the Effects of Thinning. A, Nearly 100 percent overstory stocking with little understory; B, thinning of overstory to improve growing conditions and ground cover; C, five years after thinning, the trees have bigger, more healthy crowns and well-established ground vegetation.

species; thinning is then delayed until time of development. The new overstory should be well stocked (fifty percent or more), thrifty in external appearance, and at least twenty-five feet high prior to site development. This height should encourage well-established trees with good canopy size, yet allow adequate room below the canopy for normal movement of people and vehicles. If the overstory is desirable and still in its biological prime, remove the understory and thin the overstory.

If the species are not wind firm, pre-development thinning should probably be done in two stages, starting five to ten years prior to development. The first thinning should remove approximately twenty to twenty-five percent of the crown canopy, and the second phase should open the canopy to the desired level.

Sanitation Cutting. Sanitation cutting is the removal of trees that have been affected by disease or insect attacks or have sustained mechanical injuries that would make them highly susceptible to these. Make such cuttings prior to development in order to improve the general health of the stand and reduce possible loss of live trees later on. If an insect or disease problem requires removing a significant number of trees, consider relocation. All fresh cutting, stumps, etc., should be removed, burned, or treated to eliminate any attractor of new insect infestations.

Give the stand a complete inventory to determine the degree of infestation; then individually mark each tree that you wish to remove. If the disease can be transmitted through root grafts, adjacent trees also have to be eliminated. In that case, it is advisable to burn all removed trees.

Clear Cutting. Clear cutting rights-of-way for major roads and mini-developments must be staked out to determine the types of vegetation and microclimates the road will pass through. No pre-development cutting may be necessary if microclimatic conditions are favorable, species composition is reasonably uniform, and species are wind firm. In areas where the species is susceptible to wind throw because of a shallow root system, partial removal of the overstory in the right-of-way may be more desirable; you later perform total removal at the time of development. This also allows some minimum access prior to development of the site, and you can decrease the susceptibility of the remaining trees to windthrow by feathering the edges of the clearcut.

The actual cutting of trees simply appears as thinning, and partial cuttings improve the growth of the remaining stems. Select stems for actual removal based on their position relative to other trees, visible external signs of endemic insect and disease problems, or potential for mechanical injury or necessary road access.

SILVICULTURAL TREATMENTS DURING DEVELOPMENT

Cuttings made during the development phase are similar to those made prior to it. Final thinning before development increases tree vigor, creates desired shade conditions, and improves aesthetics. The sanitation portion of the cutting removes any insect- and disease-promoting conditions. Remove up to fifty percent or more of the crown cover to allow sunlight into the site. Cutting may be uniform or variable, depending on your sun/shade requirements for specific portions of the site. For example, the campground unit may require an average amount of shade, whereas the comfort station and water-point areas may need more-than-average sunlight. When removing a high percentage of the crown cover, leave the remaining trees in clusters for mutual support from wind damage.

The final right-of-way for the access road, including the shoulders of the road bed, is allocated at time of development. If there is a dense stand of trees, feather the edge of the right-of-way to improve aesthetics, reduce wind shear, and reduce shading along the shoulder for grass establishment.

On intensive use portions of the site, prune the remaining trees along the bole from twelve to sixteen feet high after all other development cuttings have been made. This is an expensive procedure that requires close attention to detail in order to minimize mechanical damage to tree; timing and technique are important. Pruning is often criticized because it opens the tree to insect and disease attacks. On the other hand, pruning removes dead limbs and those that are injured by recreationists. Prune in the spring so that trees have an opportunity to form callous tissue over wounds immediately. If you prune in late summer after growth has ceased or during the fall, trees are more susceptible to insect attack through open wounds. In the fall, insects deposit their eggs in wounds for overwintering.

Proper technique for removal of tree limbs is to undercut the limb with a pruning saw and then remove it with a flush-out along the bole. The undercut keeps the limb from tearing the bark below. Limbs up to two inches in diameter should heal naturally without being sealed artificially; those over two inches should be sealed immediately. To encourage rapid healing of the larger wounds, light scarification with the saw around the wound may help.

The last treatment during the development phase is called mini-development. This involves preparation of such areas as an open play space at a group picnic area or a guard station at a campground. Make a small clear cutting where the mini-development is to be located, and remove all trees. You should also remove those trees that may interfere with the facility, and give consideration to the effects of root systems on foundations and sewers.

POST-DEVELOPMENT TREATMENTS

Schedule periodic surveys, using specific data collection forms, to assess the condition of the overstory vegetation. This fulfills your legal as well as professional obligation to reduce hazardous conditions due to dead or dying trees and reduce risks of further insect and disease attacks while maintaining desirable, natural aesthetics. The survey should focus on the following:

1. disease- and insect-infected trees

2. mechanical injury to tops from ice or wind
3. mechanical injury from recreational use, primarily from cutting on the bole and trampling around the root collar
4. stagheading (die-back of tree top), which may indicate severe soil compaction or biological overmaturity of species
5. general vigor and coloration of the crowns

Not all trees with negative signs must be removed immediately. Classify these as either *cut* or *watch* trees. Remove *cut* ones because they are probably a hazard to visitors or the general health of the other trees. Flag *watch* trees and observe them during subsequent surveys to determine whether or not their condition is stable. If individual trees are important in the landscape design of the site, specific treatment such as tree surgery may be recommended by an arboriculturist. The individual employed in seasonal site maintenance should also receive instructions on making and reporting casual observations while working on any site. This provides some periodic observations in between surveys.

Post-development cuttings are designed to maintain the general health of a stand of trees, to remove public hazards through the use of sanitation cutting and hazard-tree removal, and to possibly thin, though thinning is generally not necessary except on better sites. Since the crowns grow at a rate proportionate to the root system, they cannot expand very fast if the system becomes restricted by compacted soil.

One post-development treatment that has not been given sufficient attention is site expansion. If a site has been chosen to allow for future expansion, the cycle of treatments may be repeated, starting with pre-development on each new expansion; however, these treatments must be coordinated with the existing site, since the area is simply an expansion of that site. In sum, this means you must consider the overstory vegetation management program in initial site planning so that all management activities can be coordinated.

SITE REGENERATION

Ultimately managers must concern themselves with regenerating overstory vegetation in order to redevelop sites. After trees have reached their biological maturity, they begin to deteriorate. At some point, you must decide to regenerate the site or abandon it. Not much consideration has been given to this problem because most developed sites are relatively new and trees have not yet reached the point of massive deterioration. Also, little research is available about techniques for regenerating vegetation on recreational sites. A discussion of some theoretical possibilities for regenerating overstory vegetation follows.

Option 1: Relocate. If there is a minimum investment involved and if several potential sites are available, relocation seems to be the most logical choice. It causes less inconvenience to the user, it is possibly less expensive to develop, and it offers an opportunity to update the design of the site.

Option 2: Close and Regenerate. Probably the least desirable alternative is to close the site so that the overstory can be regenerated. This is inconvenient for users since the site must be closed for a number of years. Also, other sites have to absorb user demand for the seven to ten years required for vegetation to reach a sufficient height (at least twenty to twenty-five feet). Any vegetation that is smaller tends to be damaged by visitors, even with normal use.

If there are several similar sites in the area, you may only need one new site so that regeneration can be done by rotation. For example, in Figure 9-2, A_5 is the newly developed site. It replaces A_1 during the regeneration period; A_1 then replaces A_2 during the next regeneration; A_2 replaces A_3, and so on.

The regeneration method should be compatible with silvical requirements of the forest types being regenerated and with local site conditions. Natural regeneration takes too long to reestablish; therefore planting is the most logical choice. For some species, a two-cut shelter wood is desirable though it appears as a three-cut shelter wood.

Figure 9-2. Rotation of Similar Types of Sites during Regeneration. A_5 is the new site that is being used to replace A_1, while it is being regenerated, and so on. This is possible only in cases where age and site varibility will allow rotation over an extended number of years, possibly decades.

The operation is as follows:

1. In one cut, remove all competing and undesirable understory, along with approximately fifty to sixty percent of the overstory.
2. Plant older nursery stock, possibly 2-1 or 2-2 stock.* The root system is larger and therefore better able to survive and grow quickly; the remaining overstory provides protection to the seedlings during the reestablishment period (about 3 years).
3. After establishment, the remaining overstory is removed. In another four to ten years, the seedling will have grown to sapling size — the minimum necessary prior to reopening the site. Possibly fertilization and irrigation can reduce reestablishment time.

---

*2-1 refers to two years in the seed bed and one year in the transplant bed at the nursery.

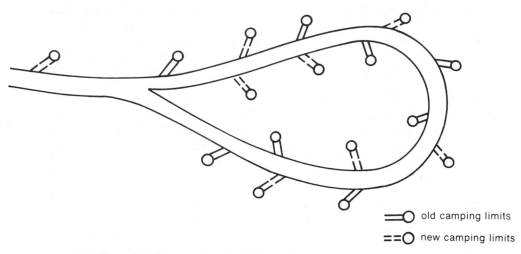

old camping limits

new camping limits

Figure 9-3. Diagram Showing Option to Re-establish or Redesign Site.

Option 3: Redesign and Re-establish. In this alternative, the entire site is not closed; however, individual units such as those in a forest campground are permanently closed and intermediate areas are then opened (See Figure 9-3.) The steps are as follows:

1. Vegetation for proposed new units is reestablished in a sufficient amount of time to grow to a minimum height of twenty to twenty-five feet prior to designing, developing, and opening new units. These must be "patch" or group selection cuttings and require a great distance in between existing units.[13] Some barriers have to be developed to minimize casual trampling.
2. The old units are regenerated — perhaps as discussed in option 2.

The arguments against this option are strong. People question why units are not developed since demand generally outstrips supply in most recreational areas. The public also decries destruction of portions of the site though timber harvesting. At the same time, the situation dictates that smaller units (openings) be regenerated one at a time rather than across the entire site, and small openings may not meet the biological requirements for adequate regeneration. Finally, Option 3 is only possible on low-density occupancy sites in which individual units are adequately separated so that they can be relocated in intermediate zones.

In sum, Option 1 (relocate) appears to be a more logical and economically efficient management strategy. However, on heavy-use sites where available open space is at a premium, the only choice may be to regenerate the site. The challenge is how to make that happen.

METHODS OF REGENERATION

There are three methods of regenerating trees: natural seeding, artificial seeding, and planting. Natural regeneration, even when associated with cultural treatments, is generally not as desirable as the other two methods for the intensive-use sites. However, natural regeneration is probably the only viable choice in dispersed use areas because of both cost and the aesthetics of maintaining the normal character of the landscape. At a number of smaller, heavily used locations in dispersed areas, some cultural treatments encourage rapid regeneration to quickly stabilize a site. However, you must also shift patterns of recreational use during the regeneration period to minimize disruption of the process. You can obtain exact natural regeneration requirements from the United States Department of Agriculture's Woody Plant Seed Manual,[15] or the US Forest Service publications on silvical characteristics for each species.[16]

Machine planting is generally not a viable alternative since the areas to be planted are usually small. If the need arises because of area size and gentle terrain, you can usually contract a local operator to do the machine planting.

Seeding can be done by either broadcasting over large openings or spot seeding. Again this method has limitations where recreation use occurs; it takes longer to regenerate the trees, and there is always the possibility of failure because of unusual environmental conditions. You can determine exact seeding requirements by using the sources that were suggested above.

For natural areas, you have no other choice but to regenerate naturally. If a species has been extirpated locally within a natural area and you wish to reintroduce the same species, collect seeds close to the point of introduction and on sites similar to that point. This is expensive but essential if you are to maintain maximum genetic integrity — just any local seed source will not do.

Of more concern to the outdoor recreation manager is an artificial means of regenerating trees — direct seeding or planting. You should base your selection of species not only on site conditions but also on intended use; i.e., the site plan may require shade trees, wind-firm trees, wildlife food, and so forth. Choose species that have those characteristics but are also adaptable to local site conditions.

The last and most important regeneration method is hand planting. Selecting and handling plant stock are important to the success of your planting program. You should obtain your stock from a local, nursery-grown, certified seed source, a seed source whose location features environmental conditions similar to those of your planting site. It is often advisable to buy transplant stock (stock that is transplanted from the seed bed) because it has a larger root system and is thus more resistant to the shock of being transplanted.

Once you obtain the seedlings, heel them in until you are ready for planting. This requires digging a V-shape trench in a shaded moist location, making sure that the sides of the trench are approximately three to four inches longer than the root systems. Open each bundle of seedlings and then spread them out along one side of the ditch. Place loose soil, with some additional organic matter, back into the ditch and water it heavily. Tamp the seedlings gently with your foot, taking care to minimize root damage.

When it is time to plant, lift the seedlings out and place them in an open container filled with sufficient water to cover their roots. The soil opening for the seedling should be large enough to accommodate the root system without bending or changing natural root conformation. Depth is also extremely important; ideally you should plant the seedling approximately one-half inch below the depth at which it grew in the nursery; planting it too deep or too shallow increases the chance of mortality.

After planting, you may need temporary fencing to protect the young seedlings from rodents, deer, etc. Additional cultural treatments such as weeding to eliminate competition from less desirable species may also be necessary particularly on the better sites.

There are two types of planting tools — the dibble (or planting bar) and the mattock (See Figure 9-4.) Either method is satisfactory; however, mattock planting is necessary on hard, heavy soils or when you're using transplant stock with large roots.

INTRODUCTION OF EXOTICS

"Exotic" simply refers to a species that does not naturally grow on a particular site. Up to this point, a good rule of thumb has been to avoid exotics, though this is not always possible. In addition, some exotics have very desirable characteristics, and you may wish to take advantage of these species. Careful review of species within a region, discussion with local experts, and trial plantings may help you

Figure 9-4. Planting Methods (From *Forestry Handbook*. K.F. Wenger [ed.]. New York: John Wiley & Sons, 1984. 2nd edition.)

Table 9-1. Trees Suitable for an Urban Environment*

SPECIES			GROWTH RATE	GROWING CONDITIONS	HARDINESS ZONES
PIN OAK *QUERCUS PALLUSTRIS* 20 to 25 METERS			MODERATE TO FAST	FULL SUN. RICH LOAMY, WELL-DRAINED, SLIGHTLY ACIDIC SOIL.	4-8
WILLOW OAK *QUERCUS PHELLOS* TO 18 METERS			MODERATE TO FAST	FULL SUN. RICH, WELL-DRAINED, ACID SOIL.	5-8
UPRIGHT GINKGO *GINKGO BILOBA* "FASTIGIATA" TO 18 METERS			SLOW	HIGHLY TOLERANT OF URBAN CONDITIONS.	4-8. INCLUDING CALIFORNIA
GREEN ASH, *FRAXINUS PENNSYLVANICA* "MARSHALL'S SEEDLESS" TO 20 METERS			FAST	FULL SUN. LOAMY, WELL-DRAINED, NEARLY NEUTRAL SOIL.	3-8. INCLUDING CALIFORNIA AND PACIFIC NORTHWEST
MODESTO ASH *FRAXINUS VELUTINA* VAR. GLABRA TO 20 METERS			FAST	TOLERANT OF DRY, ALKALINE SOIL.	5-8. PARTICULARLY CALIFORNIA AND SOUTHWESTERN DESERT AREAS
NORWAY MAPLE *ACER. PLATANOIDES* 12 to 30 METERS			MODERATE TO FAST	FULL SUN. TOLERANT OF POOR SOIL	3-10. EXCEPT SOUTHERN CALIFORNIA AND SOUTHWESTERN DESERT AREAS
JAPANESE PAGODA *SOPHORA JAPONICA* "REGENT" TO 20 METERS			SLOW TO MODERATE	TOLERANT OF POOR SOIL. DOES BEST IN NEARLY NEUTRAL WELL-DRAINED SOIL.	4-7
THORNLESS HONEY LOCUST *GLEDITSIA TRIACANTHOS* VAR. INERMIS "SHADEMASTER" TO 25 METERS			FAST	FULL SUN OR PARTIAL SHADE. TOLERATES DROUGHT AND RANGE OF SOIL CONDITIONS.	4-10
SERVICEBERRY *AMELANCHIER CANADENSIS* OR *A. LAEVIS* 7 TO 12 METERS			MODERATELY FAST	PARTIAL SUN. MOIST SOIL.	4-8
GRECIAN LAUREL *LAURUS NOBILIS* TO 10 METERS			SLOW	FULL SUN. WELL-DRAINED ACID OR ALKALINE SOIL.	7-8. INCLUDING PACIFIC NORTHWEST, NORTHERN CALIFORNIA AND SOUTHERN STATES

*From "Urban Trees," by Thomas S. Elias and Howard S. Irwin. Copyright © 1976 by Scientific American, Inc. All rights reserved.

identify the best exotics for your planting
program. A list of those that are suitable for
intensive-use sites and adaptable to specific
regions is shown in Table 9-1 and Figure 9-5.

INSECTS AND DISEASES — A CONTINUED PROBLEM

Insects and diseases are endemic in most
areas, but rarely do they reach epidemic
proportions. The best preventive measure is to
keep trees healthy, at reasonable growth rates
with minimum mechanical damage. Obviously
trees are not as healthy as they could be if a
site is not used for recreation; however, the
strategies outlined in the beginning of this
chapter should help to promote healthy trees
and reduce high risks. Some individual trees
may be valuable enough to receive special
treatment, e.g. fertilizers and water, infected
limb removal, or spraying.

You should institute some control measures
when you detect certain insects or diseases.
Unfortunately, since trees are not in an optimal
growing environment on a recreational site,
they may rapidly deteriorate and die after any
insect or disease attack. The other
consideration is that an insect or disease
problem, if not checked, may spread to areas
outside the immediate site.

In sum, the best approach is to maintain
healthy trees. Periodically inspect for any
insect or disease problem. If a major problem
emerges, use the specific, recommended
control and warn other residents and agencies
of the potential problem. Ripley, through a
synthesis of his considerable research,
prioritizes eastern species of trees based on
their ability to withstand the impact of
recreation use.[10] (See Table 9-2.)

RELATED VISITOR MANAGEMENT PROGRAMS

Management of overstory vegetation is not
complete until it has been integrated with
visitor-management programs:

Area Planning. Area planning can reduce
direct management costs after site development
if you evaluate potential sites for particular
kinds of development. Then the site you
actually choose provides the desired
recreational opportunity with minimum capital
and operational costs. When you choose a less-
stable or less-productive site, you also commit
yourself to higher operational costs in
managing overstory vegetation. To commit
yourself to less than that decreases intended
benefits of the recreational opportunity.

Table 9-2. List of Eastern Conifers and Hardwoods

Hardwoods		Conifers
1. Hickories	12. Red maple	1. Shortleaf pine
2. Persimmon	13. American holly	2. Hemlocks
3. Sycamore	14. Sourwood	3. White pine
4. White ash	15. Black birch	4. Pitch pine
5. Beech	16. White oaks	5. Virginia pine
6. Sassafras	17. Black walnut	
7. Buckeye	18. Red oaks	
8. Yellow-poplar	19. Black locust	
9. Dogwood	20. Magnolia	
10. Blackgum	21. Black cherry	
11. Yellow birch	22. Blue beech	

Note: The above conifers and hardwoods are listed in order of decreasing ability to withstand the impact of
recreation use as gauged by disease infection, insect infestation, and decline. (From Ripley, T.H. 1962. "Tree
and Shrub Response to Recreational Use." US Forest Service Note SE-171. p. 2.)

Figure 9-5. Hardiness Zones of the United States and Part of Canada. These zones show the differences in the average annual minimum temperature and thus indicate differences in the species of trees that can be expected to flourish in each zone. The map is based on a compilation and prepared at the Arnold Arboretum of Harvard University. Table shows the range of minimum temperatures. (From ''Urban Trees,'' by Thomas S. Elias and Howard S. Irwin. Copyright © 1976 by Scientific American, Inc. All rights reserved.)

Consequently area planning must not be viewed, as indicated in Chapter Three, as a site development process but as a total management process that includes all relevant programs for a particular activity. In terms of overstory management, that undertaking starts prior to development, committing you to a continual program both *during* and *after* visitor use.

One other thought is that overstory trees are what people see and equate with the generalized landscape. In some cases they are even the primary attractors, e.g. giant sequoias and Ponderosa pines — the medicine trees of the Northern Rockies. Based on this perspective, managing overstory vegetation is a much higher priority, and the process starts with area planning.

Site Planning. Site planning is as much an outgrowth of area planning as any other program. Facilities such as architectural barriers, elevated walkways, etc. can direct use to minimize soil compaction and physical damage to trees. Barriers may be vegetative or constructed of appropriate materials, and used to simply avoid zones of sensitive vegetation and soils. Just make sure that the facilities you provide reduce the impact on the overstory vegetation and are appropriate to the opportunity.

Information Programs. Much visitor damage to vegetation is done out of ignorance. People often don't understand the consequences of their actions. They tie their horses to trees while they fish. They peel the bark from around the birch trees. They cut off limbs for hot dog-sticks or bough beds. There is no end to the possible list, but the damage is not done to deliberately destroy the tree. It is done out of ignorance. Information programs, if properly developed, can reach many of these people and improve the quality of use of the site. Even with these, you may not reach some people or change their behavior.

What is needed is a better understanding of non-verbal barriers to encourage certain kinds of behavior, yet remain unobtrusive. Beyond that, we need to search for creative answers that simply can't be pulled out of a textbook.

The example of indiscriminate tree-hacking is a good one. In one park, nothing seemed to work completely. Verbal communication reduced some. Patrolling and regulation enforcement helped. Then one employee suggested "hack trees," and workers "planted" 16-foot logs at each camp unit with a sign "Please hack on me — not my live brothers and sisters." Indiscriminate hacking of live trees was reduced to a negligible amount. Hack trees? It worked.

"CREATING" A NEW RECREATIONAL ENVIRONMENT SILVICULTURALLY

Most of us tend to think in terms of how to maintain the *status quo*, to increase the health and vigor of what is already present. Rarely do we think of creating something new — a different environmental setting. This can be done by using the right silvicultural technique to convert from one forest type to another — enhancing the appeal of the site for particular recreational opportunities, increasing visual variety, and encouraging specific activities. We could go from a dense spruce forest to a spruce-hardwood mixture to increase landscape variety and allow more snow to reach the ground so the site is suitable for cross-country skiing. Or we can create natural-appearing openings to appear as forest meadows. Forests can also be converted to more pastoral-like landscapes with large, open greenspaces, and you can dam small streams to create a stronger interface between the forest and water.

Such changes can be expensive, and we give up something to get something else. Long-term management costs may also be associated with the new status. But technology is available to create these environmental settings. The question, then, is not can we, but under what circumstances should we? And the costs may not be as high as we think, particularly if we receive the revenue from the forests removed during the stand conversion, or when the benefits to the using public are greatly enhanced.

SELECTED READINGS

1. Elias, T.S., and H.S. Irwin. 1976. "Urban Trees," *Scientific American* 235(5):111.

2. Grey, G.W., and F.J. Deneke, 1978. *Urban Forestry.* New York: John Wiley & Sons, Inc.

3. Haller, J. 1957. *Tree Care.* New York: MacMillan Publishing Co.

4. Harris, R., 1983. *Arboriculture: Care of Trees, Shrubs, and Vines in the Landscape.* Englewood Cliffs, NJ: Prentice-Hall.

5. Howard, C.S. 1972. "Plants for Problem Areas of the Western States. *Yearbook of Agriculture,* p. 154.

6. Knight, F.B. and H.J. Heikkenen. 1980. *Principles of Forest Entomology.* New York: McGraw-Hill Book Co.

7. Leuschner, W.A., 1984. *Introduction to Forest Resource Management.* New York: John Wiley & Sons, Inc.

8. Neeley, D. and E.B. Himeleck. 1962. "Fertilizing and Watering Trees." Circular 52, Urbana, IL: *Natural History Survey,* University of Illinois.

9. Ripley, T.H. 1962. "Tree and Shrub Response to Recreational Use," US Forest Service Research Note SE 171.

10. Ripley, T.H. 1962. "Tree and Shrub Response to Recreational Use," US Forest Service Research Note SE 171.

11. Rudolph, P.O. 1967. "Silviculture for Recreation Area Management." *Journal of Forestry* 65:385.

12. Settergren, C.D., and D.M. Cole. 1970. "Recreation Effects on Soil and Vegetation in the Missouri Ozarks." *Journal of Forestry* 68:231.

13. Smith, D.M. 1986. *The Practice of Silviculture.* 8th edition. New York: John Wiley & Sons, Inc.

14. Spurr, S.H. 1980. *Forest Ecology.* 3rd edition. New York: J. Wiley & Sons, Inc.

15. U.S. Department of Agriculture, 1948. *Woody Plant Seed Manual.* Misc. Publ. 654.

16. U.S. Forest Service. 1965. *Silvics of Forest Trees of the United States.* Agriculture Handbook 271.

17. Wagar, J.A. 1965. "Cultural Treatment of Vegetation on Recreation Sites." *Proceedings of Society of American Foresters.* p. 37.

18. Wenger, K.F., 1984. *Forestry Handbook*, 2nd Edition. New York: John Wiley & Sons, Inc.

19. Westveld, R.H. 1958. *Forestry in Farm Management.* New York: John Wiley & Sons, Inc.

20. Young, R.A. (ed.), 1982. *Introduction to Forest Science.* New York: John Wiley & Sons, Inc.

CHAPTER TEN
MANAGEMENT OF NATURAL ECOSYSTEMS

Figure 10-1. A Natural Wildfire in Grand Park, Mt. Rainier National Park. (Photo by Glenn Powell)

In Chapter Nine, we suggested altering ecosystems to produce desired new environmental settings. This chapter looks at the other perspective — maintaining the natural ecosystem. An ecosystem is an association of plant and animal populations living together in dynamic equilibrium. In an open system of the natural setting, as with recreational opportunities in Chapter Three, we find an equilibrium not only internally affected by the interrelationships of the natural populations, but externally by changes in the environment such as climate and weather, chance introduction of exotic species, natural disasters, and modern man's activities. While probably no ecosystem has not been affected by modern man in some

way (the ones preserved through legal designations are usually only partial, with some disruption of energy flows, etc.), we typically divide them into those that are manageable as such and those that are not.

Manageable ecosystems *appear* essentially intact without the major disruptive forces of modern man, and large enough to allow the natural forces of fire, insects, disease, flood, etc. to maintain it in some less-than-climatic stage. Few of these are left, and most are probably found in the state of Alaska. Even these are not inviolate because of their legal status; on the contrary, they often suffer encroachment because of artificial boundaries or because we eliminate or modify the natural forces that maintain them. What we typically classify or are called upon to manage as natural ecosystems are vestiges that are nearly impossible to maintain as such. Worst yet, many of these are anomalies or freaks of nature such as a disjunct colony of boreal forest left when the boreal forest retreated northward after the last glacial period.

This discussion is not intended to diminish the role of management in natural ecosystems, it is only intended to point out the difficulty and complexity of striving to reach such a lofty goal. Unfortunately, such management is often equated with protecting the setting against the evils of man the recreationist, ignoring the forces of nature which shape the ecosystem and previous management actions which have encouraged existing use patterns. Recreational use typically causes only local aesthetic impact.

In sum, management of natural ecosystems is probably best summarized as:

1. protection against *external* influence of modern man's activity, i.e., keeping the landscape intact
2. protection against *internal* influences of modern man's activities such as recreation, range use by livestock, etc.
3. maintenance or introduction of forces that maintain or reestablish the dynamic equilibrium

The first two items are essential to any outdoor recreation management program, although most of us would agree that the threshold of acceptable impact lowers when we try to maintain visual as well as ecological intactness. Other chapters may reflect somewhat on those types of management programs; however, this one focuses on the third step.

NATURAL ECOSYSTEMS

There are two main parts of the ecosystem: the physical and the biological. The physical environment provides the energy, raw materials, and living space for use by the biological component. The biological compenent uses energy and raw materials to assimilate and produce biomass. Energy is passed through an ecosystem in a hierarchy of trophic levels, from green vegetation to herbivores (plant eaters) to carnivores. Eventually it is completely returned through decomposers to the soil/water. The passage of energy and nutrients through an ecosystem is a cycling process. Some plants, or parts, and some animals simply die and are decomposed; others are consumed by the next higher trophic level.

The dynamic equilibrium, in theory, is created by recycling, when raw materials and energy are maintained within the ecosystem. Remove the raw materials and/or some level of energy from the system and you have an altered ecosystem. That altered ecosystem can be natural in that it was caused by a natural disruption such as a volcanic eruption, rechannelization of a river, etc. Or it can be man-caused, like the removal of raw material or energy stored in the various trophic levels.

Here we will focus on the first trophic level — green vegetation — because all succeeding trophic levels are dependent upon it. Green vegetation fixes energy through photosynthesis, takes up almost all necessary minerals, and acts as a modifier of the environment, indirectly determining which organisms can live here. From a management perspective, the emphasis falls on agents of change in the dynamic equilibria that characterize particular ecosystems. While probably no natural ecosystem is free of the influence of modern man, these agents of change maintain the natural processes that cumulatively distinguishes one ecosystem from another. Some small ecosystems are uniquely adapted to particular microclimatic conditions and are maintained with minimum influence from agents of change. These should almost be considered as climax systems.

Many agents of change exist such as disease, flood, tectonics, altered climate, etc.; but the one force that has the predictable potential for recycling nutrients and energy and maintaining biological diversity for large areas over time is fire. This is not to insinuate, however, that fire is the primary force in all cases.

HISTORY OF
FIRE MANAGEMENT

A knowledge of the historical role of fire is important if we are to properly use fire to manage natural ecosystems. Fire has always been a primary force in shaping vegetation patterns, subsequently affecting the total ecosystem, including flora, fauna, soil, and water. During early times, fires were caused by weather cycles, particularly in places where natural fuels had built up during the intervening years between blazes. If not intense enough to kill, these fires usually caused some reshaping of vegetative structure, opening it to insect and disease attacks. A fire could completely destroy a stand of trees or create a die-back that resulted in a large fuel buildup, leading to an even more destructive wildfire.*

Indians used fire as part of their culture. They may have started fires that destroyed forests and plains, but accidentally. Fire was typically used for cooking, heating, signaling, and occcasionally driving game or waging war against an enemy tribe. The Indians' use of fire, plus the accidental starting of wildfires (usually from campfires), did affect the ecology, however, as stated by A.A. Brown and K.P. Davis:[6]

> ...firsthand testimony of old Indians of Western tribes indicates that they had great fear of conflagrations and a high respect for fire's destructiveness.

> ...It is at least a fair assumption that no habitual or systematic burning was carried out by the Indians.

During the nineteenth century, white men began to invade and settle the Midwest, the Upper Plains, the Northern Rockies, and then the West Coast. The use of fire changed drastically — abuse would be a more correct term. Forest and prairie vegetation became an obstacle to westward expansion and settlement. Native vegetation had to be cleared for farming and community development, and later for industrial development. The easiest and

cheapest means of clearing a forest was to start a fire and allow it to burn until a change in weather extinguished it. Also, settler-caused fires were thought to be an encouraging sign of progress since people felt that the forest was inexhaustible and that agriculture was part of a "manifest destiny." Unless they threatened personal property or accessible "firewood" stands, conflagrations were regarded with indifference.

In the late nineteenth and early twentieth centuries, the size, intensity, and frequency of fires greatly increased with the rise of settlements and logging. Many of the great fires in American history occurred during this time. Then the permanent reservation of land in public ownership, the introduction of German forestry, and the creation of agencies to administer lands and resources changed the official policy on forest fires. Experts agreed that forest fires destroyed valuable timber and should therefore be eliminated. Action was initiated by many states and also received presidential support at the federal level.[6]

As the benefits of increased timber production were realized, a basic fire-protection philosophy also became accepted as the proper means for maximizing timber production and protecting other resource values, including recreation. This policy has changed in recent years, particularly in designated wilderness, specific wildlife habitats, etc. Fires were once considered destructive and the policy was to immediately suppress them. Early fire education programs served primarily to prevent or reduce the number of fires. Agencies used hand tools in the early limited-suppression programs. Later, power equipment, even heavy equipment and bomber aircraft, helped to suppress almost all fires, regardless of origin or potential effects.

Since immediate elimination was the sole objective, the policy on forest fires excluded fire as a natural force in the dynamics of the ecosystems for more than three-quarters of a century. By eliminating one of the primary forces of change, we created unnatural conditions in the wildlands of the United States. However, we felt this to be necessary

*Wildfires are defined as having started naturally and burned a normal course without outside interference.

in the overall management of land and valuable resources, even in so-called natural areas. Public educational programs instituted in the 1940s promoted a fire prevention policy. Today, we still feel the effects of such concerted antifire campaigns as "Smokey the Bear." The public perceives only the need to prevent and suppress fires.

Then, in 1963, a select committee headed by A. Starker Leopold reviewed the ecosystems management programs of the National Parks and concluded that the elimination of fire had drastically altered the natural park ecosystem.[20] The dynamic succession of vegetation had been disrupted. Fire climax communities had been eliminated, and vegetation succession was moving towards the climatic climax. There was little regarding of nutrients, little dynamic recycling of successional stages, an no maintenance of a diverse age/species structure. We were attempting to stabilize the natural structure of the ecosystem through fire prevention and suppression rather than allowing normal dynamics to take place. The committee's primary recommendation was to return the ecosystem to "pre-white man" conditions.

This did not imply that a fire prevention policy is absolutely wrong, but that it is not valid in every situation — particularly in natural areas where the effects of fire can be contained naturally. Some professionals recognize the positive role of fire in the natural ecosystem but have also found that often higher administrators and the public do not readily accept this philosophy. Therefore we have been reluctant to take a forward look in our approach to the role of fire. Although we now recognize this need, we have not been very effective in implementing fire management plans in natural areas because of public criticism. At the other extreme, some overzealous managers have attempted to implement a policy of fire management through the controlled use of fire without any knowledge of its historical role in their particular ecosystem.

fire prevention and suppression have reduced the diversity of life forms, particularly in wilderness areas which are theoretically dedicated in maintaining the diversity and dynamics of the natural ecosystem. Technological advancements also make it easier to reach isolated fires and suppress them. Sixteen years ago, from his campsite in the Bob Marshall Wilderness, the senior author witnessed a fire suppression operation on Cardinal Mountain. Two large helicopters of equipment and men were flown in, and small, motorized equipment secured a fire line. The crew mopped up inside the line and the fire was quickly suppressed.

Ironically that fire, which had been burning for two days, covered less than fifty acres. Even if allowed to burn, the fire would probably have covered only one hundred to one hundred fifty acres before it reached natural boundaries that would have contained it. A walk through the burned area a few days after the suppression operation revealed that the deterioration of the site by men and equipment far surpassed fire damage — and all this occurred in an area "dedicated to the maintenance of the natural ecosystem." The same scene was repeated in 1985 on Nimrod Peak, Yukon-Charlie National Preserve, Alaska — in a zone officially designated as a "let-burn" zone in the regional fire plan.

Has the fire suppression program become a self-perpetuating juggernaut? Can we continue to afford that type of land management? Do our management strategies concerning fire fit the objectives for the area? Do we really understand the long-term effects of our management policies? Should we attempt to zone for fire management based on specific objectives? How do we properly "reintroduce" fire to the ecosystem? These questions and perhaps others, are the ones we should be seeking responses to if we are to maintain fire as a primary force in shaping our natural ecosystems.

THE EFFECTS OF FIRE

This section focuses on effects so that we may have a better understanding of the natural role of fire. Predicting the behavior of wildfires is difficult because of the tremendous variation in the conditions under which they take place. Fire behavior on the same site may differ from day to day because of changing environmental conditions. Consequently, even the fire researcher has difficulty evaluating field data because many significant factors do not remain constant. According to Brown and Davis,

> Fires respond to fuels, weather, and topography, with so many variables operating that it is nearly impossible to exactly duplicate fires in outdoor test plots, even where measured samples give assurance of reasonably uniform fuels and weather conditions and topography are carefully selected.[6]

Nevertheless, managers should attempt to understand the potential effects of a given fire, if they are to manage that fire. Even new computer simulation models can aid in understanding the probable behavior of a given blaze. (See Selected Readings.)

Effects On Overstory Vegetation. The effects of fire on overstory vegetation are significant to our discussion because the overstory tends to have a pronounced influence on the microclimate. So, too, is the relative resistance of certain species to fires of less than lethal temperatures. Lethal fires cause a complete loss of vegetation and a change in microclimate. Fires that cause extensive change through the "partial kill" are more important to managers because they are more common than lethal fires, and cause the typical ecological changes associated with earlier wildfires.

Susceptibility to Fire Damage. According to Brown and Davis, the following factors determine the amount of damage that fire can do to wooded areas:

1. *Initial temperature of the vegetation.* Foliage temperatures of over 100 °F may occur naturally, and 70 to 80 °F is common. The higher the initial temperature, the less additional heat is necessary to bring about lethal temperatures and the more quickly they can develop. This point is of importance in prescribed use of fire, since initial temperatues can be controlled by selecting the time of burning.

2. *The size of the critical tree portion exposed and its morphology.* Young trees, leaves, and small branches are easily killed because they can quickly be heated to a lethal temperature. Buds are particularly important, and their resistance to heat damage is directly related to size.

3. *The thickness and character of the bark.* Of all the protective mechanisms of the tree, the bark is the most important. This is especially true near the ground surface where most fires occur. Bark is an excellent insulating material; "bark structure, in general, is a natural design for insulation board." The insulating capacity of the bark layer depends on its structure, composition, density, moisture content, and thickness. It is known that these things vary widely by species, growth habitat, and possibly by seasons to some degree, but complete information is not available.

4. *Branching and growth habit.* Other things being equal, trees that self-prune readily and develop high and open crowns are more successful in escaping fire damage because they are less susceptible to crown fires and they accumulate less litter close to the stem.

5. *Rooting habit.* Roots have thin cortical covering and, if near the surface, are easily damaged by fire. Shallow-rooted species, like the spruces and most of the true firs, are frequently damaged by ground fires through root injury, even though the stem and crown are not affected.

6. *Organic material covering the mineral soil.* The depth and character of the organic mantle on the ground may largely control damage by surface fires to the roots, especially of the more shallow-rooted trees. If the mantle is fairly thick and the lower part does not burn, its high insulating ability will protect roots from damage. If, however, the organic mantle burns, it becomes a source of heat rather than of protection, and damaging soil temperatures are likely to result.

7. *Flammability of foliage.* Evergreens as a group, and conifers especially, are more flammable than deciduous hardwoods. There are significant differences between conifer species, though these are not of critical importance in damage

susceptibility. There are wider differences within hardwoods. The differences are least in times of severe drought, and at such times some species of both groups, mostly occurring in scrub or brush vegetative types, will burn furiously. In general, however, green hardwood foliage will not carry a forest fire except when abnormally dry.

8. *Stand habit*. Because of their greater liability to crown fires, coniferous trees that grown in dense stands or are commonly associated with abundant subordinate vegetation are more subject to fire damage than those occurring in sparsely canopied open stands with scanty subordinate ground cover. Canopy density is of little importance in hardwoods because the foliage is relatively nonflammable. Damage is controlled mostly by the flammability of subordinate vegetation and surface fuels. The volume and vertical distribution of available fuels, affecting crown-fire incidence, and the duration and intensity of the fire are closely related to stand habit.

9. *Season and growth cycle*. The seasonal stage of growth affects net damage in three ways. First, it greatly affects the total moisture content of the crown, which in turn affects its flammability. Second, new succulent growth is much more susceptible to fire damage. So growing tips and cambium are more easily damaged during the active growing stage than during the dormant state. Third, the ability of the tree to recover is affected by the food reserves in the roots, which fluctuate with the season. Fortunately, the rapid growing stage, when food reserves are low, is also the period of lowest susceptibility to crown fires.[6]

Natural Fire Resistance. The relative fire resistance of tree species is determined by basal bark thickness of mature trees, character of the individual tree crown and forest stand, and rooting pattern. (See Tables 10-1 and 10-2). Typically, the less intense fires are ground fires that may cause damage to the lower bole. Mature trees, which have thick bark on the lower bole, are more resistant to fire injury than younger trees, which have thinner bark and more succulent tissue.

The character of the individual tree crown is important since low, dense crowns are more susceptible to crown fires than higher, less dense tops. Similarly, stands of trees that grow in a very dense pattern, such as spruce or fir, are more prone to devastating crown fires than those growing in open stands, such as Ponderosa pine. Rooting patterns (deep versus shallow) obviously determine susceptibility of roots to injury.

Physical Damage. A fire that causes partial damage to an area usually leaves some basal injuries on standing trees that heal over and form scars. Since these indicate previous fire damage, you can determine the history, frequency, and intensity of fire in the existing stand from older, living trees. These scars also make trees more susceptible to insect and disease attacks due to increased ease of entry and decreased vigor of the tree.

Effects on Microclimate. The microclimate is the sum of local site factors that create a unique climate for a specific site and distinguish it from adjacent sites by factors such as soil, water, vegetation, and solar radiation. These interact to produce local air temperatures, relative humidity, soil moisture regimen, and air movement. Probably the greatest single factor in maintaining existing microclimate is overstory vegetation. If it is destroyed, temperatures rise, moisture is lost, humidity decreases, and air movement increases, accelerating the drying effect.

The degree of change in microclimate determines plant succession on the site. If the change is too drastic, plant succession is extremely slow, with potentially dramatic effects on soil, air, and water conditions.[6] Other effects may be temporary loss of wildlife and bird habitat, change in water flow and chemistry of nearby streams, and so forth. The microclimate is a complex and dynamic system that can affect large areas outside the fire's perimeter. This requires monitoring the effects of a fire on all aspects of the microclimate as well as surrounding influence areas.

Effects on Soil. The effects of fire on soil include loss of unincorporated organic material, change in physical conditions through erosion and possibly aggregation of soil particles, change in soil chemistry, and loss of soil organisms by heating. Unincorporated organic material forms a layer over the mineral soil and, as it breaks down, becomes soil nutrients. It protects the earth from heating and allows water infiltration without compaction.

Physical conditions of the soil are changed by compaction and erosion of exposed mineral soil. The force of raindrops directly hitting the ground causes compaction of the heavier soils. Fire seals the surface, causing runoff and subsequent erosion, or bakes soil particles to form larger aggregates, reducing pore space, aeration, and nutrient exchange. Fire also produces charcoal, which is black, durable, and high in heat-absorptive capacity.[6] This creates higher-than-normal surface soil temperatures that may have a lethal effect on natural reproduction of ground cover.

Fire produces chemical changes in the soil through combustion of organic material. The immediate effect of this process is the release of mineral elements into the earth, increasing available plant nutrients. The surge of nutrients stimulates revegetation of the site unless the soil is very sandy — in which case, nutrients soon become completely leached out away from the root zone. In heavier soils, the increased nutrient supply can last several years.[6] Leaching may affect the total ecosystem, including lakes and rivers within the system.

After a fire, the pH of the soil becomes more basic in the primary root zone area. This decrease in acidity causes an increase in nitrification by the immediate invasion of light-seeded, nitrogen-fixing organisms that are more adaptable to the higher pH levels. Even small changes in pH can cause significant changes in the growth of vegetation.[33]

The significant biological effects of a fire are often equated only with changes in flora and fauna. Yet other, less apparent biological effects occur in the soil. Fires that destroy the protective humus layer often reduce the number of beneficial soil organisms. In non-lethal fires, either increased soil temperatures or a change in soil chemistry may actually stimulate the productivity of soil organisms.[6]

A BASIC APPROACH TO ECOSYSTEM MANAGEMENT

Management must answer several questions. Where is a given natural area in the scheme of ecological succession? Where should it be? And what kind of management strategies move succession from where it is to where you want it to be? From a practical perspective, is such a move achievable?

In response to these questions, managers must consider several steps.

Inventory of Present Conditions. An inventory of present soil and vegetative conditions is an important first step. This tells you what stage of succession the system is in, which you then use as the baseline for judging the effects of either naturally or artificially introduced change. You should sample all components to determine the present condition of the vegetation (overstory and ground cover), fauna (vertebrate and nonverterbrate), water (open bodies and ground water), and soil (soil profile and chemistry). However, as we pointed out earlier, this sampling should focus on the first trophic level — green vegetation. Possibly a single small representative drainage can be singled out for intensive sampling.

Reconstruction of Recent Ecological History. To trace the history of an area, you must first determine the most recent period prior to the intervention of white man. You pinpoint this primarily by the alteration or elimination of significant agents of change — fire, flood, insects/diseases, etc. You then link together successional changes and the agents of such changes for the period under study. In the case of fire, it is not sufficient to simply reconstruct historical trends without some indication of their effects on vegetation succession. Reconstruction of recent ecological history should give you an indication of not only the vegetative types you can encourage, but also the primary agents nature uses to do so, the periodicity of change, and the size/shape of the areas within which dynamic equilibria were achieved. In theory, specific policy is adopted to move present conditions to the ecological

Table 10-1. Relative Fire Resistance of Selected Conifers of the Western United States (after Starker [1934] and Flint [1925])*

Species	Basal Bark Thickness of Mature Trees	Character of Tree Crown	Character of Stands	Rooting Habit	Associated Lichen Growth
Extremely resistant: (old trees only):					
Redwood (Sequoia sempervirens)	Extremely thick	High and moderately open	Dense	Deep	Not a factor
Western larch (Larix occidentalis)	Very thick	High and very open	Moderately open	Deep	Medium
Highly resistant:					
Ponderosa pine (Pinus ponderosa)	Very thick	Moderately high and open	Open	Deep	Light
Douglas-fir (Pseudotsuga menziesii)	Very thick	Moderately high and dense	Dense	Deep	Heavy
Moderately resistant:					
White and grand fir (Abies concolor and grandis)	Thick	Low and dense	Dense	Moderately shallow	Heavy
White pine and sugar pine (Pinus monticola and lambertiana)	Medium	Moderately high and dense	Dense	Medium	Medium
Lodgepole pine (Pinus contorta)	Very thin	Moderately high and open	Open	Deep	Medium
Low resistance:					
Western red cedar (Thuja plicata)	Thin	Low and dense	Dense	Shallow	Moderate to heavy
Western hemlock (Tsuga heterophylla)	Medium	Low and dense	Dense	Shallow	Heavy
Engelmann spruce (Picea engelmanii)	Thin	Low and dense	Dense	Shallow	Heavy
Sitka spruce (Picea sitchensis)	Thin	Moderately high and dense	Dense	Shallow	Heavy
Very low resistance:					
Alpine fir (Abies lasiocarpa)	Very thin	Very low and dense	Dense	Shallow	Heavy

*From Brown, A.A., and K.P. Davis. 1973. *Forest Fire: Control and Use*, 2nd Edition. New York: McGraw-Hill Book Company. pp. 52-53.

Table 10-2. Relative Fire Resistance of Selected Tree Species of the Eastern United States (after Starker [1934] and Others)*

Species and Resistance Group	Basal Bark Thickness of Mature Trees	Character of Tree Crown**	Character of Stands	Rooting Habit
Highly resistant:				
Longleaf pine (Pinus palustris)	Thick	High and open	Open	Very deep
Resistant:				
Pitch pine (Pinus rigida)	Medium	Moderately high and open	Moderately open	Medium deep
Pond pine (Pinus serotina)	Medium	Moderately high and open	Moderately open	Medium
Red pine (Pinus resinosa)	Medium	Moderately high and dense	Moderately open	Deep
Slash pine (Pinus elliottii)	Medium	Moderately high and open	Moderately open	Medium deep
Shortleaf pine (Pinus echinata)	Medium	Moderately high and open	Moderately open	Medium deep
Loblolly pine (Pinus taeda)	Medium	Medium height and density	Moderately dense	Medium
Moderately resistant:				
Chestnut oak (Quercus montana)	Thick		Moderately dense	Medium
Yellow poplar (Liriodendron tulipifera)	Medium		Moderately dense	Medium
Black and post oak (Quercus vetulina, stellata)	Medium		Moderately open	Medium
Of intermediate resistance:				
Eastern white pine (Pinus strobus)	Medium	Medium height and density	Medium dense	Medium
Jack pine (Pinus banksiana)	Medium	Medium height and density	Moderately open	Medium
Red oak (Quercus rubra)	Medium		Medium	Medium
Hickory (Carya spp.)	Medium		Moderately dense	Medium
Sweetgum (Liquidambar styraciflua)	Moderately thin		Moderately dense	Medium
White oak (Quercus alba)	Moderately thin		Moderately dense	Medium
Of low resistance:				
Sugar maple (Acer saccharum)	Moderately thin		Dense	Medium
Scarlet oak (Quercus coccinea)			Dense	Medium
Yellow birch (Betula lutea)	Moderately thin		Dense	Medium
Black cherry (Prunus serotina)	Moderately thin		Dense	Medium
Spruces (Picea spp.)	Thin	Low and dense	Dense	Shallow
Aspens (Poplus tremuloides and grandidentata)	Thin	High and open	Medium	Medium
Cedars (Thuja and Juniperus spp.)	Thin	Medium height and density	Dense	Shallow
Firs (Abies spp.)	Very thin	Low and dense	Dense	Shallow

*From Brown, A.A. and K.P. Davis, 1973. Forest Fire: Control and Use, 2nd Edition. New York: McGraw-Hill Book Company
**Not considered significant for hardwoods since fires seldom burn in crowns.

"norms" for a particular area without the interference of modern man. Those ecological "norms" vary over a large area based on differences in microclimatic conditions. You must also adopt a strategy to maintain dynamic equilibrium once the "ideal" is achieved.

Reconstruction of fire history utilizes fire dating, historic records, and interviews. Fire dating is done by examining fire scars on living vegetation or by carbon-dating charcoal layers in the soil. Standing trees can be living testimony of a natural castatrophe such as a wildfire. You can date fire scars on living trees by counting tree rings from tree cores (See Figure 10-2). However, using fire scars to date fire history has its limitations. Logging, mining, and biologically disruptive land uses have eliminated most of the older, virgin trees that could have provided a chronological fire record over several hundred years. Without these older trees, it is difficult to reconstruct the natural cycle of fire since recent fire history has been directly affected by fire suppression and other management activities. Except for isolated tracts of old timber, generally only wilderness areas and dedicated natural areas offer good chronographs of fire history. However, even most of these areas have typically been included in the universal policy of modern fire suppression. Also, destructive fires may have eliminated older trees for fire dating. This means you may have to search harder for the remaining clusters of trees that escaped the destructive fires. Even then geographic boundaries of individual fires may be difficult to determine if only clusters of older trees remain instead of the original, expansive forests.

The history of fire in a particular area should be limited to geographic boundaries so that you can focus your fire-management plan on when and where fire has been a major force in the ecology of the particular area. Also, base your procedure for reintroducing a fire artificially on specific geographic boundaries and cycle of previous fire history. Researchers are finding many areas in which fire has played only an insignificant ecological role.

Figure 10-2. Fire-dating Using Old Fire Scars In The Annual Rings. (From Heinselman, M.L. 1969. "Diary of the Canoe County's Landscape." *Naturalist* 20(1):13.)

Carbon dating can also help you to compile a fire history, and if you locate large enough pieces of charcoal, you can determine the species involved in the fire. Carbon dating of burned stump/logs can also be used to reconstruct fire history. A more sophisticated technique is to first make a pollen analysis of lake sediments in order to determine the dynamic successional changes and then to date each layer of sediment, using carbon dating.

Historical records, from newspaper clippings to trappers' diaries, are useful in dating fires for a particular locale. They can help verify tree-rings counts on old, fire-scarred trees as well as establish a fire history for locales where no living vegetation exists to serve as evidence. In that case, you should search for other written accounts, such as paintings, hospital records, and other local historical accounts, to verify the date and location of the fire. If the fires occurred within the last seventy-five years, personal interviews with early residents of the area can assist in reconstructing a detailed fire history.

Establishment of Policy. Based on a comparison of present conditions and projected ecological norms, you must establish a policy to move the existing situation toward the conditions represented by anticipated norms. In fire management, this is often called the "burn or no burn" decision. Accepted policy for areas to be burned has been that all natural fires are allowed to burn and all manmade fires are suppressed. This has moved agencies away from the "all-fires-are-bad" policy to one where natural fires are "good" and "man-caused" fires are bad. If we had good natural fire breaks and wildfires had not been suppressed in the past, perhaps such a distinction between good and bad would be an appropriate policy. However, the fire suppression policies of the past have caused significant vegetative changes and a build-up of fuel wood on the ground. Now any fire, natural or man-caused, has the potential to be a bad one because, under the right conditions, it can become so destructive or severe that in its aftermath the uniform, mature pattern of vegetation is replaced by a younger cover

offering no more ecological diversity than the original one. On the other hand, any fire has the potential to be beneficial if it produces the desired pattern of ecological diversity.

Often land-use goals conflict. When these conflicts arise, you must establish a goal-priority system to determine which decision takes priority. In areas where intensive development priorities exist, like housing, recreation, and quality-timber sites, the policy must be no burn. In other areas this distinction is not so clear. However, if the decision is to burn, then you must also determine which method to use — to let natural fires burn or to prescribe burn by introducing fires artificially in order to achieve the same objectives. These are all priority decisions that must be made a part of the fire management plan. If such policies are not established, you may choose a less desirable course of action under pressure from the public, other agencies, or higher headquarters when a major fire erupts.

A "burn or no burn" decision is the first order, and a base map can delineate no-burn zones. This means that any fire within the no-burn zone or any outside the zone that can affect it should be suppressed. Here there is no question that the proper course of action is to eliminate fire as an agent of change. However, before that decision is made a part of the fire-management plan, it is advisable to enumerate the opportunity costs (values derived from wildfires foregone when the decision is not to burn). In fact, the last management step mentioned in this chapter, interpretation of the natural role of the fire, is to direct such enumeration to the public so they, too understand the trade-offs.

Burn zones are delineated based on the historic role of fire in maintaining the ecosystem, their relationship to the no-burn zones, and the agreement among landowners that this is the proper management course. You must further separate burn zones into "let burn" and "prescribe burn." Prescribe burn subzones are so designated because there are typically insufficient natural fire breaks to guarantee that a natural fire stays within the subzone boundary. Fires within these subzones are started by management under conditions that predictably produce the desired diversity, yet are easily contained within the boundaries through appropriate management actions. By definition, wildfires are suppressed in these subzones because they are typically not containable within set boundaries. Prescribed burn subzones may never be burned because the right combination of terrain, fuel moisture, and atmospheric conditions cannot be achieved to guarantee containment. Under these conditions, some agencies have resorted to mechanical disturbances to create some diversity. Wood is shredded mechanically and allowed to rot, returning the nutrients to the soil slowly; or it is piled and burned.

Let-burn subzones pose the greatest challenge to management. Any fire predicted a threat to a no-burn zone must be suppressed. Under present modern policy, we suspect that all other wildfires should be normally allowed to run their courses with one stipulation: that the effects of all fires are predicted and, based on those predictions, that you let them run their course or suppress them. Those that produce desired diversity should be the only ones allowed to burn.

Using Alaska as an example, we can envision large areas of let-burn subzones because of the isolation, natural firebreaks, and lack of competing land values. However, when applied to other regions, it becomes very difficult to delineate let-burn subzones. Some areas obviously fit the policy requirements. Others may fit with close monitoring while being prepared for a major suppression effort if necessary. At least these areas can be recognized as part of the burn zone that requires fire as the primary element of change. Whether this is achieved through natural or man-caused activities is probably not important. The let-burn policy should simply be viewed as the least costly solution to achieving desired ecological norms, assuming that you can predict that a given wildfire will produce those results and be contained within specified boundaries.

Coordination of Fire Management. The key to fire management planning is coordination. With the mixture of landownership and thus diverse and often competing land management goals, it is essential that all affected parties work out an agreement on how to handle fires on wildlands. Negotiations on a proper course of action must take place before the fire starts, not after. These should produce a fire-management plan that establishes a basic policy for handling fires on all affected lands.

The plan should not only delineate policy direction for each zone but also agency roles/responsibilities in carrying out that plan. One of those roles is monitoring implementation to ensure compliance with policies. The state of Alaska, for example, has been divided into five fire management regions with separate fire management plans. A coordinating team consisting of representatives from all affected agencies and the private sector then develops policy direction to meet goals for specified geographical areas. Primary suppression responsibility rests either with the U.S. Bureau of Land Management or the Alaska State Department of Natural Resources. Managers of individual parcels of land within the region monitor the implementation of plans for their own lands. Once a plan is agreed upon by the agencies, it is then distributed for public input. Unfortunately public sentiment, fostered by earlier agency programs that suppressed all fires, is often against letting any fires burn. This adds to the agency's responsibility to increase the public's understanding of the benefits of fire.

Interpretation of the Natural Role of Fire. Interpretation of the natural role of fire in the scheme of wildland management is one of the keys to the successful development and implementation of any fire-management plan. This means that agencies are going to have to work with the public on a continuous basis to inform them about the natural role of fire well before any plan is presented for their comments. Without some understanding of the role of fire and the benefits to be derived, as well as being forced by time constraints to get a plan approved, the public understandably rebels at accepting the idea that fires, which used to be bad, are now good. This does not mean that everyone is going to agree and accept the plan; however, it should give the interested public a better foundation for judging a plan's merits.

A SUMMARY

Use of fire as a management tool is controversial, but where education is well-handled, support replaces controversy. The acceptance of fire-management planning appears to be directly linked to public understanding of goals such as maintaining the habitats of critical wildlife and fisheries and using wildfires in achieving that. Even then, because the system is out of kilter due to previous decades of fire suppression, all man-caused fires as primary agents of change are not necessarily bad and all wildfires good. If we had already attained a natural balance, perhaps we could make that statement. But probably a more realistic way of solving the problem is to establish ''let burn'' zones and monitor any new fires. If it appears that these create or help create the original mosaic of vegetative patterns — similar to a ''pre Columbian'' state — then let them burn. If not, put them out.

Severity is a term which refers to how severe or destructive a fire is. Very severe fires will likely replace the lack of diversity of vegetation with a new uniform carpet that shows a similar lack of diversity. By monitoring fuel build-up, fuel moisture, relative humidity, and wind conditions, you should be able to project the severity of a given fire just like it is done in a prescribe-burn situation. Prescribe burns are done where conditions do not allow natural fires to run their courses. Ecological diversity in wilderness/natural areas is important to the well-being of the ecosystem and also provides a diversity of environmental settings and thus diversity in recreational opportunities. Where other significant land values exist, the obvious course of action is to suppress all fires.

A critical link to the acceptance and implementation of fire management plans is public education. On-site information/interpretive programs are beneficial; however, it is important to use the mass media to reach large audiences potentially affected by the plan.

Cost-benefit analysis is also important. Costs are high for fire suppression, and many administrative units spend a goodly portion of their budgets on fire suppression while other areas go lacking. On the benefit side, you can estimate benefits even for foregone market and non-market values like wildlife and recreation based on the predicted outcome of the fire and cost of suppression. While estimating the benefits and costs of a particular fire may not be easy and cheap, the fact remains that the large sums of money for fire suppression should be spent efficiently to achieve public goals. It would not be unusual in Alaska, for example, to spend one to two million dollars on suppressing a single fire that protects, say thirty to fifty thousand dollars of public/private values. In the process, other public values such as improved moose browse may be foregone. We suspect that many fires in smaller natural areas can easily be handled with the cost benefit technique.

The key to ecosystems management in natural areas probably has less to do with understanding the ecological process taking place there and delineating a boundary where primary forces of nature can run their courses than resolving the conflicts between competing land uses and thus agreeing on a course of action.

SELECTED READINGS

1. Agee, J.K. 1974. ''Fire Management in the National Parks.'' *Western Wildlands* 1(3):27.

2. Aldrich, D.F., and R.W. Mutch. 1972. *Wilderness Fires Allowed to Burn More Naturally* US Forest Service Fire Control Note 33(1): Washington, DC: US Government Printing Office.

3. Anderson, H.E. 1983. *Predicting Wind Driven Wildland Fire Size and Shape.* USDA-Forest Service Research Paper, INT-305.

4. Andrews, P.L. 1986. *BEHAVE: Fire Behavior Prediction Model and Fuel Modeling System — BURN Subsystem, Part I.* USDA-Forest Service General Technical Report, INT-194.

5. Barney, R.J. 1979. *Fire Control in the 80's Symposium.* Missoula: Intermountain Fire Council and Society of American Foresters.

6. Brown, A.A., and K.P. Davis. 1973. *Forest Fire: Control and Use*, 2nd Edition. New York: McGraw-Hill Book Co.

7. Brown, J.K. 1982. *Fuel and Fire Behavior Prediction in Big Sagebrush*. USDA-Forest Service Research Paper, INT-290.

8. Cushing, E.J. 1969. "The Changing Landscape: Clues from the Canoe Country's Lakes." *Naturalist* 20(1):18.

9. Douglas, G.W., and T.M. Ballard. 1971. "Effects of Fire on Alpine Plant Communities in the North Cascades, Washington." *Ecology* 52:1058.

10. Gill, A.M. 1974. "Towards an Understanding of Fire Scar Formation: Field Observation and Laboratory Simulation." *Forest Science* 20:198.

11. Heinselman, M.L. 1966. "Vegetation in Wilderness Area." *Trends* 3(1):23.

12. Hendrickson, W.H. 1962. "Fire in the National Park Symposium." *Tall Timbers Fire Ecology Conference, Proceedings, No. 2.*

13. Holbrook, S.H. 1943. *Burning an Empire*. New York: MacMillan Co.

14. Houston, D.B. 1973. "Wildfire in Northern Yellowstone National Park." *Ecology* 54(5):1111.

15. Howe, G.E. 1975. "The Evolutionary Role of Wildfire in the Northern Rockies and Implications for Resource Managers." *Tall Timbers Fire Ecology Conference, Proceedings, Volume 14.*

16. Kilgore, B.M. 1975. "Restoring Fire to National Park Wilderness." *American Forests* 81(3):16,57.

17. Kilgore, B.M. 1984. "Restoring Fire's Natural Role in America's Wilderness." *Western Wildlands.* 10(2):2-8.

18. Kluskas, R.W. 1972. "Control Burn Activities in Everglades National Park." *Tall Timbers Fire Ecology Conference, Proceedings, Volume 12.*

19. Komarek, E.V., Sr. 1966. "The Use of Fire: A Historical Background." *Tall Timbers Fire Ecology Conference, Proceedings, Volume 6.*

20. Leopold, A.S., S.A. Cain, I.N. Gabrielson, C.M. Cottam, and T.L. Kimball. 1963. "Wildlife Management in the National Parks." *The Living Wilderness* 83:11.

21. Loope, L.L., and R.P. Wood. 1975. "Fire Management in Grand Teton National Park." *Tall Timbers Fire Ecology Conference, Proceedings, Volume 14.*

22. Lunan, J.S., and Habeck, J.R. 1973. "The Effects of Fire Exclusion on Ponderosa Pine Communities in Glacier National Park, Montana." *Canadian Journal of Forest Research* 3:574.

23. Lyon, L.J. 1984. *The Sleeping Child Burn — 21 years of Postfire Change*. USDA-Forest Service Research Paper, INT-330.

24. McLaughlin, J.S. 1972. "Restoring Fire to the Environment of the National Parks." *Tall Timbers Fire Ecology Conference, Proceedings, Volume 12.*

25. Mutch, R.W. 1970. "Wildland Fires and Ecosystems — A Hypothesis." *Ecology* 51(6):1046.

26. Mutch, R.W., and D.F. Aldrich. 1973. *Wilderness Fire Management: Planning Guidelines and Inventory Procedures*. US Forest Service, Region 1, Missoula, Montana.

27. National Park Service. 1975. *The Natural Role of Fire: A Fire Management Plan*. Yellowstone National Park, Wyoming.

28. Peek, J.M. 1981. "Thoughts on Preservation." *Western Wildlands.* 7(1):13-15.

29. Peterson, D.L., and Flowers, P.J. 1984. *Estimating Postfire Changes in Production and Value of Northern Rocky Mountain and Intermountain Reangelands*. USDA-Forest Service Research Paper, PSW-173.

30. Pyne, Stephen J. 1982. *Fire in America, A Cultural History of Wildland and Rural Fire*, Princeton, NJ: Princeton University Press.

31. Rundel, R.W. 1973. "The Relationship between Basal Fire Scars and Crown Damage in Giant Sequoia." *Ecology* 54:210.

32. Sellers, R.E., and D.G. Despain. 1974. "Fire Management in Yellowstone National Park." *Tall Timbers Fire Ecology Conference, Proceedings, Volume 14.*

33. Spurr, S.H. 1980. *Forest Ecology*. 3rd edition. New York: John Wiley & Sons, Inc.

34. Sweeney, James R. 1967. "Ecology of Some Fire Type Vegetation in Northern California." *Tall Timbers Fire Ecology Conference, Proceedings, Volume 7.*

35. Taylor, D.L. 1973. "Some Ecological Implications of Forest Fire Control in Yellowstone National Park, Wyoming." *Ecology* 54(6):1394.

36. Thompson, G.A. 1964. "Fires in Wilderness Areas." *Tall Timbers Fire Ecology Conference, Proceedings, Volume 14.*

37. USDA-Forest Service. 1985. *Fire's Effects on Wildlife Habitat — Symposium Proceedings.* USDA-Forest Service General Technical Report, INT-186.

38. USDA-Forest Service. 1983. *Proceedings — Symposium and Workshop on Wilderness Fire.* USDA-Forest Service General Technical Report, INT-182.

39. Van Nao, T. 1981. *Forest Fire Prevention and Control: Proceedings.* Timber Committee of the United Nations Economic Commission On Europe.

40. Wilde, S.A. 1958. *Forest Soils.* New York: Ronald Press Co.

41. Wright, H.E., Jr., and M.L. Heinselman (eds.). 1973. "The Ecological Role of Fire in Natural Conifer Forests of Western and Northern America." *Quaternary Research* 3:317.

CHAPTER ELEVEN

VISUAL RESOURCE MANAGEMENT

Plan in full awareness of nature's forces, forms, and features — the sweep of the sun, the air currents, the peaks and hollows of the earth, rock and soil strata, vegetation, lakes and streams, watersheds and natural drainage ways — and this awareness should obviously entail planning in harmony with the elements of nature. If we disregard them, we will engender countless unnecessary frictions and preclude those experiences of fitness and compatibility that can bring so much pleasure and satisfaction to our lives.[16]

Approximately eighty-seven percent of our perception of the landscape is based on sight. If we are to enjoy the aesthetic beauty of the environment, we must protect these important visual elements. Where possible, we can also manipulate viewing distance, lighting, and vertical position, so that the observer's enjoyment of the landscape is enhanced. Too often, however, planners interpret this approach in the context of the superlative view and forget the typical one. Unfortunately most people participate in recreational activities on typical, regional landscapes. If we agreed with this interpretation, we would be remiss in our jobs as recreation managers since very few superlative landscapes exist and we are already protecting many of those. At the same time, we are rapidly losing the typical landscape to incompatible and often destructive changes. This in turn lowers its quality and desirability as a place for living as well as for recreational activities. We do not mean to imply that all incompatible land uses must cease. However, to protect the treasured beauty of our surrounding landscapes, we must alter many existing land use practices. In some instances, this may mean renovating the landscape to produce an acceptable visual environment.

In most cases, there are no simple answers. Innovative approaches are necessary because of the conflict in public interest, from aesthetic to economic, over existing and proposed land uses and the potentially high cost of maintaining or renovating landscapes. But with a minimal investment, a midwest city was able to turn "eyesores" (i.e., old gravel pits) into beautifully landscaped, open-space areas for water-based recreational activities. The municipal government even bought up gravel reserves outside its jurisdiction so that, as the city expands, water-based parks can become an integral part of any new neighborhoods — at zero cost.

Thus, Visual resource management is a term that refers to the way in which the visual qualities of a landscape are handled in order to produce the maximum aesthetic response. This is only achieved by first understanding what people are responding to in the landscape, and then mitigating the impact of man's activities on those elements.

MODEL OF AESTHETIC RESPONSE

Several models attempt to describe how people respond to the landscape. (See Selected Readings.) Many of these focus on landscape elements and simply disregard the observer. Other models are based on personal biases without any theoretical reasoning as to relationships or predictability. Some researchers have translated peoples' responses to the

*Parts of this chapter have been adapted from *National Forest Landscape Management,* Vol. I, 1973, US Forest Service, and "The Visual Management System," *National Forest Landscape Management,* Vol. II, 1974, Washington, DC: US Department of Agriculture.

landscape into quantitative terms. However, the basic model of aesthetic response is more than a function of a static, unchanging landscape; it is a response based on the dynamic relationship of many classes of variables, from environmental to social. The following equation describes this response:

$$VP = f \ (BO, \ E, \ CO, \ OLR),$$

$VP =$ the aesthetic response of the observer,

$BO =$ the background of the observer,

$EC =$ the environmental conditions under which the observation takes place;

$CO =$ the character of the object being observed; and

$OLR =$ the observer/landscape relationships.

How people respond to their visual perception of the landscape depends on the background of each individual, i.e, previous learning experiences to which that individual has been exposed. These experiences shape attitudes toward certain environmental stimuli. For example, people who live in high-density areas may perceive gateway towns to national parks as desirable settings that accommodate their needs, whereas someone who wants to aesthetically experience and enjoy the unmodified landscape of a natural park may see these towns as manmade disasters. The haze in the valley from the cement processing plant may be perceived as an aesthetic disaster by one person and economic prosperity by another. We respond not just based on conditioning from previous experiences, but also on our motivations at the time. It is only after more mundane needs are met, such as the financial survival of the family and perhaps the community, that we are able to view the haze from the cement plant as potentially harmful or aesthetically undesirable.

Environmental conditions for observation can vary considerably, often during the course of a single day. Perception of the landscape is affected by these changes, from the obvious such as direct sunlight or fog to the more

subtle, such as temperature inversions which trap smoke and smog but are only visible above the inversion layer.

Observer/landscape relations are further discussed by Litton.[7] He claims that the relationship of the observer to the observed is important to visual resource management. The landscape is more than just a state of mind; it is an array of environmental stimuli bombarding the individual. Each person reacts to this stimuli according to his or her state of mind and the conditions under which the observation takes place.[10]. Thus, to be effective in management prescription, managers must be able to describe the landscape — both its physical aspects and the observer's response — in tangible terms. Doing this should provide a firmer grasp of the effects of landscape manipulation on the aesthetic experience of the user. If a response is predictably negative, the project can be redesigned, relocated, or eliminated in order to maintain the appeal of the landscape.

Sometimes environmental manipulations enhance the aesthetic appeal of an altered landscape, depending on existing conditions from past land uses and the state of mind of the observer. Removing offensive sights like junkyards, or removing vegetation to create natural-appearing openings in a mundane forest landscape, are examples of enhancing aesthetics.

LANDSCAPE TYPES

There are four primary landscape types and three secondary ones. Panoramic, feature, focal, and enclosed are primary, or macro-landscapes, referred to in the basic management model in Chapter Three as "generalized." The secondary ones — detail, canopied, and ephemeral — occur at specific points within this generalized landscape.

1. *Panoramic Landscape*. A panoramic landscape features a 360-degree view limited by the continuous line of the horizon, such as you might find on a flat, continuous surface like a large body of water. On land, the

panorama is often limited to 180 degrees or less because of changes in landscape composition, limits of peripheral vision, or natural side screening. The basic dimension is horizontal, with little feeling of boundary or visual restriction. This landscape stimulates the greatest feeling of distance and openness, with no single dominant feature.

2. *Feature Landscape.* This landscape is visually dominated by a singular or closely related group of features, natural or manmade. There is a great diversity in the types of dominant features, scale (relative to other items around it), configuration (shape), orientation (vertical or horizontal), and position relative to the observer and other potentially dominant elements. You must consider all of these variables if you plan to feature a given element for the observer. If you feature too many elements, the dominance you hope to present may be obscured. Similiar shapes, orientation, and other factors may confuse the observer. Also, objects in the near-viewing zone may appear larger than the high mountain peak in the distant-viewing zone — the item you might have wanted to emphasize in the landscape.

3. *Enclosed Landscape.* In this landscape type, vertical sides enclose a base plane. Sides in a natural landscape are formed by either vegetation or topographic features, and the base generally approaches a horizontal plane. The water's edge can form a conspicuous junction with vertical walls composed of vegetation or steep topography and a horizontal base composed of flat water. The enclosure is then created by well-defined limits of space; if the base (body of water, meadow, etc.) is enlarged to the point that vertical walls become insignificant or even visible, then the feeling of enclosure is lost. The landscape then approaches the panoramic type.

4. *Focal Landscape.* This type of landscape is structured by a series of parallel lines, or aligned objects, which converge or tend to converge on a focal point in the landscape. According to R.B. Litton,

> Both point convergence and feature terminus may occur with or without side enclosures; that is, either may be overlaid

on an open panoramic landscape or can occur as corridors on a flat plane. Portal or self-enclosure compositions can occur only in the context of enclosed landscape...A stream course or a road tangent are the most likely places to look for the focal landscape. Perhaps the most commanding or effective focal composition occurs when a landscape feature is present as a visual terminus.[7]

5. *Secondary Landscape Types.* These are part of the basic landscape types, are smaller in scale, and generally have more detail because of their closeness to the observer:

a. *Canopied landscape.* Vegetative canopies tend to limit viewing and are relatively small scale. Thus the landscape is easily seen and observed by the pedestrian, but the vehicle operator, because of his closeness, speed of travel, and focus on the road, is not able to grasp the detail. Roads within a canopied situation may be the closest contact that many auto visitors have with the out-of-doors. These rapidly moving observers can sense three sources of contrast in the canopied landscape: changes in general vegetation types, marked changes in size, class and condition of vegetation, and spatial definition of the canopied enclosure. There are three basic canopied postures: broad open corridors of major highways; medium closure corridors of secondary, moderate-speed roads; and small corridors or completely enclosed vegetative tunnels on slow-speed, minimally improved roads. We can create a feeling of contact with the natural landscape by bringing the edge of the road to the forest edge and minimizing or lowering road cuts and fills. On the other hand, we can create a feeling of detachment by separating the road from the forest edge and increasing cuts and fills. We can also increase vegetative contrast by running roads or portions thereof somewhat perpendicular to major topographic features, since changes in topography generally reflect changes in vegetation. As Litton states:

Transferring the characteristics of the lower-speed road to high speed roads has little chance to succeed. Lane division and use of broad median areas can help maintain contact with forest stands. But we should recognize that each road type imparts a different scenic quality to the stand — more light or less; more enclosure or less. One is not better than the other. Each offers a difference which should be retained for variety and contrast.[9]

b. *Detail landscape.* A detail landscape is part of a basic landscape that focuses on specific detail close to the observer. The detail requires pedestrians to proceed at a slow pace to seek out the natural, artistic amenities in the detail. Patterns, forms, and symbolism the observer perceives can offer personal satisfaction. These may be unique, symbolic, or merely reflective of the total landscape composition. Such detail may be composed of plants, rock deposits, water, and other features; however, the position of the observer in terms of background, lighting, and changing weather can cause him or her to focus attention on specific detail while creating a sense of changing landscape through small changes in light, weather, and other conditions. Thus observers may want to return again and again to receive the full continuum of visual opportunities from the specific detail landscape. Also, this type of landscape can be used as a relief and transition from one observer position to another in a given basic landscape, or between basic landscapes. This situation is similar to using foreground detail as a transition scene in a play while the larger background scene is being changed.

c. *Ephemeral landscape.* The ephemeral landscape depends on temporal or transitory effects that may last a few seconds or perhaps several days. Five types of influences affect ephemeral detail in the landscape: atmospheric conditions, projected and reflected images, displacement, signs, and animal presence. Produced by cloud and fog formation, precipitation, changing light, and wind motion, atmospheric conditions are the most extensive effects. Projected and reflected images are secondary images created by light shadows or reflections on water. Reflections are more conspicuous than shadows because they mirror the image of a real form even though the color may be somewhat darker. Under suitable conditions, a secondary image can be complete and can enhance recognition of objects. Signs are indications of former life or occupancy by animals or plants. Animal tracks, bird nests, spider webs, chewed trees, feathers, or bubbles from feeding fishes indicate that animals were recently present. Animal presence has a transitory influence on the landscape, generally in the near-viewing zone of subtle secondary landscapes available mostly to pedestrians. Although impossible to control, the ephemeral landscape is important and extremely stimulating to many observers who seek out subtle transitory natural elements. Timing is often important and observers should be made aware of its importance to these elements.

MANAGING THE VISUAL RESOURCE

Basic Concepts. You must understand three terms to manage a visual resource. All geographic areas have *charactertistic landscapes* with a normal amount of *variety* or natural variation. Man's activities cause *deviation* from that characteristic landscape. With a firm understanding of these three terms, you should be able to synthesize a workable visual-resource management model.

Characteristic Landscape. Each landscape, regardless of the size or segment being viewed, has an identifiable character created by its unique combination of visible features such as land, vegetation, water, and structures. To classify a landscape you must describe its physical elements in terms of their visual effects. A recommended classification is:

$$\text{Characteristic landscape} = f \begin{cases} \text{Dominance elements} \\ \text{(Primary descriptors)} \\ \text{Principles of Dominance} \\ \text{(Secondary descriptors)} \\ \text{Perception Variables} \\ \text{(Context of observation)} \end{cases}$$

Variety. Variety in the landscape is a desirable visual quality. Monotonous landscapes are not pleasing to the user and discourage the observer, creating a minimal perceptual response to existing environmental stimuli. The question is, how much variety is enough? For a given area, it can range from zero (low appeal) to an acceptable level. Beyond this level, appeal may decrease until it again reaches zero. Planting trees on an open hillside may increase variety and visual appeal, but at some point adding more may in fact reduce the effect of both qualities. Planting could continue until the hillside is entirely covered with trees, creating a new monotonous landscape.

Deviation. Deviation refers to manmade alterations in the characteristic landscape. Most land has been subjected to some use and/or development. Thus deviation, including that created by recreational developments, occurs and will continue to occur on the landscape. Deviations that emulate the elements of the natural landscape or create desirable variety may be acceptable to the observer. Unfortunately in the past decisions about these matters have often been made without considering landscape aesthetics. Nevertheless, more people are becoming aware of the appeal of the landscape, and although they realize some modification is necessary to provide needed goods and services for our modern society, they still feel that deviations should affect visual qualities as little as possible. In most cases, too little attention has been paid to visually disruptive land use allowing unacceptable deviations to occur. Given proper concern, we can make alterations acceptable and even enjoyable for users.

Dominance Elements. Four elements that compete for dominance in any landscape are form, line, color, and texture. It is important to analyze their relative strengths in an existing landscape and the possible effects proposed developments may have on them.

Developments should generally complement, or at least not detract from, more dominant elements. If alterations supplant them, they may destroy the natural harmonious appeal of the landscape or, worse, create a landscape that people react to negatively.

Form. Form is the mass of an object or of a combination of objects that appears unified. When viewed in two dimensions, it is referred to as shape.

Line. Line is the intersection of two planes. In nature, it occurs in shorelines, timberlines, meadow edges, avalanche paths, vegetation boundaries, ridgelines and tree trunks.

Color. Color patterns of landscapes are important in differentiating objects. Your perception of color often depends greatly on your position; distant colors appear muted while foreground colors seem stronger and more dominant. This contrast is especially obvious when you view the same color from varying distances. Color can be described in terms of hue, such as blue and green, and value such as the tonal quality between light and dark. Value tends to dominate hue, except in very close viewing; however, a detectable variation gives greater clarity to the elements of a landscape — the golden yellow of a dandelion meadow in contrast with the brilliant blue of a mountain lake, for example.

Texture. The dominant texture, or grain, of a landscape varies with distance. From short distances, individual trees or leaf patterns may show more than the rough texture of bark or clusters of leaves. From greater distances, stands of trees may be dominant and appear to have a medium texture. From extreme distances, the texture of the entire viewing area may appear homogeneous and relatively smooth.

Principles of Dominance. Six principles affect the visual dominance of form, line, color, and texture in a landscape:

Contrast. Contrast is important in discriminating form. In areas dominated by heavy texture and little variation, any change in the landscape produces a sharp contrast and is quickly recognized by any observer.

Sequence. There are two aspects to sequence: sequential landscapes and sequential experiences. Sequential landscapes are those in which the dominant elements of form, line, color, and texture are repeated in the specific area. Potential developments or activities for an area should thus be evaluated according to their visual effect on the continuity of these elements. Any development or activity imposed on a specific area should complement its landscape sequence. Otherwise, the development will most likely appear incongruent or out of sequence.

Sequential experiences are also important: "A well-planned sequence of visual experiences can enrich viewer appreciation."[20] Since most people travel by developed transportation systems such as roads or trails, we might try to maximize a hiking or driving experience by utilizing sequence. Perhaps the focus of a trail is St. Mary's Peak. Exposing the peak to hikers at given distances through trail location and/or vista clearings should heighten their anticipation of the next exposure as well as increase their appreciation of this dominant feature. With constant exposure to the peak, however, change may be so continuous and gradual that it is difficult to really appreciate.

Axis. Axis is the main line of focus created by converging lines toward some central point. Observers focus secondary attention on the lines of approach to a focal point. An axis can be natural, such as a river, an elongated ridge, or a narrow valley, or manmade, such as a road, a fence line, or a bridge. It can also be used intentionally to focus attention on natural or manmade objects of interest. For example, the tunnels on the road through Mt. Rushmore National Memorial Park form the axes which focus attention on Mt. Rushmore. In identifying axes and focal points for visitors, managers should try to maintain the continuity of the axis, the immediate landscape around the axis, and the background of the particular landscape. If this continuity is disrupted, attention may be directed away from the primary object, diminishing visual aesthetics for visitors.

Convergence. In convergence, several axes meet at a single focal point. Regardless of which axis you focus on, all ultimately lead to a focal point. Thus the area around a point of convergence is a dominant part of the landscape, and any development in this area should blend with the character of the landscape. Even then, development in these locations should serve as a backdrop to activities and/or facilities such as visitor centers.

Multi-dominance. Multi-dominance is created by two or more similar features in a landscape view. This may occur naturally in something like a series of rock outcroppings, but occasionally results from manmade activities such as timber harvesting or mining exploration. If the series of objects are competing for landscape dominance, they can distract the viewer and create an inferior view.

Enframement. Enframement occurs when vertical axes such as rock walls or timber edges intercept a flat plane such as a valley, road, or lake. It often reinforces other dominance principles.

Variable Factors. Eight environmental factors influence the way in which we perceive dominant elements. These often can be indirectly controlled by manipulating the observer. In analyzing the influence of these variable factors, it is important that you choose environmental conditions which create the greatest contrast between the land use activity and the characteristic landscape.[10] Although these factors may vary considerably, their occurrence and influence are generally predictable. The motion of water plummeting over a waterfall is breathtaking in early summer; by fall, this motion may be reduced to a trickle of water. Knowing that when the motion of the water is high the visual experience is more intense gives the manager a level of predictability that he or she can incorporate into management planning.

Motion. Motion can be influential in capturing the visual interest of the observer. Water is probably the most important source of motion in the natural landscape, others being wind, rain, snow, and avalanche. Motion can attract and hold the attention of observers and draw their attention to or away from various land use activities. In some places, it may be difficult to control the negative effects of land use or to screen these effects with intervening topography or vegetation. Possibly the natural motion in the existing landscape can divert attention away from a negative scene.

Light. All objects reflect sunlight to some degree. Natural light varies daily and seasonally, producing a contrast that affects visitors' visual perception of a landscape. We know that variety is important in producing an aesthetic response; we also need to understand how light can enhance this response by emphasizing or masking particular landscape elements.

For a scenic road corridor, we may choose light conditions that maximize contrast in the landscape and increase visual perception of forms, lines, colors, and textures. We can also choose reduced light intensity and reflection; this subdues the elements of the landscape so that the more negative land uses are less apparent along a corridor.

Determined by the time of day, the season of the year, and the position of the observer relative to its source, the direction of the light is also important. Backlighting — i.e., facing into the light — obscures details so that only a general outline is discernible. Frontlighting — facing away from the light — tends to produce less contrast and consequently less interest in the scene. Shadows tend to be shorter and fall away from the observer, and more surface tends to lay in direct sunlight.

Sidelighting generally produces the greatest contrast; thus it is usually best for evaluating scenes for visual acuity or manmade activity (visitor centers, road layouts, and so forth). This information can aid us in selecting overlooks, trail locations, etc. that maximize visual experience. Consider the time of day the observation would normally take place, and remember that the angle of the sun and the intensity of the light vary with each season.

Atmospheric Conditions. These often have a masking effect on dominance elements. The visual impact of a scene is reduced by cloud cover, fog, or precipitation, thus you should not evaluate the landscape under those conditions. Some atmospheric phenomena can accent landscape form, line, color, texture. Water on the opposite side of a mountain peak may affect the creation of a fog or a cloud bank that can serve as a backdrop to accent particular elements. An impressive scene that is usually obscured by fog or clouds may become even more dramatic to the observer when seen in the abrupt contrast of gleaming brilliant sunlight. Mount McKinley is an example of this type of effect. Although we personally visited Mount McKinley National Park several times in the 1960's, our only glimpse of the peak was from a commercial jetliner at 27,000 feet. As the clouds abruptly parted, the peak was exposed. Then, just as quickly, the clouds again covered the mountain. We remember it as being one of the greatest visual experiences we have ever had, yet it lasted only a moment.

Distance. Color value affects the visual qualities of the landscape. As distance increases, color value decreases because of the scattering of light rays. At great distances, the landscape is reduced to uniformity of both color value, usually blues or grays, and relief, or less perceived vertical change. The distance at which an object can no longer be identified depends on two factors: the size of the object and the degree of contrast with its surroundings. Sample viewing zones were established with criteria that included an overlap of distances (See Figure 11-1). These zones and their characteristics are shown in Table 11-1.

Observer position. Observer position is the vertical location of the individual in relation to the object being observed. The three positions are normal (at the same level as the object observed), inferior (below the object observed), and superior (above the object observed). Superior and inferior positions are only important in areas having reasonable topographic relief. The superior position offers opportunities for maximum viewing orientation to the total landscape. Also, more surface area of a given object is exposed here than in the normal position. The least surface area is exposed in the inferior position, and that is easily screened by intervening vegetation. For

Figure 11-1. Photo Showing Distance-viewing Zones (US Forest Service)

Table 11-1. Viewing Zones*

Foreground Characteristics	Middleground Characteristics	Background Characteristics
• Presence — the observer is in it. • Maximum discernment of detail — in proportion to time and speed. • Scale — observer can feel a size relationship with the elements. • Discernment of color intensity and value seen in maximum contrasts. • Discernment of other sensory experiences — sound, smell, and touch are most acute here. • Discernment of wind motion. • Aerial perspective absent.	• Linkage between foreground and background parts of the landscape. • Emergence of overall shapes and patterns. • Visual simplication of vegetative surfaces into textures. • Presence of aerial perspective — softens color contrasts. • Discernment of relation between landscape units.	• Simplification-outline shapes, little texture or detail apparent, objects viewed mostly as patterns of light and dark. • Strong discernment of aerial perspective-reduces color distinction, replaces them with values of blue and gray. • Discernment of entire landscape units- drainage patterns, vegetative patterns, landforms. • Individual visual impacts least apparent.

	Foreground	Middleground	Background
Distance	0 to half-mile	one-quarter to five-mile	three to five miles—infinity
Sight capacity	detail	detail & general	general — no detail
Object viewed	rock point	entire ridge	system of ridges
Visual	individual	textures (conifers	patterns (light & dark)
Characteristics	plants & species	& hardwoods)	

From US Forest Service. 1973. *National Forest Landscape Management,* Vol. I. Washington, DC: US Department of Agriculture, p. 57.

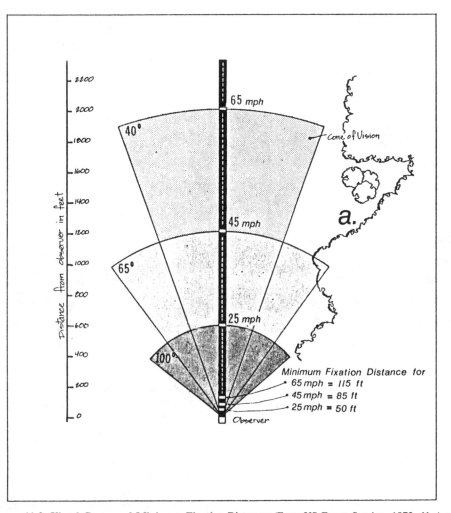

Figure 11-2. Visual Cones and Minimum Fixation Distances (From US Forest Service. 1973. *National Forest Landscape Management,* Vol 1. Washington, DC: US Government Printing Office, p. 63.)

example, you can locate an interpretive center in a superior position so that visitors can see entire plant communities and interpret the total ecosystem.

Scale. Scale means measuring the relative size of an object, and viewing distance affects scale relationships. Objects viewed closely are often measured in proportion to the human figure. In intermediate and distant viewing zones, an object is seen in proportion to the total scene. When a person looks at a pipeline corridor from a one-quarter mile distance, the irregular feathered edge of surrounding vegetation may be visually acceptable to him or her. But when the same scene is viewed from several miles away, the corridor becomes lost within the general texture of the landscape.

Time. This refers to the length of time in which observers view a point of interest. The longer the time, the more detail they see. "Seeing takes time — up to three-tenths of a second is needed for the eye to fixate."[20] This means that the auto driver, as speed increases, concentrates his or her vision on fewer objects at greater distances. The time factor primarily pertains to visitors who are in their

Figure 11-3. Landscape Character of the Alpine Zone, Summit Lake, Yosemite National Park (Photo by B.W. Twight)

automobiles. When on foot visitors generally concentrates on the landscape, thus increasing their perception of detail. Visual cones and minimum fixation distances are shown in Figure 11-2.

Seasons. Season of use is important because the contrasts that accent landscapes vary considerably through weather changes. In the summer when leaves are fully developed, landscapes may offer little variety because the heavy texture of the trees predominates. The colors of newly emerging leaves in the spring or frost-colored leaves in the fall may break up the monotony of a landscape; they can also decrease the visual impact of a development and cause the line, color, form, and texture of manmade structures to blend in more naturally with the surrounding area.

Snow tends to strengthen form and line through maximum contrast; thus winter is often the best time for evaluating potential visual impact.

Summary of Landscape Classification. The following examples summarize analysis of

landscape character, giving you an opportunity to apply the above information on landscape classification.

Figure 11-3 is a landscape characteristic of the Alpine zone as viewed from fore- and middle-ground zones. It has tremendous visual variation, which makes it attractive to observers. This land has strong form in the granite outcropping, strong line in the ridges and shoreline of the lake, and excellent textural variation in vegetation, snow, and rock outcroppings.

Any management practice should consider the strong line, texture, and form. Trails should be located so as not to detract from the ridgeline on the horizon or along the lake. Primitive campsites should complement texture and form and avoid disrupting the strong lines around the lake. All development should be avoided at the focal point — the upper reach of the lake.

Figure 11-4 is an enclosed landscape dominated in the foreground by the line of the lake, the interface of forest and meadow, and the variation in texture. Management practices

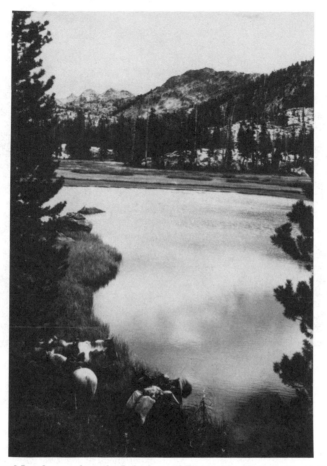

Figure 11-4. Enclosed Landscape along the Lakeshore of Tilden Canyon Lake, Yosemite National Park (Photo by B.W. Twight)

should consider the strong lines and the strong attraction of the water; the lake should be made visually accessible for the enjoyment of the casual user since any kind of intensive use or development would be too distracting. Intensive developments such as roads, trails, and campgrounds should be screened within the spruce-fir forest. There are also ecological factors to consider in these types of decisions.

The best features of the landscape in Figure 11-4 fall completely in the foreground and are dominated by the shoreline and the texture of lakeside vegetation. Any management action should preserve the existing line and texture if visual integrity is to be preserved for those using the lake.

Campgrounds and picnic stops should be located away from the lakeshore.

This landscape (Figure 11-5) is dominated by smooth texture in the foreground and by background lines at horizon and spur ridges, along with the dominant mountain peaks in the background. One other major feature is the line of vegetation at the interface of foreground and background. Very little middle ground is visually accessible.

Any intensive land-use development is better located in middle ground where it can be screened and blended with vegetation. Any development in the foreground should blend with the texture and not disrupt the dominance of the mountain range.

Figure 11-5. Snow-capped Sawtooth Mountain Range, Sawtooth National Recreation Area. Sawtooth National Forest (Photo by B.W. Twight)

APPLICATION OF VISUAL RESOURCE MANAGEMENT

This discussion covers scale of application, the visual resource management model, and mapping techniques.

Scale of Application. In visual resource planning, scale of application is divided into three major levels — regional, area, and site. *Regional Landscape.* The regional landscape is delimited by physiographic provinces. For example, the major physiographic provinces in southeastern Wyoming — from east to west the eastern plains, Laramie Mountains, Laramie Basin, Medicine Bow Mountains, Platte River Basin, and the Sierra Madres — describe the characteristic regional landscapes. Major developments such as transportation and utility systems should be evaluated in terms of their general affect on the regional landscape. Properly locating developments ensures minimal visual impact at the regional level. *Area Landscape.* The area landscape is delimited by the visual corridor, or the

envelope of space enclosed by land forms.[8] Detailed visual resource management planning is usually done on an area basis. At this level you make judgments about the specific effects of a given development on the visual experiences of visitors. Most recreational use occurs along roads, trails, water courses, or at specific sites. Managers should give priority to any portion of a landscape readily viewed by visitors, but this should not be interpreted as a "green light" to exploit the remaining areas. *Site Landscape.* Site landscape refers to the area on which you locate a recreational development. It is important to maintain a visually pleasing environment thoughout the site, and this is generally accomplished during the site-planning phase. The visual effects of site development on casual observers passing through the area should also be considered under area-landscape management. All site developments should conform to the requirements of the stated visual-quality objectives, which are covered in the succeeding section.

Figure 11-6. Visual Resource Management Model (From US Forest Service. 1974. ''The Visual Management System.'' *National Forest Landscape Management*, Vol. II. Washington, DC: US Government Printing Office. p. 9.)

Visual Resource Management Model. The basic visual resource management model is illustrated in Figure 11-6. Here a visual resource is inventoried according to the character, variety, and affect of the landscape. Note the feedback loop which suggests that we should periodically test the professional judgements made in the VRM plan against the preference/perceptions of the clientele. Ultimately, a resource's ability to absorb development must be coordinated with the sensitivity of observers in order to establish visual-quality objectives. These objectives affect the location, type, and level of development allowed in an area.
Landscape Character. First, character type and subtypes of the resource must be identified and mapped. The Laramie Mountains in southeast Wyoming are one example of character type. Subtypes are areas of significant size with visual differences that distinguish them from others within an overall character type.

Next, you should establish the variety classes of each subtype, of which three are recognized: 1.) distinctive — those landscapes having outstanding visual qualities such as a mountain peak, a deep gorge, or a glacial

field; 2.) common — those having a variety of basic landscape elements but no outstanding features; and 3.) minimal — those having little variety in basic elements such as an unbroken canopy of lodgepole pine or a grain field.

Finally, you should draw up a chart that classifies the basic features of each subtype into distinctive, common, or minimal. To illustrate this idea, an example is shown in Table 11-2, which uses the Western Cascades as a landscape character type and steep mountain lands as a subtype. You can use vertical aerial photos in conjunction with the criteria established in the variety class chart to delineate distinctive (A), common (B), and minimal (C) classes. Then you can transfer the information to a base topographic map (See Figure 11-7).

To obtain the necessary detail needed at the subtype level, managers may be forced to establish a priority system, phasing in the visual resource management program over several years. Typically, distinctive landscapes are recognized and visual aesthetics protected. This is as it should be; however, we should also devote more attention to the common landscape, which is where most people

Figure 11-7. Mapping Landscape Variety Classes A, B, and C. *Top,* Vertical photos, particularly in stereo pairs, are an excellent tool in judging the broad variety classes. *Bottom,* Prepare a detailed base map at the same scale as those currently being used for Multiple Use planning units. Prepare an overlay as shown to illustrate the variety class determination. Information on the base map will be used for all aspects of the Visual Management System process and should include but not be limited to: Topographic data (best available); land ownership boundaries; existing and proposed (within 10 years) travel routes, and bodies of water. (This would include but not be limited to roads, trails, low-level commercial air routes, passenger rail routes, etc.) Information can be obtained from local, state and national route studies and transportation plans. (From US Forest Service. 1974. ''The Visual Management System.'' *National Forest Landscape Management,* Vol. II. Washington, DC: US Government Printing Office. p. 9.

Table 11-2. Chart of Landscape Features of Resource Area — Western Cascades Character Type, Steep Mountain Slope Subtype*

	CLASS A	CLASS B	CLASS C
	DISTINCTIVE	COMMON	MINIMAL
Landform	Over 60 percent slopes which are dissected, uneven, sharp exposed ridges or large dominant features.	30-60 percent slopes which are moderately dissected or rolling.	0-30 percent slopes which have little variety. No dissection and no dominant features.
Rock Form	Features stand out on landform. Unusual or outstanding, avalanche chutes, talus slopes, outcrops, etc., in size, shape, and location.	Features obvious but do not stand out. Common but not outstanding avalanche chutes, talus slopes, boulders and rock outcrops.	Small to nonexistent features. No avalanche chutes, talus slopes, boulders and rock outcrops.
Vegetation	High degree of patterns in vegetation. Large old growth timber. Unusual or oustanding diversity in plant species.	Continuous vegetative cover with interspersed patterns. Mature but not outstanding old growth. Common diversity in plant species.	Continuous vegetative cover with little or no pattern. No understory, overstory or ground cover.
Water Forms, Lakes	50 acres or larger. Those smaller than 50 acres with one or more of the following: (1) Unusual or outstanding shoreline configuration, (2) reflects major features, (3) islands, (4) Class A shoreline vegetation or rock forms.	5 to 50 acres. Some shoreline irregularity. Minor reflections only. Class B shoreline vegetation.	Less than 5 acres. No irregularity or reflection.
Water Forms, Streams	Drainage with numerous or unusual changing flow characteristics, falls, rapids, pools and meanders or large volume.	Drainage, with common meandering and flow characteristics.	Intermittent streams or small perennial streams with little or no fluctuation in flow or falls, rapids, or meandering.

*From U.S. Forest Service, 1974. "The Visual Management System." *National Forest Landscape Management*, Vol. II. Washington, DC: US Department of Agriculture, p. 13.

participate in recreational activities. Most landscapes fall into the common category; therefore, we should give more attention to managing the common landscape if we are to provide adequately for aesthetic and recreational needs. Minimal landscape may absorb intensive developments because of dense overstory vegetation; however, some prairie and desert lands which are classified as minimal cannot absorb any development without maximum disruption of landscape elements.

Viewer Sensitivity. Viewer sensitivity is a composite of attitudes and viewer distance. Ideally, you should survey the attitudes of those who use the specific management area to evaluate their level of sensitivity. In the absence of such information, use Table 11-3 as a guideline. Now combine your survey with viewer distance — foreground (FG), middle-ground (MG), and background (BG), shown in Table 11-1 — in order to determine the overall level of viewer sensitivity. At level 3, it is not necessary to divide into foreground, middle ground, and background because of the low sensitivity level. For mapping viewer sensitivity, prepare an overlay of all viewable areas for all travel routes using areas and bodies of water. This can be done with a large-scale topographic map since all you need is the distance and elevation from the potential viewing point. Plot foreground, middle ground, background, and viewer sensitivity in terms of attitude for each road, trail, recreational development, and body of water, including streams. In the past, only roads have been given consideration in relation to viewer sensitivity; however, travel on water and trail is increasing and should therefore be given equal consideration. Overlays for all travel/use areas should then be superimposed to produce a composite overlay. (See Figure 11-8.)

Note the multiple classifications for most zones since many are viewable from more than one distance zone or viewer sensitivity level as classified in Table 11-3. For zones in which multiple classifications occur, the more restrictive sensitivity classification should always be used. To determine which classification is most sensitive, refer to the matrix shown in Table 11-4.

Visual Quality Objectives. Viewer sensitivity and landscape variety must be integrated into visual quality objectives. Do this with the matrix in Table 11-5; you can see the result in Figure 11-9. Visual quality objectives are as follows:

1. *Preservation (P).* The intent is that only natural, ecological changes are allowed since some local impact from recreational use may occur. These are roadless areas where the main development is the trail system and possibly some primitive campsites; all should be designed to blend with the visual resource.

2. *Retention (R).* Retention refers to planning developments so that they are not evident to the casual observer. You should maintain existing form, line, color, and texture in the landscape as viewed from the same point(s) where most people casually observe.

3. *Partial Retention (PR).* To achieve partial retention, make developments subordinate to characteristic landscape features. Try to imitate landscape elements, but realize that no development can completely blend into the background. The goal is to make the view acceptable for observers by preserving or complementing the landscape.

4. *Modification (M).* With modification, man's activities may visually dominate the characteristic landscape, but even these activities should borrow as much as possible from the elements of form, line, color, and texture so that it appears congruent with the setting.

5. *Maximum Modification (MM).* Man's activities, including alteration of land forms by timber harvesting or major development, may dominate the landscape and seem somewhat incongruent within foreground or middle ground viewing distances. Yet when viewed as backgrounds, these forms should blend in. Viewing distance is therefore important, and the duration of the visual impact should be minimal through either rehabilitation or enhancement (secondary objectives).

Note that there is such a thing as unacceptable modification that does not blend with the character of the landscape regardless of viewing distance. Activities such as contour strip mining and large symmetrical clearcuts often have a lingering effect that cannot be mitigated. Modification or enhancement may improve the visual quality of the activity, but the activity often remains unacceptable. In any situation, you should not tolerate unacceptable modification. Note the amount around you. If you recognize it on the ground, the picture is more vivid than any photo could reproduce.

Rehabilitation is a secondary, short-term, visual-quality way to improve the landscape. Enhancement, another secondary, short-term objective, is aimed at increasing visual appeal by creating variety in a monotonous vista.

Visual Absorption Capacity (VAC). VAC is the relative ability of the landscape to absorb a

Table 11-3. Summary of Sensitivity Levels*

Summary Table for all Sensitivity Levels:

Use	1	2	3
Primary Travel Routes, Use Areas and Water Bodies	At least ¼ of users have MAJOR concern for scenic qualities	Less than ¼ users have MAJOR concern for scenic qualities	
Secondary Travel Routes, Use Areas and Water Bodies	At least ¾ of users have MAJOR concern for scenic qualities	At least ¼ and not more than ¾ of users have MAJOR concern for scenic qualities	Less than ¼ of users have MAJOR concern for scenic qualities

Level 1-Highest Sensitivity
Level 2-Average Sensitivity
Level 3-Lowest Sensitivity

*From U.S. Forest Service. 1974. "The Visual Management System." National Forest Landscape Management, Vol. II. Washington, DC: US Department of Agriculture, p. 21.

Table 11-4. Chart for Determining Most Restrictive Sensitivity Level*

	fg1	mg1	bg1	fg2	mg2	bg2
bg2	fg1	mg1	bg1	fg2	mg2	bg2
mg2	fg1	mg1	mg2	fg2	mg2	
fg2	fg1	mg1	fg2	fg2		
bg1	fg1	mg1	bg1			
mg1	fg1	mg1				
fg1	fg1					

fg1 — Foreground Level 1
mg1 — Middle ground Level 1
bg1 — Background Level 1

*From U.S. Forest Service, 1974. "The Visual Management System." *National Forest Landscape Management,* Vol. II. Washington, DC: US Department of Agriculture, p. 25.

Figure 11-8. Composite Overlay of Viewer Sensitivity Based on General Visitor Attitudes (Table 11-3) and Viewing Distance Zones (Table 11-1). A is a composite overlay before adjustments have been made, B is the final overlay showing the most restrictive sensitivity levels as in Table 11-4.

Table 11-5. Visual Quality Matrix**

Variety Class

		Sensitivity Level						
		fg1	mg1	bg1	fg2	mg2	bg2	3
	class A	R	R	R	PR	PR	PR	PR
	class B	R	PR	PR	PR	M	M	M* MM
	class C	PR	PR	M	M	M	MM	MM

SYMBOL	OBJECTIVE
R	Retention
PR	Partial Retention
M	Modification
MM	Maximum Modification

*If a 3B area is adjacent to a *Retention* or *Partial Retention* visual quality objective, select the *Modification* visual quality objective. If adjacent to *Modification* or *Maximum Modification* objective areas, select *Maximum Modification.*

**From U.S. Forest Service, 1974. "The Visual Management System." *National Forest Landscape Management,* Vol. II. Washington, DC: US Department of Agriculture, p. 43.

given land use without visual impact. When you implement a given Visual Quality Objective (VQO), adjust the prescription to achieve it within the constraints of the VAC.

There are *no* absolute absorption values in management decision-making. It is, however, important to recognize the need to adjust land-use developments according to the relative absorption of a given landscape. This relative absorption is a function of landscape character — primarily topography and vegetation. The adjustment in management prescriptions must also reflect proposed land use/development because some of it may not be absorbable, even though a particular landscape has a high VAC. Two other factors affect relative absorption — distance from the viewer and user perception or sensitivity. However, these are already accounted for in the basic visual-resource management model.

VISUAL RESOURCE MANAGEMENT — AN INTERPRETATION

We have just discussed a system used by an agency whose interest in land management is multi-faceted. Some modification of the system is obviously necessary at the local level, depending on the perceptions of the user population. User perceptions have sometimes differed from professional ones. Also, the legislative mandate, agency goals, and complexity of programs may determine the visual quality objectives that you select. Regardless of agency or situation, what is presented is a basic model that managers can use to arrive at the specific objectives for a resource-management prescription. If you understand the underlying concepts of characteristic landscape, variety, and deviation, then specifics within a model can be modified to suit an individual manager's needs or a new model can be developed.

Objective Map

Symbol Objective   Code
R   RETENTION
PR   PARTIAL RETENTION
M   MODIFICATION
MM MAXIMUM MODIFICATION

Preservation does not appear on the
chart but is indicated by:

P   PRESERVATION

Assign Preservation Objective to all existing and
proposed (within 10 years)
Specify Classified Areas.

Figure 11-9. The application of visual quality objectives, integrating landscape variety and viewer sensitivity. Note those areas in need of either rehabilitation or enhancement by the appropriate symbol beside the quality objective, *e* for enhancement and *reh* for rehabilitation. Rehabilitation should be noted when management activities in a particular area do not conform to an agreed upon quality objective. Enhancement notation should come from a detailed landscape management plan for a particular area. The Visual Resource Management System thus produces an area map showing visual quality objectives.

SELECTED READINGS

1. Alexander, C., and S.I. Chermayeff. 1964. *Notes on Synthesis of Form.* Cambridge, MA: Harvard University Press.

2. Arnheim, R. 1974. *Art and Visual Perception. A Psychology of the Creative Eye.* Revised edition. Berkeley, CA: University of California Press.

3. Birren, F. 1982. *Light, Color, and Environment.* Revised edition. New York: Van Nostrand Reinhold Co.

4. Ekbo, G. 1969. *The Landscape We See.* New York: McGraw-Hill Book Co.

5. Elsner, G.H. and R.C. Smarden (eds.). 1979. *Proceedings of Our National Landscape: A Conference on Applied Techniques for Analysis and Management of the Visual Resource.* USDA-Forest Service General Technical Report PSW-35.

6. Litton, R.B., Jr. 1973. *Landscape Control Points: A Procedure for Predicting and Monitoring Visual Impacts.* US Forest Service Research Paper PSW-91.

7. Litton, R.B., Jr. 1968. *Forest Landscape Description and Inventories — A Basis for Land Planning and Design.*

8. Litton, R.B., Jr., R.J. Tetlow, J. Sorenson, and R.A. Beatty, 1974. *Water and Landscape.* Port Washington, NY: Water Information Cente, Inc.

9. Litton, R.B., Jr. and R.H. Twiss. 1967. "The Forest Landscape: Some Elements of Visual Analysis." *Proceedings of Society of American Foresters.* Portland, OR: Society of American Foresters, p. 212.

10. Lowenthal, D. (ed.). 1967. *Environmental Perception and Behavior.* Geography Research Paper No. 109. Chicago: University of Chicago Press.

11. Mitchell, W.J. (ed.). 1972. *Environmental Design: Research and Practice.* Los Angeles: University of California at Los Angeles.

12. Nighswonger, J.J. 1970. *A Methodology of Inventorying and Evaluating the Scenic Quality and Related Recreational Values of Kansas Streams.* Topeka, KS: Kansas Department of Economic Development, Planning Division.

13. Peterson, G.L., and E.S. Neamann. 1969. "Modeling and Predicting Human Response to the Visual Recreation Environment." *Journal of Leisure Research,* 1(3):219-237.

14. Rutledge, A.J. 1986. *Anatomy of a Park.* 2nd edition. New York: McGraw-Hill Book Co.

15. Shafer, E.L., J.L. Hamilton, and E.A. Schmidt, 1969. "Natural Landscape Preferences: A Predictive Model." *Journal of Leisure Research* 1(1):1.

16. Simonds, J.O. 1983. *Landscape Architecture.* Revised edition. New York: McGraw-Hill.

17. Steintz, C., and D. Way. 1970. "A Model for Evaluating Visual Consequences of Urbanization on Shoreline Landscapes." US Army Corps of Engineers. Washington, DC: US Government Printing Office.

18. Tunnard, C. 1978. *A World With A View, An Inquiry into the Nature of Scenic Values.* New Haven: Yale University Press.

19. US Forest Service. 1974. *National Forest Landscape Management, Volume I.* Agriculture Handbook 434. Washington, DC: US Government Printing Office.

20. USDA-Forest Service. 1974. *National Forest Landscape Management,* Volume II, Chapter 1, (The Visual Management System), Agriculture Handbook 462. Washington, DC: US Government Printing Office.

21. USDA-Forest Service. 1975. *National Forest Landscape Management,* Volume II, Chapter 2, (Utilities), Agriculture Handbook 478. Washington, DC: US Government Printing Office.

22. USDA-Forest Service. 1977. *National Forest Landscape Management,* Volume II, Chapter 3, (Range), Agriculture Handbook 484, Washington, DC: US Government Printing Office.

23. USDA-Forest Service. 1977. *National Forest Landscape Management,* Volume II, Chapter 4, (Roads), Agriculture Handbook 483. Washington, DC: US Government Printing Office.

24. USDA-Forest Service. 1980. *National Forest Landscape Management.* Volume II, Chapter 5, (Timber), Agriculture Handbook 559. Washington, DC: US Government Printing Office.

25. Vernon, M.D. 1962. *The Psychology of Perception.* Baltimore. Penguin Books.

26. Zube, E.A., R.O. Brush, and J.G. Fabos, 1975. *Landscape Assessment: Values, Perceptions, and Resources:* Stroudsburg, PA: Dowden, Hutchinson, and Ross.

PART III.
VISITOR MANAGEMENT

To reiterate what was presented in Chapters Two and Three, the total management program is the combination/interaction of three subsystems — resource, visitor, and service. The particular combination of all programs for a given area constitutes the *recreational opportunity* being provided. Part II focused on the resource management programs, or the subsystem. Part III covers the visitor management programs. These are aimed at directly or indirectly manipulating visitors to protect/enhance their recreational experiences and/or to protect, enhance, or rehabilitate the resource base. Thus, as stated before, no one program can be judged good or bad, appropriate or inappropriate, a success or a failure by itself. It must be judged in relation to the opportunity being provided.

Included in Part III are discussions about the following programs: distribution of use, information, interpretation, and public safety. Redistribution is a perennial problem that exists because we have not understood the linkage between specific management programs and the resulting user response, macro-behavioral patterns. In other words, the need to redistribute use is often created by failing to achieve a given equilibrium, described in Chapter Three, or overestimating the ability of a resource to sustain that equilibrium over time. The chapter on distribution of use deals with the principles and techniques, not on how

to achieve a given equilibrium.

Information programs have three functions: 1) to provide visitors with sufficient information to make a rational choice between competing recreational opportunities; 2) to manage visitor use patterns by clearly establishing norms of behavior and warning of potential hazards; and 3) to explain the necessity for specific management actions. The first two are obvious, but the last is often overlooked. If the public does not understand the need for a given program, such as the value of fire in maintaining a given ecosystem, it may react very negatively to a new program and thwart or negate your efforts.

Interpretive programming deals with translating the natural history of the landscape into something that is meaningful to visitors. The goal is simply enhanced appreciation of the natural setting, which should also enhance the recreational opportunity for the typical visitor. Principles, methods, and media for doing so are presented here.

Public safety is an important consideration, and the character of the program reflects its relative location along ROS. Safety is often an implied goal or simply seen as a constraint on management; however, it should be realistically viewed as an integral part of any recreational opportunity. As such, public safety goals should become part of the written management prescription.

CHAPTER TWELVE

DISTRIBUTION OF VISITOR USE

Figure 12-1. The Effects of Concentrated Use in a Backcounty Zone: Schreibers Meadow, Mt. Baker National Forest (Photo by B.W. Twight)

How to obtain a reasonable distribution of use over existing recreational areas and sites has always been a management concern. However, as suggested in Chapter Three, people tend to concentrate at particular attractions within a landscape — sometimes to the exclusion of the rest of the landscape. Other managerial and user input also affects points of visitor concentration, so this chapter focuses not only on techniques of dispersal but also on conditions that make each onc most effective. The common ideal of spatially and temporally redistributing use is also appraised.

PRINCIPLES OF DISPERSAL OF VISITOR USE

You can disperse use on a local, area-wide, or regional basis. Local or area-wide programs are easiest because land typically falls under the jurisdiction of one agency and programs can often be implemented without the approval of higher authority. Typically, road and trail access can be controlled or redirected in local zones, and, as shown in Chapter Three, access is a primarily manager-influenced attribute which affects users' perceptions of the opportunity.

Figure 12-2 shows the three principles of

visitor dispersal in ascending order. If you want to change existing use patterns, you should first try voluntary dispersal through either information programs or changes in the physical design of the setting. Changes in physical design are most effective. Limiting parking space, erecting physical barriers, etc. are non-confrontational compared to permit or regulation enforcement. When these programs fail to achieve your objective, you may still have to limit use in order to protect the recreational opportunity and the environment in which it takes place. When you begin to limit use, you may also be detracting from the very opportunity you are trying to preserve. As suggested in Chapter Three, voluntary dispersal through physical design should generally not detract from the opportunity, but implementing a confrontational limited-entry system to redistribute use may have a negative impact on perception of the opportunity. It may also attract a new clientele group. Even in the most carefully considered program, you may have to close a certain locale to recreational use to allow it to recover or to protect, on a long-term basis, its unique, fragile environment.

Dispersion is considered a voluntary redistribution of recreation use over an area. This should really be the manager's first alternative when overuse occurs on some sites while others remain underused. Assume that there are planned, physically available substitutes and that you are simply publicizing them. Note that crowding, or density of use, is not targeted as a justification for dispersal from the visitors' perspective. Density should reflect the opportunity to be provided, and it is better

and more naturally achieved by altering access, facilities, and services.

As shown in Chapter Three, people who want certain density levels choose opportunities which have the greatest probability of providing them. Even within those limits, management can use some sort of feedback mechanism, such as a report card, to enhance recreational opportunities for the existing clientele.[16] That is the reason this chapter is entitled "Distribution of Visitor Use" rather than "Redistribution." Management tries to create certain recreational opportunities and to stabilize these over time. If they do not become stable over time, you end up with constant social succession rather than simple adjustments to achieve and maintain the desired balance. Under those conditions, management constantly confronts the public it is trying to service.

In order to maintain public confidence, stability of recreational opportunities is essential. The agency also has some self-interest in stability because supportive clientele and budgeting for future years are results of management programs that are well-defined and have been refined over time.

A program should disperse use voluntarily through information services. This may be very effective where there is a lack of information and/or the networks through which people seek information affect existing use patterns. (See Chapter 13.) Better information may not achieve optimal dispersal from the manager's perspective, but it may provide sufficient redistribution to reduce problems of overuse on specific sites. Through this approach, you cause minimal disruption to normal visitor participation

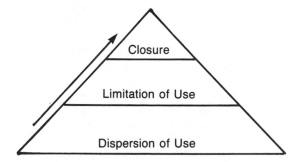

Figure 12-2. Principles of Visitor Dispersal, in Ascending Order of Implementation

patterns. Visitors do not feel forced into changing their itineraries, yet may find other sites more enjoyable. In fact, providing more information on available recreation opportunities allows users more variety.

Such a technique may also help to eliminate ''off-site'' users. For example, suppose some horsemen drive two to three hours from the Butte, Montana area to the Anaconda-Pintlar Wilderness, in order to go horseback riding. They have been assured that there will be no encounters with noisy trail bikes during their ride because of the wilderness designation. They do not seek a wilderness opportunity; they only desire a respite from trail bikes. You can possibly eliminate these ''off-site'' users and simultaneously enhance their experience by providing information on bridle paths or trails zoned for horse use only that are within easy driving distance of Butte.

Limitation means restricting the number of people who may participate in a particular activity at a particular location. It involves determining a site-capacity limit beyond which use cannot be permitted. Such limits are often arbitrary, based on managerial judgement, but they can also take very specific criteria like water-quality standards into account. There are several ways of limiting use; the most desirable is one closely aligned with normal visitor-use patterns that minimizes disruption. Perhaps this may seem a somewhat idealistic approach, but by using it you can often discover the existing social mechanisms that tend to separate users into compatible patterns.[25]

Closure is usually the last alternative for changing recreational use patterns, and it may be either temporary or permanent to protect the resource base. Attempt permanent closures only when no other means are available for protecting a valued resource. The size of the area involved should be no larger than necessary when you do this.

Under certain circumstances, closure may logically be your first alternative. For example, perhaps you have located a pair of nesting bald eagles along the river in your park. You may wish to close the general area to recreational use and not allow people to get out of their

boats along this stretch. You also may want to limit the number of people or the size of the craft on this portion of the river. Through your information program, you may even attempt to direct people voluntarily to other rivers and streams or to other portions of the same river. In other words, you can simultaneously employ all levels of visitor redistribution for a specific problem in a recreation area. As the preceding example illustrates, the problem for management becomes much more complex when you try to incorporate resource and social variables into your decision; therefore it is important to follow the hierarchy to redistribute recreational use.

Technique — Dispersion. There are three general techniques for obtaining voluntary dispersal: regional and area planning, regional information management, and area information systems.

Regional and Area Planning. On a regional or area basis, patterns of use are primarily determined by transportation systems like roads and trails. Since nearly all recreational use is associated with road or trail access, the type, character, and location of either or both generally determine the type and amount of recreational use a given place will receive. Use is concentrated on environmental attractors associated with these transportation systems.

The type and character of roads or trails encourage or discourage certain recreational uses and patterns of use. For example, a scenic road can be designed to slow people down so that they enjoy the view of the surrounding landscape. If we design the scenic road for high-speed through traffic, we may encourage undesirable behavior and create conflict between users. Even if the road has been properly designed in terms of speed, its character must still be considered. The presence of large cuts and fills or widely cleared areas for rights-of-way may detract from its character and discourage sightseeing. Location can also influence use — whether a road features a wide variety of scenery or masks negative sights like dumps and junk yards.

As indicated in Chapter Three, the above

example suggests that macro-patterns of use are directed by the location and character of access. Hopefully we encourage certain uses and patterns of use through a positive process rather than discourage use through negative means like unpleasant landscapes or poorly designed road or trail systems. Or we can improve access and services and then simply allow use to increase to a point where the site is no longer desirable for social or environmental recreation. People then move on to other sites that have not yet been overused.

This scenario is reminiscent of the early days of farming in this country. When the soil was worn-out, farmers simply moved onto new lands. Today, while there may be a scarcity of truly unique recreational opportunities and/or a disparity between where people live and the location of public lands, space *per se* is still generally not limiting. However, there may be limits or shortages of unique natural attractors or budgets for certain types of opportunities. Thus we should try to optimize existing space *within the constraints of the dedicated recreational opportunity,* which requires a positive approach to the distribution of people over the landscape. In sum, there is a limit to the amount of land and facilities the public is willing to maintain for intensive recreational use. Consequently, if we wish to maintain or improve the quality of the experiences provided at these dedicated intensive use areas, dispersal of use is necessary.

Given a particular transportation system, the character of the adjacent landscape and the type, character, and location of specific site developments determine patterns of recreational use. While more valued portions of the landscape attract and concentrate users, who is actually attracted is often determined by the type of site development associated with the means of access. Everyone has different preferences for specific site developments. For example, campers must choose between primitive auto campgrounds versus modern ones. Character is really the quality that distinguishes one development from another, given a specific type of site. Thus it can encourage or discourage certain types of uses.

The location of a development can also

directly affect use patterns.[14] If location adversely affects normal visitor behavior, substitutes may be sought. For example, a transient campground located away from the main through route will not be used for the purpose it was originally intended. And informal, transient camping often occurs near the access to a through route because dedicated sites are not available.

Regional Information Management. After development, the most effective management tool for obtaining voluntary dispersal is an information system that reaches visitors before they arrive at their destination. Ideally, you should reach the recreationist in the planning stage so that he or she has sufficient information on which to make the best personal choice. By the time you contact visitors on the site, it is often too late to better disperse use since plans are less flexible at that point.

Area Information Systems. Area distribution or redistribution can be accomplished through specific visitor-information programs. Information programs at the area level can be aimed at direct visitor contact through signing, information centers, on-site contact, and brochures.[4,14] By making specific information available to users, managers do influence the distribution of people over an area and may also affect redistribution of visitor use by making information available on existing patterns, points of overuse, and conflicts. (See Figure 12-3). However, information is most effective during the trip planning phase. [13,15,20] You may cause some on-site redistribution through information programs, but such programs may also increase impact by attracting new users. Intensive on-site contact has been found to improve redistribution.[18] Many people feel that socially this is a more desirable approach to redistribution than limitation or closure programs.

Technique — Limitation. Limitation of use is *not* predicated on determining the carrying capacity of a site. It is a matter of discovering at what point the impact of recreational use becomes unacceptable. Laws and regulations may establish these limits sometimes. At others

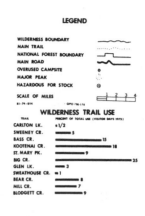

LEGEND

WILDERNESS BOUNDARY
MAIN TRAIL
NATIONAL FOREST BOUNDARY
MAIN ROAD
OVERUSED CAMPSITE
MAJOR PEAK
HAZARDOUS FOR STOCK

SCALE OF MILES

WILDERNESS TRAIL USE

TRAIL	PERCENT OF TOTAL USE (VISITOR DAYS 1973)
CARLTON LK.	1/2
SWEENEY CR.	5
BASS CR.	15
KOOTENAI CR.	18
ST. MARY PK.	9
BIG CR.	25
GLEN LK.	3
SWEATHOUSE CR.	1
BEAR CR.	8
MILL CR.	7
BLODGETT CR.	9

Figure 12-3. Informational Map Showing Existing Use Patterns on the Stevenville District of the Selway-Bitterroot Wilderness Area (From a US Forest Service Brochure)

professional judgements do. Such judgements should reflect the opportunity being provided. Too often, as suggested by F.E. Boetler, the manager who needs to limit use has searched for some "magic" capacity to justify his or her decision.[1] There is no good substitute for professional judgement in terms of limiting use. Probably as important is the decision on *how* to limit it. Once you decide to steer visitors away from an area, you should try to understand those factors — particularly those under your control — which have created the existing recreational pattern. Knowing them, you can judge the reversibility of such patterns with regional and area planning. If it is not feasible to reverse the process, then look at some sort of limited entry system or simply live with the new equilibrium created.

Recreational Use Zoning. This is probably the most common method of limiting use — and also one of the most appropriate.[18] It consists of clustering compatible recreational activities in selected zones to limit them within an area. This type of zoning has been employed successfully on large bodies of water in order to separate activities like motorized and nonmotorized boating, boating and swimming, and fishing and waterskiing. Perhaps zoning should be your first step since this is essentially what is meant by area planning — i.e., allocating space for specific recreational uses and locating that space, based on some pattern or system, within a given area.[14] If existing physiographic features such as waterfalls on rivers, lack of road access, or steep topography constrain recreational use, you can incorporate these into the area recreation plan so that desired patterns of use are encouraged without having to actually zone and enforce zoning regulations.

Time Limitation. Time zoning is a means of controlling use during peak periods, reducing conflicts between users, and ensuring adequate turnover rates so that opportunities are available for everyone. The actual time limit can be daily, weekly, seasonal, or annual. The time frame that you choose depends on the activities, the season of use, the concentration during certain periods, and the efficiency level that you wish to attain in redistributing use over the area. Where competition for open space is high, time zoning can assist in redistribution by limiting visitor stays. This forces some users who want to stay longer to seek other alternatives or change their use patterns on that particular site. If the program is to be reasonably successful, visitor-use alternatives must be available because time zoning often forces some users to abandon a particular opportunity in favor of alternative ones.

Ideally, time zoning fits the normal behavioral patterns of users as closely as possible. For example, a small lake near the coast of North Carolina was being used by fishermen and water-skiers. Conflict occurred between users because the lake was oval-shaped and not large enough to handle both types. An observational study showed that the fisherman typically used the lake from daybreak until about 9 am, returning around 5 pm until dark. Water-skiers usually arrived around 10 am and stayed until 4 pm. Conflict arose over the times when the fisherman stayed late and/or the water-skiers arrived early. The final policy decision limited the fisherman to a period from daylight to 9 am and from 5 pm until sunset; water-skiers were allowed on the lake from 9 am to 5 pm. Minimal monitoring of transition times was all that was necessary to ensure a successful program.

Most situations are not that simplistic but regardless of the problem you should consider existing user behavior. Time zoning is better adapted to shorter time frames like days or weeks. Seasonal or annual periods are usually too long to effectively redistribute use for either ecological or sociological purposes. You should also consider specific time frames as different recreational opportunities and managerially treat them as such. Since the basic management model is an open system,

responsiveness to public input or changes in other social factors can create different opportunities at different times on the same site — summer versus winter, a three-day Fourth of July weekend versus any other summer weekend, etc. A good example is a newly designated wild river in Alaska. Heavy use concentrates around the Fourth of July weekend, which also coincides with the peak of the salmon runs. If one avoids that time frame, there are very few people on the river. However, management has decided to try to redistribute use over the entire summer. Bon chance!

Space Limitation (Use per Unit Area). Space limitation, or density zoning, is a relatively new concept that has been applied to surface waters and roadless areas.[2,12] Desirable density levels are functions of the type of opportunity to be provided, the durability of the resource, and the perception of users, and are established as the upper limit for various management zones. Once these densities are reached, use is shifted to less populated zones. To be effective, this measure requires a well-supervised limited-entry permit system.[24]

Quota or Service Limitation. Quota limitations are established for developed sites based on their capacity to handle a given number of people at any one time. Capacity may be limited by the size of the facility, by the service loads of supporting facilities, or by legal criteria such as fire codes. Often the quota system is referred to as a "bed count" (for overnight facilities) and a "head count" (for day-use facilities). If no overflow camping is allowed, service limitation is the total number of camping units located in developed sites. Camping is usually regulated on a unit basis rather than by number of individual campers.

Technique — Closure. Closure simply means closing an area to recreational use. No matter what the reason behind its use, managers need to identify closure as temporary or permanent since these are entirely different programs. *Temporary Closures.* Temporary closures are implemented on a particular site for specific objectives and for a given amount of time.

Their primary purpose is to renovate a worn-out site or to protect the resource during periods of maximum vulnerability — such as high precipitation periods in areas with heavy clay soils, nesting times for particular bird species, or gathering seasons for grizzly bears or other large mammals.

Obviously you should employ other techniques to reduce visitor concentrations before attempting a temporary closure program. Seasonal closures generally relieve pressure on a resource from visitors during critical periods. Many times, the situation is a self-correcting one. For example, times of heavy rain, when soil compaction is highest, also discourages visitor participation, though some activities such as four-wheel driving and hunting may not follow this trend.

Ultimately, managers may have to make unpopular decisions to close areas or sites during a particular season. In doing so, they realize the need to sustain resources over time rather than having them depleted by visitor use for short periods. When you use this approach, a concomitant information program is also mandatory so that people understand what you are attempting to do and become aware of available alternative sites. Without this program, you may face a greater, long-term problem — visitor dissatisfaction with any new management program because of a lack of confidence in management that stems from poor communications.

Temporary closures do not necessarily have to be obstrusive. For example, the road leading to a campground located in a sub Alpine zone was snow plowed during the early camping season so that people could use the site. Because of the semi-open forest cover, the campground was freed of snow but the soil was saturated by snow melt. Early use was causing problems such as soil compaction, loss of vegetation, and sheet erosion of the soil surface. The decision was made to discontinue plowing since the timing of the natural snow melt on the road would allow the site to dry out before campers could get into it. This was less obstrusive than continued plowing with a sign stretched across the entrance to the campground stating that no camping would be allowed until after July 1.

After reviewing many impact studies, D.N. Cole concludes that regardless of the site, the greatest cumulative impact is from limited initial use.[9] Thus in backcountry areas rest and rotation are not very effective because management tends not to be intensive (people may continue to use a closed site) and deterioration is typically faster than recovery. More and more sites have to be allocated under such a system. The other consideration is the attributes of these alternatives in terms of natural attractors. Simply closing one and opening another does not guarantee that people will obey the rule and shift to the new site(s). If use does not shift, resource allocation costs increase because the closure has to be stringently enforced.

Permanent Closures. Permanent closures may be needed to protect people from environmental hazards or to protect a very sensitive resource from any recreational use. Determine the need for such a measure during the area planning process. Generally, problems requiring closure are more easily handled by not locating roads, trails, or sites near suspect areas. Locating the new sites, roads, and trails away from problem points creates more of a psychological barrier than a physical one. More significant problem locations such as sink holes or rare or endangered vegetation, may still need physical barriers to deter the public from general recreational use.

APPRAISAL OF DISPERSAL MANAGEMENT

Much consideration has been given to dispersal of use. Often defined as the redistribution of use over a given geographical area or time period, or both, neither are ideal goals. Recreational use tends to concentrate naturally at more valued portions of the landscape — the natural attractors — whether they be a Mount Denali or a small, midwestern lake. Society also makes particular time periods attractive for visits — Memorial Day weekend, summers after schools close, work weeks that become four 10-hour days, or whatever.

You might argue that access to Mount

Denali or the midwestern lake should not be allowed to the point where attractiveness or the quality of the resource is significantly reduced. We would all agree on that point. But the answer is not trying to redistribute use over an entire geographical area; it is in designing management actions, particularly the access transportation system, to maintain a level of use commensurate with the capability of the resource to sustain that use, and to maintain the desired recreational opportunity.[14]

You could make the same argument for attempting to redistribute times for use. Many factors beyond management control affect chronological distribution, such as flexible work schedules, designation of holidays as three-day weekends, internal allocation of family vacation time, and so on. On the other hand, resource attributes themselves often determine visitation times — like the spring chinook salmon run, the changing of the leaf colors in the fall, etc.

The newly designated wild river example used earlier points to the problem of trying to redistribute use which coincides with the summer king salmon run, around the fourth of July weekend. The river is accessible via road, but once you get on the river it takes three days to float back to the road system. Many Alaskans are given three-day weekends for the fourth of July celebration. Thus the concentration of people on the river during that period is a product of circumstances not directly controlled by a managing agency. Yet the agency has expressed a desire to redistribute river use because it exceeds social carrying capacity. From a social standpoint, we would doubt that very many people are disappointed with their fourth of July float/fish trips, unless the fishing is lousy. Since fish stocks have not been affected by the "pressure" it may not be possible to cause a voluntary movement to other rivers or other time periods on the same river.

Perhaps limiting use would cause some redistribution, but this would also require an expensive enforcement program. Such action may be unjustified if the resource is not being measurably affected and users are satisfied with the recreation opportunity they are experiencing. Ironically, management's perceived need for redistributing use fails to account for the unique circumstances that cause such concentrations, including a previous management action that improved access to the upper river after it was designated a wild river.

While the literature on distribution of use is limited, Jubenville and Becker suggest that visitors naturally concentrate at natural attractors within the generalized landscape, and that the level of use and type of user attracted result from development norms applied by management in order to provide access and facility accommodations.[14] To suggest that we can redistribute use voluntarily, without modifying the development norms already in place, implies that visitors are choosing recreational opportunities under maximum uncertainty — that they are not aware of what they are getting into and/or alternative choices, or that they are not looking for a particular set of resource attributes.

Studies by E.E. Krumpe and P.J. Brown in the backcountry of Yellowstone National Park,[13] R.C. Lucas in the Selway-Bitterroot Wilderness,[17] and J.H. Schomaker[23] indicate that two factors must be present in order to effectively redistribute use voluntarily: 1.) novice users, *inexperienced* at either the activity or the geographical area; and 2.) people who can be reached at the point in their planning process where they can incorporate such information into their decisions. J.W. Roggenbuck and D.L. Berrier feel that some redistribution can be accomplished through intensive on-site contact programs, but these can be very expensive.[21] They also caution against impact from the program itself.

In sum, voluntary redistribution of use based on an information program would probably not be very successful unless the circumstances are similar to those outlined above. The redistribution of use through regulation, probably a limited-entry permit system, is not very effective unless monitored and enforced. A. Plaeger and P. Womble,[20] and J.W. Van Wagtendonk and J.M. Benedict[25] found that over fifty percent of those who received a backcountry permit deliberately violated its provisions because there was no monitoring. You could close an area permanently or temporarily, but such a move would likely come under close public scrutiny. Justification would have to be overwhelming and generally related to the protection of the resource.

From a more pragmatic viewpoint, the dispersion technique is a tool of modern management. This technique is used regularly to maintain the potential for a particular experience via equal opportunity, protection of desired social or resource attributes, or pressure from existing user groups to maintain the status quo. However, unless circumstances are similar to those cited previously, you should not invest much in *voluntary* redistribution.

Rather than viewing the above as redistribution of use, we prefer the term "distribution." The geographical pattern of use is really a response to the total number of attributes a recreational opportunity has. Thus, if there is a problem with current distribution, it is most likely the result of some previous management action. A logical management direction would be to examine the link between present use and past management actions, then seek the least costly solution that maintains the desired pattern of use.

Because of equity issues, some opportunities may be artificially supported by increasing access, yet regulating numbers and patterns of use. Blazing trails for the physically handicapped is an example of this. Social equity is also the main justification for not charging the full per capita costs for recreational use of public resources. Yet many managers have become interested in charging users full fares, or at least more of the base cost. The neoclassical economist would consider this the appropriate direction, letting the signals from the marketplace direct the allocation of resources and thus the distribution of recreational use. Probably some compromise will be established for public lands where less-than-fair-market-value fees are charged, but users will be expected to supply many needed services such as trash disposal, firewood, etc.

For the more primitive user, "sweat equity" will likely be touted as a substitute for price. With "sweat equity," rather than charge

a hard-to-collect fee and then provide facilities such as footbridges, trail maintenance, etc., users are provided minimal access and expected to reach their destinations within roadless areas through their own physical effort. Some people create their own trails, bridges, campsite developments, etc. in order to reduce or average the amount of "sweat equity," particularly if they use an area more than once. This is simply a cost averaging. Unfortunately the ideals of such a "sweat equity" program may not be achieved unless we closely monitor such activity in relation to the impact on the opportunities being provided, which in turn increases the cost of the program.

SELECTED READINGS

1. Boteler F.E. 1984. "Carrying Capacity As a Framework for Managing Whitewater Use." *Journal of Park and Recreation Administration.* 2(2):26-36.

2. Brooks, L. 1963. "Zoning as a Step in the Planning of Natural Parks." Second Federal-Provincial Parks Conference Proceedings, Ottawa: Canadian National and Historical Parks Branch.

3. Brockman, C.F., and L.C. Merriam, Jr. 1979. *Recreational Use of Wildlands.* 3rd Edition. New York: McGraw-Hill Book Co.

4. Brown, P.J., and J.D. Hunt. 1969. "The Influence of Information Signs of Visitor Distribution and Use." *Journal of Leisure Research* 1(1):69.

5. Bureau of Outdoor Recreation. 1966. *National Conference on Policy Isues in Outdoor Recreation.* Washington: DC: US Department of Interior.

6. Canon, L.K., S. Adler, and R.E. Leonard. 1979. "Factors Affecting Dispersal of Backcountry Campsites." USDA-Forest Service Research Note NE-276.

7. Clawson, M., J.L. Knetsch. 1966. *Economics of Outdoor Recreation.* Baltimore: The John Hopkins University Press.

8. Cowgill, P. 1971. "Too Many People on the Colorado River." *National Parks and Conservation Magazine* 45(11):10.

9. Cole, D.N. 1981. "Managing Ecological Impacts At Wilderness Campsites: an Evaluation of Techniques." *Journal of Forestry* 79(2):86-89.

10. Douglass, R.W. 1983. *Forest Recreation.* New York: Pergamon Press.

11. Godfrey, E.B., and R.L. Peckfelder. 1972. "Recreation Carrying Capacity and Wild Rivers: A Case Study of the Middle Fork of the Salmon." *Western Agricultural Economic Association Annual Meeting, Proceedings.*

12. Jackson, R. 1971. "Zoning to Regulate On-Water Recreation." *Land Economics* 45(4):382.

13. Krumpe, E.E. and P.J. Brown. 1982. "Redistributing Backcountry Use through Information Relating to Recreational Experiences." *Journal of Forestry* 80(5):360-362.

14. Jubenville, A. and R.H. Becker. 1983. "Outdoor Recreation Management Planning: Contemporary Schools of Thought." *Recreation Planning and Management.* Lieber, S., an D. Fesennaier (eds.). State College, PA: Venture Publishing, Inc.

15. LaPage, W.F. 1968. *The Role of Fees in Campers' Decisions.* US Forest Service Research Paper NE-118.

16. LaPage, W.F. 1983. "Recreation Resource Management for Visitor Satisfaction." *Journal of Park and Recreation Administration* 1(2):37-44.

17. Lucas, R.C. 1981. *Redistributing Wilderness Use through Information Supplied to Visitors.* USDA-Forest Service Research paper INT-277.

18. McEwen, D., and S.R. Tocher. 1976. "Zone Management: Key to Controlling Recreational Impact in Developed Campsites." *Journal of Forestry* 14(2):90.

19. McGill, A.W. 1974. "Dispersal of Recreationists on Wildlands." *Outdoor Recreation Research: Applying the Results.* US Forest Service General Technical Report NC-9.

20. Plaeger, A., and P. Womble. 1981. "Compliance with Backcountry Permits in Mount McKinley National Park." *Journal of Forestry* 79(3):155-156.

21. Roggenbuck, J.W., and D.L. Barrier. 1981. "Communications to Disperse Wilderness Campers." *Journal of Forestry* 79(5):295-297.

22. Schlatter, J. 1972. "Great Smokies Trails: The Backpacking Permit System." *National Parks and Conservation Magazine* 46(9):13.

23. Schomaker, J.H. 1975. "Effect of Selected Information on Dispersal of Wilderness Recreationists." Ph.D. dissertation (unpublished). Colorado State University.

24. Stankey, G.H. 1973. *Visitor Perception of Wilderness Recreation Carrying Capacity.* US Forest Service Research Paper INT-141.

25. Van Wagtendonk, J.W., and J.M. Benedict. 1980. "Wilderness Permit Compliance and Validity." *Journal of Forestry* 78(7):399-401.

26. Wagar, J.A. 1964. *The Carrying Capacity of Wild Lands for Recreation.* Forest Science Monograph 7, Society of American Foresters, Washington, DC.

27. Wilson, G.T. 1969. *Lake Zoning for Recreation: How to Improve Recreation Use of Lakes.* American Institute of Park Executives, Washington, DC.

CHAPTER THIRTEEN
INFORMATION SERVICES

Figure 13-1. Information Is Important Both for Management of the Recreational Opportunity and Improved Decision-making by Visitors (Photo by B.W. Twight)

From a management perspective, information programs ensure the success of all other programs. Their primary purpose is to inform visitors of behavioral norms, to guide visitors' resource use, and to explain *why* certain actions are necessary. Explanation is essential to understanding the problem and supporting the agency.

Information *per se* is not a stand-alone program; it is the binder that pulls together the total recreational opportunity. As such, it links other visitor management programs. Making particular recreational opportunities available, closing backcountry zones to protect a resource, warning of hazardous water conditions, improving wilderness user etiquette,

and so on are management actions that require information programs. We think it is safe to state that public support for recreation programs is often affected by associated information programs.

By giving visitors adequate information and using the information program to protect the quality of the recreational opportunity, agencies build a committed clientele who support them in the long run. In essence, this program is a marketing strategy that insures an agency's survival and growth.

In sum, information programs serve visitors. They provide information that improves personal decision-making, promotes general welfare, and protects the resource where the activity takes place. Information is essential to the success of most agency programs. Informing visitors and encouraging feedback to management provides cues to keeping those programs on target.

There is no guarantee that any particular information program will be an instantaneous success. Understanding applied communication can obviously help, but we must recognize that communication is a two-way street. You must offer some type of feedback mechanism to determine if a program meets visitors' needs and presents your message clearly. If they do not understand or you do not reach them, you can make adjustments. Too many management programs fail to satisfy the public because they lack a proper feedback mechanism or management fails to make adjustments after receiving visitor feedback.

Think about your own experiences. Have you ever visited a park where you were handed a four-page, single-spaced brochure and told to read it because you must abide by the rules? Observe other users under those circumstances. How many pull their auto over to the side of the road and read the brochure? How many stop at the first coffee shop to read the brochure? Simply handing out information is no guarantee of success. If you are sincerely interested in guiding resource use and enhancing visitor experiences, then you must become more sophisticated at designing, implementing and monitoring information programs.

APPLIED COMMUNICATION THEORY

People seek information for two reasons: 1.) as an end in itself to increase their knowledge about some particular subject of interest and 2.) as a means to an end. In this situation, people seek specific information to help make personal decisions. While they may accept information about some natural feature such as a thermal pool, what most visitors need is assistance in choosing a form of recreation. In the broadest sense, people want information about recreational opportunities so they can

maximize their outdoor experience. This is an ongoing process for anyone before, during, and after participation. Getting information before participation is obviously preferable. However, most people continually accept and respond to information while engaged in an activity to conform to rules and norms and to adjust to situational conditions. Future decisions are affected not only by this stored information, but also new data received later on.

The form the information takes — verbal or non-verbal — is extremely important. Our formal programming often focuses on verbal communications, yet much of what we communicate to users is non-verbal. In fact, some of our non-verbal communications are so strong as to override the verbal ones. For example, a sign can say ''No Motorized Use.'' but the design of the trail head and trail can say ''Trail bikes and three-wheelers welcome!'' These are typical causes of constant conflict, where additional dollars are required to enforce a no-motor policy and solutions are rarely lasting. When you design access facilities, you non-verbally communicate the nature of the recreational opportunity for that particular setting. And as R.A. Hinde states, non-verbal stimuli may be so strong that people either miss any verbal message or dismiss it as a mistake or inappropriate.[11] In sum, the strength of an information program lies in proper non-verbal communications and alignment of the verbal message with the non-verbal.

You must also consider *how* people seek information. Styles of participation affect what people need to know and how they try to obtain this knowledge. Most RV campers want information on camping facilities, but the local RV'er already knows about these. This individual has a greater interest in the condition of the access road, whether the fish are biting, the anticipated weather pattern for next weekend, or the marauding black bears that sometimes patrol the campground. The non-local RV'er may want to know about the types of environmental settings, the local attractors within each, and the RV facilities available to enjoy those things. Or perhaps, if a particular activity is of interest, such as lake fishing, what particular lakes are available within a given distance of camp or along a given travel route.

The non-local may choose Site A because it offers fishing, is accessible by RV, has RV camping facilities, and falls within limits of distance. The local user may choose Site A for all of the above reasons but utilize additional, more refined information to, as much as possible, eliminate the uncertainty of not catching good-sized fish at the lake. Non-locals tend to seek the more general information already available to locals and choose recreation based on that information. If they participate and find the fishing poor, the reason may be timing. If they need to arrive a month earlier, they use this information for future trips to the lake. Perhaps you can locate a local resident to find out fishing conditions, such as a marina owner. Or, after a sufficient number of "trial and error" trips, you may gather much more detailed information about Site A that the locals use. Thus what you seek and how you seek it depend on what you already know.

As suggested in Chapter Five, *how* we seek information is based on sources that are known to us and how familiar and trustworthy we perceive those sources to be. People perceived as "experts" are trusted, and the more familiar we are with an individual, the more willing we are to trust his or her information. If we find no experts on available sources, familiarity with the source may become the overriding factor in accepting the message.

The *how* is probably best described by the term "networking." To choose a type of recreation, you may use a single network or a whole series of networks, depending on how important your decision is to you, the networks available, and how much uncertainty you are willing to live with. For generalized participation decisions, people typically use formal information networks supplied by the agency which manages the resource base, or some affiliated group such a RV association or sport-fishing group. For more specific information, people typically rely on informal networks: friends, acquaintances, or mutual friends.

Standing or acceptance within a network is essential to getting desired information. In the formal networks, you may already have standing as a member of the general public (public sector) or association (private sector). In the informal networks, you obtain standing through familiarity and trust. You can often penetrate a network through a mutual friend who is already involved. The senior author faced that very problem trying to gather information about bighorn-sheep hunting in a particular drainage in Idaho. He drew a once-in-a-lifetime permit and used formal networks to obtain all the generalized information available. However, in order to get detailed information, he needed to communicate with the local hunters, taxidermists, etc. who are knowledgeable about bighorn sheep habits and patterns in that drainage. Mutual friends either sought this information or legitimized entrance into their networks.

Dividing users into locals and non-locals is a classic illustration of networking. Other divisions based on participatory style include guided and non-guided visitors, groups and individuals, etc. What management must recognize are formal and informal networks. The agency's formal network is only one source of information, and for many users not the most important, particularly for more detailed, refined participation decisions.

Next you must consider *when* people seek information. Clawson's five stages of the recreational experience suggest that stage one — the Planning Stage — is when people use information to make decisions. The plan can be very abbreviated, like one based on a comment by the "Dean of the Bass Fishermen" who says, "The big ones are biting in the north arm," or very involved, like the one for the RV camper-fisherman who lives a thousand miles away and invests considerable time and expense to catch a "big one." The *when* is important to management, as suggested in Chapter Twelve, because it affects the type of information needed and how visitors seek/accept that information.

To put it into context, local users are already knowledgeable about an area and tied into informal networks. A formal information program is probably of no use to this individual unless some recent change has been introduced by either management (change of regulations, rerouting of the road) or some exogenous input such as a flood. Consequently, management should rely on local informal networks and non-verbal communications to inform locals, then use on-site verbal communications to encourage proper use patterns where non-verbal and local informal networks are not sufficient. Management can take advantage of these networks simply by "passing the word" to a few key links — the postmaster, the bait-shop owner, the bartender, etc.

Most people are ethical and respond to verbal messages from management.[8] For those who are not, the only effective communication appeals to their sense of moral costs and benefits. What is the probability of getting caught, and what is the cost if they do? Off-site communications, if desired, can also be accomplished through other formal networks that locals might use, such as the Valley Sportsman's Association or an area chapter of an RV association, or perhaps even a nearby radio or television station. Where use is rationed and monitored closely by an agency, local users may take advantage of a formal information program to obtain detailed news. Where such contacts become routine, an agency may use a recorded phone message which can be quickly updated. Mass media such as newspapers, radio, and television also help reach local users on either a regularly scheduled basis to announce the latest information on local conditions or on a periodic basis to warn users of abrupt changes in local conditions or inpending regulatory changes.

Non-locals use formal information programs more because they do not possess all the general data known to locals. If this group constitutes a considerable portion of the user population, your off-site program becomes more important. Printed material, particularly maps showing activity sites and written descriptions called recreational opportunity guides (ROG's), are an essential part of the program. Potential local users, if they take advantage of the formal program, have needs

similar to non-locals. They may, however, seek information differently — by calling on the phone or stopping at the office. Some agencies try to improve this effort by conveniently placing ROG's in the local library or other public areas. Non-local non-users are people who may travel to an area for a given purpose and seek information about available opportunities. These individuals confront the same problems as local non-users, finding it difficult to enter a formal network because of public and private ownerships in a given area and difficult to locate agencies and access their information programs. Many states and multi-state regions have established specific informational programs, including regional visitor centers, to help this type of person make decisions and to increase access to specific agency-information programs.

REGIONAL INFORMATION SYSTEMS

There are two potential planning stages in individual decision-making: 1.) the macro-level, region or general zone of participation, and 2.) the micro-level, the specific recreational opportunity within a general zone or area information program.

Some people choose a region or general zone, travel to that zone, and then select specific opportunities. While it may appear that such a planning process leaves much uncertainty, people typically choose a region because it offers a number of *desired* recreational opportunities. They go prepared with sufficient skills, equipment, and information about the area in order to take advantage of what the region has to offer.

Others choose a region and a given opportunity simultaneously. They select the specific activity and focus all of their additional planning and trip preparation on that activity. Thus they need maximum information because they are likely to have less flexible schedules and locations if some problem arises. Still others focus all their planning on the specific activity or micro-level.

Regional Programs. The regional informational network is designed to enhance macro-level decision-making by providing base data on available opportunities and an agency contact for obtaining more detailed information. Regional information systems can be holistic and offer an entire gamut of opportunities, public or private, within a region. Under those conditions, the information has to be relatively general so people can assimilate it quickly and make choices. The state or some private company typically provides this type of publication/service.

Or the regional system can focus only on one agency. Parks or recreation areas under its jurisdiction are identified, and the information program describes only recreational opportunities within these units. A system can also delineate a theme such as colonial history, trout fishing, or wilderness hiking, then build a regional program around that theme. Typically the private sector offers this type of service.

Regionalization. It is important to gather and disseminate information on a regional level to minimize discrepancies due to variation in data collection methods, units of analyses, and models of actual participation.[5] Many people agree on this point; however, the problem becomes one of defining regional boundaries. Some feel that each state should be divided into regions, but this is not a large enough geographic area to describe normal visitor travel and behavioral patterns and disseminate this information to the using public. The geographic area should be larger — much larger. Since use patterns and demands for information often exceed state and even multi-state boundaries, these regional boundaries should cover an area as large as six to ten states, and the regions should be interconnected for information exchange. Probably the best way to delineate boundaries is to base them on the primary physiographic areas of the United States that have been adjusted to the political boundaries of the states. (See Figure 13-2). Alaska and Hawaii, not shown, would be separate regions.

Probably as important as any single phase of a regional information system is actual operation. Other systems are usually limited to

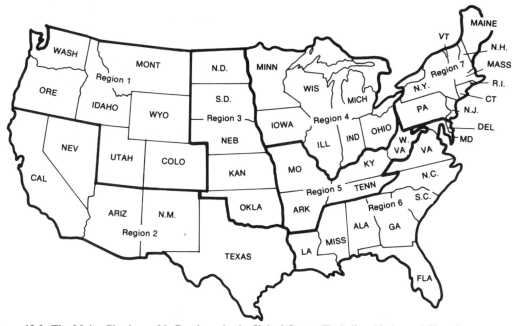

Figure 13-2. The Major Physiographic Provinces in the United States (Excluding Alaska and Hawaii). These represent general recreational opportunities.

a single agency that does not show visitors the total spectrum of available opportunities. Consequently, visitors often have limited options but sufficient information with which to make a choice. Increased information helps people make the best possible choices.

This requires constant updating of information if the system is to be effective. Every agency should use the same vehicles, the same units of measure, and so forth to feed new data into the system. Such an operation is ideally computer-based because of volume and the need for constant updating.

Some broad-range systems are already in operation, such as that used by AAA; however these simplified information systems generally inform people about limited opportunities/ services. A more sophisticated, nationwide operation might be devised where individuals go to their local branch offices, plug in their computer cards, and obtain all the information needed for visits to southern Florida during December or the North Slope of Alaska in July.

There are many drawbacks to a regional information system, including the following:

1. information overload at the macro-level of decision-making
2. lack of participation by agencies and organizations
3. current availability of much of the information, often in fragmented form
4. competition from existing private endeavors
5. lack of acceptance by the public
6. attempts to reduce uncertainty when it is really a part of the recreational experience[6]

Many agencies are looking closely at the regional information system for outdoor recreation management. A contemporary concept and very controversial, it is worth considering, but we should proceed slowly. People need information to make decisions, but if it requires an extensive new infrastructure, data collection and updating, and/or long-term commitment from agencies already experiencing severe budget reductions, then you have to question the desirability of such a system. We suspect that many people who have to travel long distances to get to a region will only rely on an agency for general information and other sources, including formal networking through clubs, organizations, etc., for detailed information. Detailed information about areas within a region or specific opportunities within a given area is the function of an area information program. Thus, while most agencies continue to search for ways of reaching people at the macro-level, the micro-level continues to be the primary focus of agency programs.

AREA INFORMATION SYSTEMS

Area information systems are designed to focus on micro-level decision making. As previously indicated, they offer more refined information in greater detail so participants can make more informed choices. But managers must remember that timing the receipt of information and networking through associations other than the agency are important. Rather than repeat the concepts discussed with regional information systems, I will summarize the ones applicable to area information systems during the actual participation period:

1. While part of the program aims at assisting people in macro decision-making, much of it is directed at the micro-level.
2. Nonverbal communication is important to convey the type of recreational opportunity participants should expect.
3. Verbal communication must be aligned with nonverbal so no mixed signals confuse participants.
4. The onsite information program is a simple reminder of what to expect or what rules govern participation. Simplicity is the key.
5. Types and level of information provided should reflect where that activity falls on the recreational opportunity

Figure 13-3. Ohanapecosh Visitor Center, Mt. Rainier National Park (Photo by B.W. Twight)

spectrum. The more primitive the opportunity, the less specific the information. Under these conditions, risk, uncertainty, and self-reliance become more essential to the experience. Thus the area information program becomes an important management tool, much more so than the regional one.

Information Media. Since the area information program is directed toward specific opportunities with specific geographical boundaries, necessary information is more easily identified, updated, and transmitted. Media for transmitting these verbal communications are as follows:

1. *Visitor Centers.* Probably the most traditional means of transmitting information to visitors is through on-site contact at a visitor center. The visitor center is usually located at the main access point of the area so it is easily identifiable and accessible to visitors as they enter the area. Or it is located at some critical point in the visitor's path, like near a mountain pass, where he

or she can seek information about several surrounding areas.

Cost efficiency depends on user population and the users' need for that type of detailed information. In sum, there have to be a relatively large number of recreation participants, primarily non-locals, who use the visitor center. Capital and operating costs for any center should reflect the concern for getting information to visitors as cost efficiently as possible. From a design perspective, visitor centers should be stationary, easily accessed, and readily available. They should not disrupt visitors who are not interested in using them. Site planning should not create traffic problems or facilities that are visually incongruent with the landscape. Based on observations, it is amazing how auto and pedestrian traffic flow and the appearance of centers affect visitor participation. A center that is properly located along main access routes, has easy ingress/egress, and fits the surrounding landscape is more casually and continuously used than one that does not possess these characteristics. Thus the

Figure 13-4. An Example of an Area Information Sign, Wapiti Valley, Shoshone National Forest (Photo by B.W. Twight)

original plan has tremendous effect on a visitor center's success.

Facilities should fit the situation. They may be very simple or complex, yet we often provide expensive facilities at visitor centers. A simple, one-room building with parking is sufficient in some situations; others may call for a major complex to handle high visitor loads. You can also offer additional services and information like comfort stations, emergency phones, interpretive programs, overnight accommodations, and reservation systems. This improves the availability of all services by increasing accessibility. By housing them together in a single facility, it is also more economical to provide a combination of services.

2. *Area Signing*. Use signing to provide visitors with information as they travel through the area. An area sign or a map showing road and trail systems, available recreational opportunities, and developed facilities should be strategically placed at major access points to quickly familiarize visitors with the area. (See Figure 13-4). This type of area information sign is becoming more popular in relatively large regions where there is no visitor information center. Ideally visitors can understand the message with minimum time and inconvenience.

Post additional signs in an area for information, education or warnings, but carefully scrutinize use and location. Below are some rules of signing that you should remember:

a. Do not overload the visitor with informational signing.
b. Identify need at specific location.
c. Convey only one message per sign, and make the message as simple as possible.
d. Where possible, use international symbols which have been adopted by most major park systems.

3. *Publications*. Publications are important sources of information; however you should follow the basic rules of signing and not overdo them. Consider conducting follow-up

FLOATING THE SNAKE RIVER IN GRAND TETON NATIONAL PARK

THE NATIONAL PARK SERVICE
U.S. DEPARTMENT OF
THE INTERIOR

MILEAGE LOG AND TRAVEL TIME. The following chart gives the river mileage between all major landings. The location of these landings is shown on the Snake River map.

Major Landings	Jackson Lake Dam	Pacific Creek	R.K. O. Site	Deadmans Bar	Lower Schwabacher
Jackson Lake Dam	0				
Pacific Creek	4.5				
R. K. O. Site	8.5	4.0			
Deadmans Bar	15.0	10.5	6.5		
Lower Schwabacher	20.0	15.0	11.5	5.0	
Moose	25.0	20.0	16.5	10.0	5.0

Travel time on the river is highly variable depending on many factors, such as rate of water flow, type of craft, speed and direction of wind and rate of rowing and paddling. Suffice to say that the entire 25 mile trip from Jackson Lake Dam to Moose can be made in one day under all but the most unfavorable conditions.

Figure 13-5. A Simple But Effective Brochure (National Park Service brochure, illustrations by Scott M. Coburn.)

studies to determine the effectiveness of publications, particularly those that are not sold at publication cost. Often we spend considerable amounts of money on brochures that are used very little by visitors, reach the wrong audience, or are misunderstood.

Brochures passed out at entrance stations are often wordy and difficult to read, so visitors just scan and discard them. Therefore such publications are frequently an ineffective information medium because people are not interested in reading extensively while pursuing outdoor leisure activities. They prefer a minimum of inconvenience.

Assuming this is true, managers must seek more innovative means of getting necessary information to visitors. Sometimes agencies are more concerned with meeting legal and administrative requirements in their publications than communicating with visitors, as discussed in the beginning of this chapter. Thus, as previously indicated, you shouldn't oversell the role of publications.

At the same time, a brochure that is done well can be very effective. When developing one, consider the following variables beyond specific managerial goals:

a. *Overall appearance.* The overall appearance should invite the user to read. (See Figure 13-5.) Too often, we are more concerned with the technical aspects of the message rather than whether it will be read. Packaging is as important as product.

b. *Attractive cover.* The cover creates the initial impression. If done well, it may encourage visitors to open the brochure and read further. The title should clearly state the subject presented. Remember that you never get a second chance to make a good first impression.

c. *Proper size and shape.* Proper size and shape can encourage continued use. For the backpacker to refer to a brochure during a trip, it should easily fit into a shirt pocket; otherwise it will not be convenient to use. If it is to be mailed to visitors prior to arrival, it should be the right shape for mailing.

d. *Conciseness.* Use as few words as possible in your message. People at their leisure are generally unreceptive to lengthy messages.

e. *Pictures and diagrams.* Pictures and diagrams can clearly convey a message with minimum distortion, regardless of audience. In addition, you reduce the amount of time needed to read and understand.

f. *Eliminate agency rhetoric and bias.* Don't try to impress others with technical jargon and artificial eloquence. Also try to be factual, eliminating agency bias and personal values.

g. *Local contact.* Provide a local contact if desirable. Too often, we attract people's interest only to frustrate them by not including an address, phone number, or schedule for those who want more information.

h. *Management problem.* If your brochure focuses on a management problem, mention the regulations designed to alleviate it, but don't dwell on the subject. Also indicate the reasons for these actions and rewards for the user.

4. *Radio Gadgetry.* Special radio programs can provide information to visitors. The mobile visitor may receive a signal on an auto radio from a remote, short-distance transmitter usually within a one-mile transmitting radius. A foot traveler receives it through a headset receiver. Remote radio transmitting is done with a continuous taped program easily change at the site. Usually a short and concise presentation works best because of time limitations as people pass through the transmitting radius.

For walking visitors, headset receivers operate from a very short distance — sometimes less than one hundred feet. Usually these gadgets work best in well-developed, controlled areas like historical sites or museums. On-call radio transmitters, on which you push a button to receive information over an open speaker or headset, may also be available.

5. *On-site Contact.* On-site visitor contact is a very personal and often very necessary means of transmitting information — information that is an integral part of a visitor-safety program, for example. However, as a general program, on-site contact, tends to be ineffective and inefficient unless large numbers of visitors converge on a developed site. For dispersed use, the cost of such a program far exceeds the benefits: however, personnel who are actually performing other on-the-ground services may contact people informally.

6. *Mass Media.* Mass media such as radio, television, and newspapers are a legitimate means of disseminating information to large numbers of people. Too often this is deplored as being impersonal and consequently is not used. However, the media may be the only means to reach large numbers of people, who do not consider this method impersonal at all since we receive much daily information in this manner anyway. Whenever mass media are used, receivers should be made aware of direct communication channels for follow-up.

7. *Group Contact.* Continuous contact with groups — conservation, recreational, business, or otherwise — is an excellent means of communicating. Today more people belong to various recreational organizations and special-interest groups who participate together. It is important to maintain open communications with such groups to understand their motives and

concerns. At the same time, you can express the concerns and contemplated actions of your agency. The contact between agency and groups simply provides a forum for open discussion.

Group contact is often spurned by the politically naive as having no real benefit for the agency or is envisioned as "consorting with the enemy." If such contacts are to be made, they should be done on a continuous basis with a variety of organizations in order to maximize information exchange and maintain the groups' confidence in management. Being extremely selective in choosing groups for contact is self-defeating because, in doing so, you lose the attention and respect of other organizations. It appears that you are listening only to those groups whose values you personally agree with.

8. *Public Hearings.* Public input into decision-making has been covered in Chapter Five. It should be emphasized that public hearings are excellent opportunities for communication; however, too often managers treat them as one-way information flows rather than exchanges of ideas. If handled correctly, these sessions can enable you to clear up unfounded concerns and any misinformation. As indicated in Chapter Five, people are often polarized because they don't understand the views of others or are suspicious of their motives. Public hearings alleviate some of this with objective information and discussion.

SUMMARY

Sometimes we forget that information management involves communications — a continuous interchange of information. Both agencies and visitors must reassess and adjust their own programs, modes of behavior, and so forth. Management adjusts the prescriptions for a particular area to obtain the desired equilibrium, as discussed in Chapter Three, or to enhance an already stable opportunity. This communication can be formal and informal, verbal or nonverbal. Unfortunately such programs are sometimes undertaken without

any regard for public reception and response. When this happens, channels of communication often become restricted and the public loses confidence in management. These channels can only be re-established after the public agency has done something to redeem public confidence.

The following are types of communication that agencies should encourage:

1. information to users on available recreational opportunities and feedback from users on the quality of the experience
2. information to users on existing activity patterns and feedback
3. information and feedback on major problems or proposed plans being considered by agencies
4. open channels for continuous interchange of information.

Item number four is vital to any organization and the public. As indicated in Chapter Five, projects or programs can often be delayed or stopped when there is no *interchange of information.* An uninformed public loses confidence in an agency and subsequently withholds support — even for a very sound, rational program. It is important that all people feel they can use open channels; otherwise we may discourage the interchange that we wish to encourage. We already have too many people talking to those who agree with them and not enough people talking to those who do not.

SELECTED READINGS

1. Berlo, D.K. 1960. *The Process of Communications: An Introduction to Theory and Practice.* New York: Holt, Rinehart and Winston, Inc.

2. Bleiker, H., and A. Jubenville. 1977. "The Freedom of Choice Issue in Outdoor Recreation." Laramie, WY: University of Wyoming, unpublished.

3. Budd, R.W. 1972. *Approaches to Human Communications.* New York: Spartan Books.

4. Burch, W.R., Jr. 1970. "Recreation Preferences as Culturally Determined Phenomena." *Elements of Outdoor Recreation Planning.* School of Natural Resources, University of Michigan. Ann Arbor, MI: University of Michigan Press.

5. Burdge, R., and J. Hendee. 1972. "The Demand Survey Dilemna: Assessing the Creditability of State Outdoor Recreation Plans." *Guideline* 2(6):65.

6. Clawson, M., and J.L. Knetsch. 1966. *Economics of Outdoor Recreation.* Baltimore: Johns Hopkins Press.

7. Donaghy, W.C. 1980. *Our Silent Language: An Introduction to Nonverbal Communication.* New York: Cambridge University Press.

8. Dustin, D. 1984. "To Feed or Not to Feed The Bears." *Parks and Recreation* 20(10):54-57.

9. Eisenberg, A.M., and R.R. Smith, Jr. 1971. *Nonverbal Communications.* New York: Bobbs-Merrill Co., Inc.

10. Hendee, J.C., and R.J. Burdge. 1974. "The Substitutability Concept; Implications for Recreation Research and Management." *Journal of Leisure Research,* 6:155.

11. Hinde, R.A. (ed.). 1972. *Non-verbal Communication.* New York: Cambridge University Press.

12. Howard, C.J., and R.F. Tracz. 1984. *Contact: A Textbook in Applied Communications.* Englewood Cliffs, NJ: Prentice-Hall.

13. Kasschau, R.A. 1982. *Information Technology and Psychology: Prospects for the Future.* New York: Praeger Publishers.

14. McAvoy, L.H., and D. Dustin. 1983. "Indirect Versus Direct Regulation of Behavior." *Journal of Park and Recreation Administration* 1(4):12-17.

15. Rapoport, A. 1982. *The Meaning of a Built Environment: A Nonverbal Communication Approach.* Beverly Hills, California: Sage Publications.

16. Ross, T.L., and G.H. Moeller, 1974. *Communicating Rules in Recreation Areas.* US Forest Service Research Paper NE-297.

17. Schramm, Wilbur L. 1982. *Men, Women, Messages, and Media.* 2nd edition. New York: Harper and Row, Inc.

18. Wagar, J.A., and B.W. Twight. 1983. "Communication and Public Involvement." *Section 23, Forestry Handbook.* 2nd edition. Wenger, K.F. (ed.). New York: John Wiley and Sons.

CHAPTER FOURTEEN
INTERPRETIVE SERVICES

Figure 14-1. A Guided Nature Walk, Yellowstone National Park. (Photo by B.W. Twight)

It is not so much what we see in
nature but how we interpret what
we see

— John Burroughs

Interpretation may have many meanings. In
park management, it is essentially the act of
demonstrating meaningful relationships among
the natural phenomena around us. F. Tilden
considers interpretation to be more than mere
communication of information; it is "an
educational activity which aims to reveal
meanings and relationships through the use of
original subjects, by first-hand experience, and
by illustrative media..." He further states that
"the chief aim of interpretation is not
instruction, but provocation."[26] These citations
summarize the role of interpretation. Through
it, we can reveal the meaning of natural
phenomena to visitors on a first-hand basis
with common, easily understood examples that
illustrate the interrelationships of various
phenomena. In addition, it is hoped that our
examples motivate readers into searching for
greater meaning and understanding in nature.

Interpretive services must adequately tell
the story of a specific park, ecosystem, or
historic/cultural artifact. A total program
designed to portray a whole story, interpretation
usually breaks the event into parts intended to
reach a variety of audiences. Variety is a key
word; we must use many different methods and

media to reach a variety of users since they have diverse interests and ways of using parks. Most failures in interpretive programs result from a lack of understanding about the role of interpretation and a lack of understanding about the role of interpretation and a lack of sufficient variety within the total program.

G.W. Sharpe lists three objectives for interpretation programs:

> The first or primary objective of interpretation is to assist the visitor in developing a keener awareness, appreciation, and understanding of the area he or she is visiting. Interpretation should help to make the visit a rich and enjoyable experience.
>
> The second objective of interpretation is to accomplish management goals. It can be done in two ways. First, interpretation can encourage thoughtful use of the recreation resource on the part of the visitor, helping reinforce the idea that parks are special places requiring special behavior. Second, interpretation can be used to minimize human impact on the resource by guiding people away from fragile or overused areas into areas that can withstand heavier use.
>
> The third objective of interpretation is to promote public understanding of an agency and its programs.[22]

Many agencies have developed their interpretive programs around these objectives. If you look at the umbrella program called interpretation, you find that it includes not only history and natural-history interpretation but also public information, behavioral modification (manipulation through information), and public relations. While all these programs are certainly important, the original meaning of interpretation in terms of history or natural history is sometimes lost or at best relegated to a position of lesser importance.

Our concern is to maintain the purity of programs that interpret natural history and contribute to our national and international park heritage by not becoming confused with visitor-management and related public-relations programs. We are *not* saying that other aspects under the general umbrella are not as important, but rather that they should not be confused with interpretive programs. Others have stated a similar view most eloquently:

> Our interpretive efforts must be designed to complement an area, to tell its story, and at the same time utilize the purpose and values of the area to stimulate better understanding and the appreciation of this place — earth — our home.[25]

— Tom D. Thomas

> To excite curiosity, to open a person's mind — there is a challenge for anyone who seeks to communicate ideas. I know of no one more sensitive to the challenge than the interpreter, for he is a teacher in the purist sense of the word. He works with people who are at leisure, at the special places of beauty and history which have been dedicated and set aside. He seeks to translate, vividly, the language of the earth, and of the earth's inhabitants.[26]

— Freeman Tilden

> When technology has nothing more for man, then nature will go on showing him her wonders.

— Eduardo Arango

There is the world around us, the complex society in which we live, and our increasing detachment from nature. Then there are interpreters. For them to tell a story we can understand and appreciate is a real challenge.

BASIC INTERPRETIVE MODEL

The basic interpretive model is presented in Figure 14-2. The park is the microcosm in which interpretation takes place, and it is hoped that the effects of the program extend beyond that microcosm. Interpretation is necessary for people's understanding of natural phenomena. From this need evolve the principles of interpretation. Certain methods facilitate the art of interpretation — personal services, self-guiding programs, and now

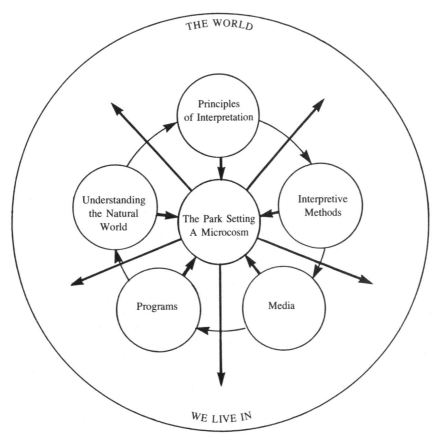

Figure 14-2. The Interpretive Model

electronic gadgetry. The media associated with these methods has also become more sophisticated, including the modern interpretive center, the interpretive trail, and radio and television. The special programs aim at children, environmental education in public schools, junior rangers, urban awareness, and so forth. The ultimate goal is that the visitors can relate this information to the world in which they live.

While we all tend to glorify idealism, to want to have some impact on the world beyond our park, it is awfully naive to think of our efforts as saving or even having a meaningful impact on that world. Rather than dwelling on the grandiosity of the interpretive model, then, it is better to go back to the basics of history/natural history interpretation.

People personally grow through the experiences that they have with other people, situations, and even the natural wonders of the world. That growth evolves in three stages: appreciation, understanding, and knowledge. Certainly we cannot expect people to grow much in understanding and knowledge if we offer a fairly simplistic explanation of a very complex phenomenon presented over a very short period of time. What we should expect interpretive programs to cause is greater appreciation of that phenomenon. Maybe the intellectual arousal stimulated by the program leads you to more detailed readings, perhaps even formal courses to fully develop your knowledge. But hopefully what most people leave with is simply a heightened appreciation of a particular part of nature.

As part of the basic model, we would like to explore the concept of appreciation from a managerial perspective. Appreciation means to recognize, be sensitive to, and enjoy. Assume that people are at a given location to participate and enjoy a particular recreational opportunity. The activity could be an auto tour of Banff National Park or a wilderness backpack trip in the Arctic Wildlife Refuge. Now, from the users' perspective, classify the recreational perceptions they receive as a "larger experience." Within that "larger experience" may be several smaller exposures to particular natural phenomena — a view of a glacier-covered mountain, a moose feeding on aquatic vegetation, or perhaps the rich bouquets of Alpine flowers. These informal contacts with the full force of nature, though usually viewed and enjoyed in the abstract, are really informal interpretive programs because they promote appreciation of nature, reach more people, and reveal more in reality than our formal programs.

From a managerial perspective, we should, within limits, offer more opportunities for "larger experiences" because visitors are better able to find suitable recreational niches to enjoy. In the process, they can find more suitable and varied "smaller experiences" to heighten their appreciation of nature, to awaken curiosity, and perhaps to seek more formal programs, if desired, to satisfy that curiosity. Through design we can help visitors capture these smaller experiences.

We put much emphasis on the formal, concrete program; yet, as suggested by Tilden, enjoyment of the landscape in the abstract may be more rewarding and stimulating.[26] If we recognize the goal of interpretation to be appreciation, perhaps we can, and already do, reach and stimulate many more visitors than we actually count in formal programs. The way to make this happen is to emphasize the larger experience, to let people find their own stimulating smaller ones, and to be prepared through a well-publicized formal, concrete interpretive program to enrich this appreciation.

The best example of such planning is the road between Banff and Jasper in two Canadian national parks. It passes through some of the most spectacular scenery in North America and attracts people from all over the world. One subtle design feature, a paved parking lane on each side of the road, allows visitors to stop and enjoy a myriad of "smaller experiences" along the way — a gnarled lodgepole pine, a lazy riffle in a brook, a colorful rock outcropping, or a coyote stalking a vole. Everyone can find something in the landscape that tingles their imagination and causes them to linger and reflect, which in turn may lead to increased appreciation. Some of those "smaller experiences" may actually inspire people into searching for deeper understanding, but certainly that should not be our goal. Possibly formal programs directed at improving observational skills would be of benefit in this appreciation game.

Many people recognize historic interpretation as a pure form because the story to be told is well-delineated, involving a period of time, an event, a building, etc. What actually happens is that, to the participant, the "larger experience" and "smaller experience" become essentially inseparable. You visit a historic site because of the associated history for which it was dedicated, and not generally for other activities. Even then, if allowed to browse, you may find numerous "smaller experiences" on which to cogitate.

PRINCIPLES OF INTERPRETATION

Tilden summarizes these principles as follows:

1. Any interpretation that does not somehow relate what is being displayed or described to something within the personality or experience of the visitor will be sterile.
2. Information, as such, is not interpretation. Interpretation is revelation based on information, but they are entirely different things. However, all interpretation includes information.
3. Interpretation is an art which combines many arts, whether the material is scientific, historical or architectural. Art is in some degree teachable.

4. The chief aim of interpretation is not instruction, but provocation.
5. Interpretation should aim to present a whole rather than a part, and must address itself to the whole, rather than any phase.
6. Interpretation (say up to age twelve) should not be a dilution of the presentation to adults, but should allow a fundamentally different approach. To be at its best, it will require a separate program.[26]

These principles are as meaningful today as when they were written, and the fourth one best summarizes the intent of interpretive programming: as an attempt to stimulate curiosity, awareness, and appreciation for an environmental setting. Program planning pulls it all together to present the whole, the total, picture. Individual interpreters may add to this picture, but there are many concepts and skills you need to become a bona fide interpreter of the environment. Probably none is more important than the basic philosophy of interpretation developed in the first two sections and summarized in the above principles.

PROGRAM PLANNING

As a process interpretive planning is probably not much different than other planning. You inventory what you have, select pertinent environmental themes, establish specific programs and activities to fully capture themes and develop necessary infrastructure, hire personnel to conduct programs, train them, and then monitor their presentations. Simple? Not really, but those are the basic steps.

Typically, overseers of the individual park or recreation area first develop an overall *resource management plan* which includes an inventory of natural or historical resources. Then they compose a *statement of interpretation* which identifies the basic interpretive themes from the inventory and the amount of programming the agency intends to do. This is a very concise document that simply establishes scope. The actual *interpretive plan* comes next, identifying

necessary facilities, activities, and locations for presenting themes and making them meaningful to the public. The annual *activity plan* is what the staff interpretive specialist prepares, within budgetary limits, for the logistics of annual interpretive activities. Thus what visitors enjoy as an interpretive program is really just the tip of the iceberg. R.K. Grater offers a detailed outline of the total interpretive prospectus.

Methods. There are three methods of interpretation:

1. Personal services, which include talks, demonstrations, and walks.
2. Self-guiding, by which the visitor is directed through the program with special self-guiding materials and facilities.
3. Gadgetry, by which the interpreter uses electronic devices to communicate to the public.[14]

Personal Services. Communicating directly with visitors is important; these contacts may be formal or informal. Informal interpretive programs are conducted by all park personnel — from the information specialist to the law enforcement officer. Visitors expect all park employees to be able to answer questions about an area, and employees should ideally be able to respond to these questions. If they are unsure, they should refer visitors to a place where questions can be answered. Informal contacts usually occur on a one-to-one basis at points of visitor concentrations. Point duty generally consists of answering questions, but you can also interpret surrounding wildlands in the process.

Formal personal-service programs include:

1. *Talks.* As indicated by G.W. Sharpe, interpretive talks involve the...translation of technical and often complex language of the environment into nontechnical form, with no loss in accuracy, so as to create in the listener sensitivity, awareness, understanding, enthusiasm, and commitment.[22]

These talks should accommodate the level of understanding of the audience and are usually more effective when you add illustrations or real examples. For example, it is much more effective to show a weathered replica of an early horse-drawn wagon that depicts life on the trail during westward expansion than to merely describe it.

2. *Demonstrations.* Demonstrations enhance appreciation with minimal verbal communication. They can inform by recreating history. For example, suppose a living-history program illustrates the lifestyle and hardships of early settlers. When using this technique to show a natural ecosystem, you should display a model so that the audience can see the entire system and any changes in the system that you wish to demonstrate.

3. *Walks.* Guided interpretive walks are what we consider the classical interpretative approach. They are probably most interesting and motivating for visitors because they can learn through first-hand experience and ask questions about what they see. Personal interactions are greater on interpretive walks because of the informality and the small group size. Also, a capable interpreter is reassuring to people who visit a new and strange environment for the first time. At ease, they can focus more attention on the environment around them.

Self-Guiding. Self-guiding refers to unattended, interpretive programs that are usually designed to interpret a particular landscape, environmental variable, or unique species. Self-guided programs are propelled by printed brochures or signs. On the long walks, a brochure is typically provided to interpret natural phenomena for the visitor. For point-specific opportunities such as an overlook, interpretation is usually conveyed through signs and displays.

Gadgetry. Interpretation has reached the age of advanced communications. We now use radio contact from remote stations, short-distance radio contact requiring headsets, electronically controlled moving displays, and educational television. This type of gadgetry has made it easier to reach more people. The questions to ask are how far do we go, and at what price?

Interpretive Media. Although some of these have been mentioned previously, this is an appropriate place for enumerating and discussing the various media available to managers.

Interpretive Centers. Interpretive centers should be relatively accessible to all park visitors and generally connected with a variety of other services such as information areas, rest stops, possibly a special permits center, or transportation centers. It is listed as a prime medium in which interpretation takes place because, as a complex, it is usually one of the focal points of visitors' itineraries.

Interpretive Trail. The interpretive trail facilitates the nature walk. If a trail is purely interpretive, its design enhances the interpretive program so that each stop along the way tells part of the story. By the end of the walk, visitors should have received the entire message that you wished to convey.

Signs and Displays. Signs and displays can reach visitors along the road, trail, or water routes. They can very effectively present simple ideas to visitors, particularly at points where it is difficult or inefficient to have an interpreter. (See Figure 14-3.) The only word of caution here is to keep the message simple since there is no one to answer any follow-up questions about the phenomenon.

Publications. Brochures and lengthier publications have been used as primary media since the beginnings of interpretation. Possibly millions of dollars are spend annually on printing information related to the use of our parks, recreation areas, and open spaces; yet little effort goes into evaluating these programs.

Too often, we immerse ourselves in the natural history of an area without effectively communicating our ideas to visitors. First, we need reliable communication techniques in our publications; second, we should periodically evaluate how well the public is receiving and using this information.

Radio, Television, and Other Special Devices. These are being used more and more as interpretive media because they can reach large numbers of people quickly and efficiently. Radio and television have some limitations. Usually the receiving range is limited; at times you may have to restrict this range even further to reduce possible overlap during transmission.

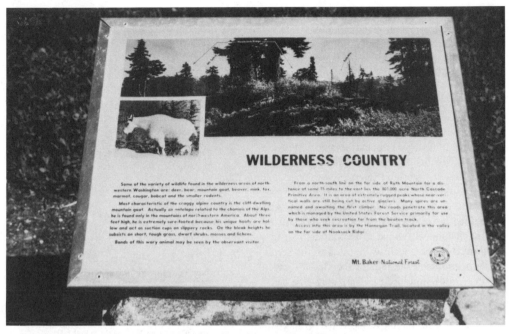

Figure 14-3. An Example of An Interpretive Sign (Photo by B.W. Twight)

There also are some legal concerns involving overlap with commercial frequencies. With more public education channels, these concerns are minimized.

Special devices may include a tape series that visitors use while driving through the park or a battery-operated headset that picks up short-distance, continuously playing radio programs as one passes from one point to another on a trail or historic site. New gadgetry is continuously being developed, especially for interpretation purposes. Watch the market in the next few years as we proceed through the space age of communications.

A FINAL THOUGHT

This chapter focuses on developing interpretive programs — *not* presenting them. There are three managerial concerns:

Evaluate the total interpretive program.
Typically, interpretive programs start out as a few presentations and limited facilities and grow from there. Evaluation occurs incrementally as additional presentations are proposed. Periodically evaluate the total program to ensure that the entire story and the themes within the story are adequately covered.

You should also evaluate how effectively your message is received and understood. Baseline data on the use of any program are essential to a long-term evaluation. However, these only indicate patterns of visitor use. You need more to determine the effectiveness of communication and visitors' reaction to it.

Quality control of presentations is also important. This starts with your procedures for hiring seasonal employees — who conduct most of the presentations — and the training you provide them. Quality control continues through periodic review of individuals.

Don't overdo the formal interpretive program. Too often we feel that we *must* reach visitors with our programs, yet many may wish to have minimal "interference" in their leisure activities and rebel at being overtly "forced" into enjoying nature. As suggested earlier, you should emphasize the informal interpretive program where people can be exposed to something in the landscape that touches each personality and stimulates each individual. The formal program becomes a focal point for enhancing appreciation acquired through informal contact with nature.

Maximize budgetary efficiency of the formal program. By first emphasizing informal programs and then capturing increased interest at critical points, you should be able to provide more for visitors at less cost. These critical points, dubbed Optimal Interpretive Opportunities (OIO's), are where people normally concentrate within the landscape. As described in Chapter Three, an OIO consists of a combination of unique natural attractors and improved access, such as the road to the scenic vista overlooking the falls of the Grand Canyon of the Yellowstone River. They may also be strategically located facilities such as visitor centers near park entrances. By identifying OIO's, you can maximize participation in your formal program at some fixed cost because these are points where visitors would normally concentrate and seek information about the environmental setting.

Lastly, the interpretive program is a system component, a very special way of communicating with system clientele, improving the quality of their experiences, and increasing their support of an agency and its programs. This provides you with a way of stimulating curiosity and interest in particular environmental settings. A by-product of this relationship may be transforming visitors from ''shoppers'' to ''clients.''

SELECTED READINGS

1. Arango, E. 1982. ''Interpretation Around the World.'' *Interpreting the Environment.* Ed. G.W. Sharpe. New York: John Wiley and Sons, Inc.

2. Ashbaugh, B.L. 1963. *Planning a Nature Center.* New York: National Audubon Society.

3. Ashbaugh, B.L. 1963. *Trail Planning and Layout.* New York: National Audubon Society.

4. Baker, D.R. 1969. ''Nature Interpretation.'' *Trends* 6(2):14.

5. Boulanger, F.D., and J.A. Smith. 1973. *Educational Principles and Techniques for Interpreters.* US Forest Service General Technical Report PNW-9.

6. Boulanger, F.D., and J.A. Smith. 1971. ''Principles, Methods, and Techniques for Teaching in Recreational Areas: A Primer for Interpreters.'' project report, Pacific Northwest Forest and Range Experiment Station.

7. Cahn, R. 1968. ''Will Success Spoil Our National Parks?'' *Christian Science Monitor.*

8. Collins, J. 1968. ''The Braille Trail.'' *Trends* 5(2):1.

9. Conway, M.R. 1968. ''Petersburg-Living History.'' *Trends* 5(4):1.

10. Dick, R.E., E. Myklestad, and J.A. Wagar. 1975. *Audience Attention as a Basis for Evaluating Interpretive Presentations.* US Forest Service Research Paper PNW-198.

11. Erskine, D.J. 1964. ''A-V Materials in the Interpretive Programs,'' *Trends* 1(1):11.

12. Food and Agricultural Organization. 1976. *Planning Interpretive Programs in National Parks.* Rome: United Nations.

13. Gantry, J. 1968. ''Touch and See Trail.'' *Science and Children* 6(2):20.

14. Gibson, W.H. 1897. *Eye Spy: Afield with Nature among Flowers and Animate Things.* New York: Harper and Brothers.

15. Grater, R.K. 1976. *The Interpreter's Handbook.* Globe, AZ: Southwest Parks and Monuments Assn.

16. Grove, H.J. 1971. ''Interpretation in the National Wildlife Refuge System.'' US Department of the Interior. Washington, DC: US Government Printing Office.

17. Leopold, A. 1949. *A Sand County Almanac.* New York: Oxford University Press.

18. Mahaffey, B.D. 1968. ''Interpretation — The Missing Ingredient?'' *Trends* 5(3):9.

19. Mills, E.A. 1911. *The Spell of the Rockies.* Boston: Houghton-Miffin.

20. McCurdy, D.R., and L.K. Johnson, 1967. *Recommended Policies for the Development and Management of State Park Systems.* Southern Illinois

University Agric. Pub. No. 26. Carbondale, IL: Southern Illinois University Press.

21. National Park Service, 1965. *Interpretive Planning Handbook.* Washington, DC: National Park Service.

22. Pile, J. 1962. ''Enjoyment and Understanding.'' *First World Conference on National Parks.* Washington, DC: US Government Printing Office.

23. Sharpe, G.W. 1982. *Interpreting the Environment.* New York: John Wiley and Sons, Inc.

24. Shiner, J.W., and E.L. Shafer, Jr. 1975. *How Long Do People Look at and Listen to Forest Oriented Exhibits?* US Forest Service Research Paper NE-325.

25. Shoman, J.J. 1968. *Manual of Outdoor Interpretation.* New York: National Audubon Society.

26. Thomas, T.D. 1968. ''The Challenges of Interpretation.'' *Proceedings, Recreation Management Institute.''* College Station, TX: Texas A&M University.

27. Tilden, F. 1967. *Interpreting Our Heritage.* Chapel Hill, NC: The University of North Carolina Press.

28. Wagar, J.A. 1974. *Interpretation to Increase Benefits to Recreationists.* US Forest Service General Technical Report, NC-9.

29. Webb, E.J. 1971. *Unobtrusive Measures: Nonreactive Research in the Social Sciences.* Chicago: Rand McNally and Co.

30. Wiley, E.A. 1951. *John Burrough's America.* New York: Devin-Adair.

CHAPTER FIFTEEN
PUBLIC SAFETY

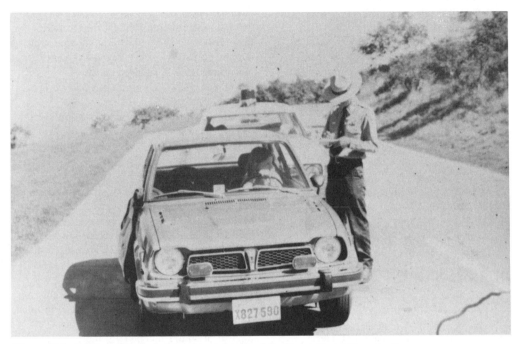

Figure 15-1. Public Safety Is An Important Aspect of the Recreational Opportunity (Photo by Gordon Wissinger)

Broadly defined, public safety means using public lands without harm or risk. Too often, managers adopt a paternalistic approach, attempting to eliminate all potential safety problems and control participant behavior to prevent accidents. By this approach we assume that man is not rational and cannot make reasonable choices when faced with personal risk. In some instances this may be true. However, this attitude creates a very sterile environment for recreationists because free choice is taken away. Such an attitude may even modify visitors' perceptions of a setting so much that it is no longer desirable to pursue activities there. And many activities are undertaken because of the risk involved and the challenge they present.[1,8]

As land managers we are responsible for public safety, but we should develop reasonable programs to ensure this. These programs must balance the safety of visitors with their level of sophistication, the type of activity, and the potential consequences of a decision. The activity itself should dictate the need for a general safety program. Certain activities require maximum safety standards; others, such as wilderness recreation, require only a minimum (usually information). You should also consider the level of knowledge or experience required for a particular activity. Visitors with less experience should be encouraged to participate with those who have more until they develop the necessary skills. Possibly, in potential life-threatening situations, only those individuals possessing requisite skills should be allowed to participate. However, it is often difficult to define that level of expertise with any accuracy. More commonly, programs feed up-to-date information to users and allow them to make their own decisions.

Since programs must also focus on protecting the resource from deliberate abuse and destruction by visitors, safety is really a two-way street. We try to provide a risk-free, enjoyable experience for visitors, but must also protect the natural resource base and developed facilities from overuse and abuse.

Public safety, as a management objective, is often implied and consequently not delineated as a separate program. To ensure adequate safety control, it is better to state objectives for public safety and develop specific safety programs that eventually are integrated into all other programs.

PUBLIC SAFETY AND ROS

Public safety fits very well into the ROS concept. As stated in Chapter Three, all programs should be aligned with a chosen anchor point on the recreational opportunity spectrum. As you move toward the modern portion of the spectrum, your public safety program becomes more intensive and sophisticated. Barriers are erected, regulations increased, and rules enforced to increase visitor safety. On the other hand, as you move toward the primitive end, programs bcome more simplistic, relying on information programs and subtle design features such as with few or primitive trails from which fallen trees are not removed. Visitors must assume a greater burden of the risk and deal more personally with the uncertainty of this kind of environmental setting.

At the extremely primitive portion of the ROS, visitors assume complete responsibility for their own welfare. L.H. McAvoy and D.L. Dustin suggest that we have a *no* rescue zone

to accommodate such visitors.[13] Participants should rely strictly on their own skills to cope with hazards and extricate themselves from dangerous situations. Many feel that this is appropriate, but that "no rescue" is unacceptable.[1] Probably the best way to philosophically deal with the primitive end of the recreation continuum is to maximize potential uncertainty — leave the area totally undeveloped, minimize public information flow, and sever the umbilical cord connecting users with management via two-way radio monitoring, and schedule registration.

Obviously we are all human enough to respond to distress calls. Thus, where warranted, we should maintain our ability to respond with search-and-rescue operations. We should not simply pass by an injured climber, ignoring the plea for help, because he or she is responsible for his or her own actions. Neither should we try to make every area safe by eliminating hazards and the uncertainty of the environmental setting. However, to improve user decision-making and preclude lawsuits, risk-takers must be adequately warned about "the hazards inherent" in pursuing activities within a particular area.

This chapter focuses on law enforcement and search-and-rescue operations. Keep in mind that the type of program, intensity, and sophistication are functions of the opportunity being provided. Failure to align public safety programs with this opportunity either alters the activity or has dire consequences for naive, unsuspecting visitors.

LAW ENFORCEMENT

As a visitor management program, law enforcement is purposely included under the category of public safety since it is a primary activity of any public safety program. (Hazard management is handled in the succeeding chapter.) As managers, we try to reduce safety violations and improve the ways in which visitors treat the landscape. These efforts not only utilize information programs, but must be backed up by law and the authority to enforce it. It may be wiser to use the term "public

safety'' here; too often people are turned off
by ''law enforcement'' because they associate
the words with police action after a crime has
been committed. ''Public safety'' is more
acceptable because it connotes a genuine
interest in visitors and the protection of those
values that originally attracted them to a site.

Each park or recreation area generally has
its own public safety problems. The actual
number of law-enforcement programs reflects
its particular needs. Therefore several types or
levels of law enforcement may operate within a
given management structure.

Scope. There are really two basic guidelines
for law enforcement in parks/recreation areas:

1. Protect the resource from the visitor.
   Assuming that the system is designed so
   that overuse cannot occur, vandalism causes
   the most harm even though some site
   impact results from visitor ignorance.
   Information and education eliminate
   ignorance. Vandalism, a real management
   concern, is covered in more detail later in
   this chapter.
2. Protect the visitor from the visitor. This
   means high-profile law enforcement, from
   traffic control to criminal investigations. In
   this chapter, we address the issue primarily
   from the management planning perspective,
   not that of normal daily operations. You can
   find material on daily operations in various
   books on police patrol, rules of evidence,
   enforcement tactics, etc.

Both guidelines are important in any park
operation. Certainly the welfare of the visitor is
paramount; however, as suggested previously,
how you actually provide for that welfare is a
function of the recreational opportunity. In the
process, you must protect the resource base and
make realistic trade-offs between the two.
Again, if we were to look at the extreme
positions on the ROS, trade-offs would be
easy. The difficult ones fall in the intermediate
positions along the spectrum where we
deliberately permit large numbers of people to
use an extremely sensitive resource. There are
no simple answers, but under these

circumstances you must consider trade-offs in
the planning stage and account for all factors
and their impacts in relation to your overall
goals for an area.

Levels of Law Enforcement. The three
primary levels of law enforcement for park and
recreation agencies consists of the following:
High Profile. High-profile programs enable you
to supervise and enforce existing laws and
regulations. This may involve highly visible
monitoring, e.g., road and trail patrols, facility
surveillance during periods of visitor use, and a
communications network for receiving and
responding to distress calls. It also may include
investigation, apprehension, and prosecution of
criminals. While the public equates such
programs with the typical police action of most
cities, it is absolutely necessary in light of the
many law and regulation violations in most
park and recreation areas. Because of highly
specialized requirements, actual investigation
and follow-through on major crimes like
felonies and high misdemeanors are usually
handled by a staff specialist or an outside law-
enforcement agency — depending on who has
legal jurisdiction.

Managers frequently assume that this type
of program requires the regularly visible
presence of emergency flashing lights, special
law-enforcement vehicles, special training, and
sidearms. Where required by law, as in the
National Park Service, this may be warranted,
but in others it may not be necessary or even
desirable. Agencies must uphold law and
agency regulations, but too much identification
with law-enforcement programs creates false
fears of crime and an impression of
regimentation, reducing the overall
effectiveness of the general public safety
program as well as the quality of visitors'
experiences. There is a fine line between the
two, and one that varies according to the
particular agency and its legal and
administrative mandates. But it is not a trivial
matter to consider when planning an effective
program.

Low Profile. In low-profile programs, we
try to either encourage or discourage certain
types of visitor behavior by design, continuous

monitoring and improvement of safety conditions, or information aimed at improved visitor cooperation. If we can anticipate problems in visitor conduct during the planning phase, we may be able to design a road, a trail, a recreation site, or even an entire system, such as a river system, so that it promotes the intended types of use and discourages others. In this respect, we are often our own worst enemy. We create a lot of management problems when we, for example, develop a poorly designed site with many access roads and no entrance control, then implement an intensive, high-profile law-enforcement effort to alter the use patterns created by the design. To even a casual observer, this appears a rather expensive way to make a poor design actually work. On-site enforcement is very expensive and often difficult to implement without good facility design.

For instance, a number of trails and trail heads led into certain wilderness and backcountry areas where considerable illegal and uncontrollable vehicle use was taking place, along with vandalism. Typically, the agency attempted to catch the culprits. When that proved nearly impossible, they asked nonvehicular travelers to report any violations (the agency would follow up any reports). When this approach also did not work, the agency gave up on the problem. In most cases, the real problem was poor design. Widened trails, low gradients, removal of barriers, and casually placed occupancy sites had been located adjacent to the trail head. They encouraged casual trail bike use that could have been discouraged by natural barriers, steep grades, and fencing.

We can also manipulate the social environment to deal with problem situations. We can separate conflicting and competing uses to reduce tension, such as limiting horseback riding and hiking to separate trails. Possibly, we can also limit the size of parties, require them to register, and work with interest groups to plan their itineraries for a more manageable situation.

Visitors can even police themselves. For example, a state park was having trouble with large motorcycle gangs abusing the parkscape and harassing other users. The park agency developed a plan whereby all large groups were required to register twenty-four hours in advance so that facilities could be reserved. In addition, a group member had to register as a trip leader. Problems from the gangs diminished drastically because of these reasonable controls exercised by the manager. Ultimately the gangs began to police themselves.

Continuously monitoring potential problems and developing mutual-aid agreements, contingency plans, and up-to-date training for law enforcers help managers maintain law and order in parks. This type of planning was exemplified by training Yosemite National Park's road crews, trail crews, and other normally non-law enforcement personnel in the use of riot-control tactics in the 1960s and 1970s. Such training proved most helpful in the famous "Battle of Stoneman Meadow" in 1970, when more than two hundred drug-using unlawful campers were arrested and jailed.

Educational. The educational approach improves quality of use by making people aware of important park values and the individual's role in protecting these values. For example, the very survival of the grizzly bear in Glacier National Park may depend on educational programs to reduce the number of undesirable encounters between man and bear. In such an encounter, the bear ultimately loses to man. We can issue citations for camping in the wrong area, leaving food to attract the bears, etc., or we can relocate trails and campsites to reduce the probability of an encounter. Beyond that we still must educate users, or the program is not effective. All levels of law enforcement must be operable in order to have a total program; however, to protect the parkscape, we must work with visitors before they commit violations — with a positive approach that emphasizes education and environmental design.

Consider establishing other related public-safety programs for emergencies and search-and-rescue. Both are important and require good management, good planning, and regular training to be effective; facilities, well-maintained equipment, skilled personnel, good communications and mutual-aid agreements with other agencies are all necessary for programs to succeed. These must be considered in a management plan so that you know how to respond before a problem situation arises. It is easier to be logical and objective in decision-making without the tension and pressures of an emergency situation.

Organizational Framework. You manage the way you are organized for management; this axiom is especially true in law enforcement. You have to be prepared to respond to specific law-enforcement problems rather than just react to particular circumstances. The organizational framework is the first step in management planning. If you are not organized properly, you are not very effective no matter what you do. Your plan should be thought out well in advance; then you should carry out realistic training operations with serviceable equipment and sufficiently trained personnel to see if it is properly organized.

Problems caused by a poor organizational framework are shown in the following example. A state park division is part of the state's Department of Natural Resources. It is organized into seven districts, each with a district supervisor. The conservation law-enforcement division of the department is not organized into districts but small areas in which a conservation law-enforcement office reports directly to the division chief at the state level. If a problem arises, the park superintendent has to call his district supervisor, who then relays the problem to the park division chief at the state office. The chief then asks the law enforcement division chief to respond to the problem by calling the local field officer.

Needless to say, there is much inefficiency here, and many problems receive no response. In fact, the situation has become so frustrating that the state park division chief has armed and trained his own personnel in some of the troublesome parks. Because of the difficulty in getting the proper authority to respond, these park personnel, with limited training and experience, have taken over the primary law enforcement program. Some poorly trained park

personnel have become so ''gun-happy'' that many of the charges they bring against violators are dismissed, and people have become upset and angry. Because of the officials' behavior, all management programs suffer.

In delegating responsibility within your organization, you should consider separating areas of responsibility as follows:
Crime (Felonies and Major Misdemeanors). A person in a staff position should investigate, arrest, and assist in the prosecution of major crimes that occur within the park. He/she needs to complete all the training and experience required to handle this type of law enforcement. Where there is shared legal jurisdiction, this role is often handled by the other legally authorized law-enforcement agency — state troopers, the sheriff's office, the FBI, etc.
Traffic Accidents, Minor Misdemeanors, and Rule Violations. This should be the responsibility of the management staff assigned to patrol duty, where the emphasis is on reducing accidents, investigating park violations, and handling emergency situations as well as educating the using public. Investigating traffic accidents and issuing citations is secondary but necessary in certain situations.

Park staff members are typically the first officials at the scene of a crime or an accident. Although they may not directly handle the problem, they should still supervise (e.g., obtain witness statements, take pictures, seal off the area, and detain people) in a proper legal fashion until the staff law-enforcement officer or the other agency sharing jurisdiction arrives. Thus all management personnel should have at least minimal training in law-enforcement practices and be familiar with the standard operating procedures of the agency.
General Safety Management Problems. All staff members, including those in the lowest positions, should have some public-safety training in general law enforcement, first aid, and public relations. Many times the maintenance worker or similar technician is present when a problem arises. He or she needs minimal training to handle the situation

until other assistance arrives on the scene.

While some organizations are large enough to have staff diversity in public safety, you should generally consider the above three levels of law enforcement and try to organize your agency to respond accordingly. Even so, you must understand the legal responsibilities involved and attempt to maximize your legal role while cooperating with other agencies that may have specific law-enforcement functions within park boundaries. For the major national parks, these functions are defined in enabling legislation that describes the jurisdiction of the federal government and state law-enforcement agencies. These laws are written in US Code Titles 16 and 18. If all responsiblities for law enforcement are delegated to the federal agency, it is called *exclusive jurisdiction.* If the states have not ceded their jurisdiction back to the federal government, which is not necessary if the park predates the state, then the jurisdiction may be either *concurrent* or sometimes only *proprietary.*

A Conceptual Program. Based on the previous discussion, a law-enforcement program should respond to two kinds of behavior — crime and park violations.

Crime is an important part of a total program, particularly in our larger parks and recreation areas. Some of these areas have tremendous crime problems that have been difficult to combat. Thus much of their management budget has gone toward crime-prevention efforts. However, the law enforcement staff must still be made aware of and properly trained for several related programs.

Crime Prevention. Crime prevention is very important and includes roving and point patrol, installation of building and recreation-site security equipment, and public information/education efforts. Through information and education visitors can help discourage or report suspected crime to a degree.

Detection and Arrest Procedures. Detection is best accomplished by direct observation, electronic surveillance, and reports of violations by visitors. This requires the manager to identify and concentrate on potential crime

areas, yet respond to crime in all portions of the park or recreation area.

Arresting someone requires special training and a knowledge of proper procedures. This involves informing people of the violation they are being charged with and advising them of their rights. By law, the manager making an arrest is not allowed to use excessive force; at the same time, he/she should be extremely cautious about personal safety. Don't do it alone; get some help first.

Criminal Investigation. Successful prosecution of a crime depends on good investigation. This begins as soon as the first park staff member arrives at the scene. Seal off the area immediately and record the names, addresses, location, and auto license numbers of all potential witnesses. If you do not take these steps, evidence may be destroyed or testimony lost. Only qualified investigators should handle evidence and interview witnesses. Investigations may take weeks or even months; thus the staff investigator or outside law-enforcement agency must have time to examine the problem.

Assistance in Prosecution. An investigation is not finished until the prosecution is completed. Management personnel and investigators must work with the local prosecutor or United States attorney, understand court procedures, and be able to properly present testimony in court.

Coordination with Other Agencies. Coordination with other law-enforcement agencies and the prosecuting attorney is essential to developing a viable program, and must be planned so it can immediately be implemented at the local level. That way criminals can be apprehended and prosecuted with minimal delay. Sometimes federal, state, or local statutes, or written cooperative agreements, outline parameters for coordination, but at no time should it be merely implied or assumed. Get acquainted with the prosecuting attorney and judges before you have to go to trial.

Park Violations. Three subprograms involve park violations and types of protection:

Protecting People from People. We should try to maximize the enjoyment of each visitor. This often requires rules that reduce conflict between users. Through management, we minimize harassment and confrontation, and this is becoming more important as the number of visitors increases. With more people there is more social contact and greater diversity of interest. Crowding leads to social conflict if we try to provide too much variety in too small a space, and a feasible area plan and site design can reduce tension between user groups.[3,20] Enforcement of rules is still necessary to minimize social tension. In addition, many recreation areas are prime targets for predation by professional thieves, so park authorities must be constantly alert and warn the public about them.

Protecting People from the Park. We can encourage or discourage certain types of use patterns in order to minimize potential harmful effects to the visitor — whether from grizzly bears, hot springs, or automobiles.

Protecting the Park from the People. An important, traditional role of law enforcement, this kind of protection requires a set of rules for visitor conduct and a means of making visitors aware of these rules. If the rules are broken, many of the features for which the park is established and maintained are destroyed.

Try to remain objective and respond according to the actions of visitors, the consequences of their actions, and causal relationships. Intentions are often not as significant as you first imagine, and people may act out of ignorance or at least a lack of awareness. Don't overreact. Don't be hasty or harsh. Do be firm in your handling of the individuals involved. Remember that this is an opportunity to informally educate visitors on the effects of their behavior. If you can change someone's behavior, you also increase the future treatment of the landscape. Often anything more than a verbal warning and explanation are unnecessary. The mere act of stopping adult visitors is generally quite embarrassing, and a few friendly "words to the wise" make a lasting impression and a park supporter.

Vandalism — A Special Problem. As pointed out by Sharpe, Odegaard, and Sharpe, vandalism means malicious or ignorant destruction of public or private property.[20] Thus vandalism is seen from the perspective of the property owner or manager. Whether it detracts socially or environmentally, any act of destructive or malicious behavior obviously affects users' perceptions of a recreational opportunity and ultimately the experiences they derive from it. Most problems and managerial responses are logically covered by the umbrella of public-safety law enforcement, so why does vandalism have to be treated separately? Probably because it is one of the significant budget items of most park and recreation agencies, and its allocation has increased while budgets decrease. Thus, while it has always been a problem, the percentage of operating budgets allotted for correcting vandalism has reached alarming proportions.

Now managers are asking what they can do. How do you deal with these acts? How can you reduce budget impact to a more acceptable level?

Management Programming. Consider three areas of programming when dealing with vandalism:

1. *Objectives.* Your goal is to reduce the costs of vandalism, to free up declining budget dollars, to enhance existing opportunities, or to add new ones. Objectives, then, are specific statements of what you propose to achieve for a given recreational opportunity, site, or facility. These can be a reduction in the number of incidents, actual dollar costs, or percentage of budget.[6] The important thing to recognize is that while it may be philosophically desirable to eliminate vandalism, it may not be practicable or cost efficient to actually do so. Vandalism occurs in many forms and has no universal solution. Therefore managers need to isolate significant forms of vandalism within parks or recreational areas, analyze what is happening and the probable perpetrators, and direct management programs where the greatest budget savings can be realized.

At the same time, you should also look at vandalism in a holistic manner. What is its impact on the recreational opportunity? Minor acts that cost little may have a dramatic effect on users' perceptions of the opportunity and ultimately the value of that opportunity. In

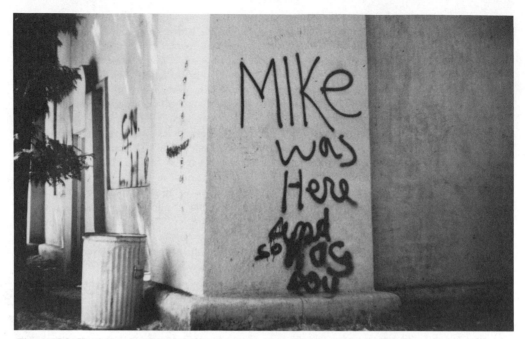

Figure 15-2. Vandalism is a Major Management Problem (Photo by B.W. Twight)

other words, you can greatly increase net benefits to society but spend very little on repairs. Perhaps early morning fishermen have been cleaning their fish on picnic tables. The smell has driven away many afternoon picnickers. A few simple signs may solve the problem at very little cost. Or, for more money, perhaps a fish-cleaning facility can enhance the opportunity. There are no savings; only expenditures. But strategy can solve problems and enhance the recreational experience for family picnickers and fishermen.

In terms of ROS, there are obviously greater potential budget consequences at the modern end of the spectrum. Here there are more facilities, more intensive management, and more people, particularly casual users. However, the impact of vandalism on the perception or opportunity can be great over the entire spectrum. Consequently, specific program objectives that deal with vandalism should be a part of your total recreational planning process. From a more positive perspective, the effectiveness of any vandalism program starts with initial planning of specific opportunities — What facilities are needed?

What about location? Design? Vandalism control does not begin after the act, and management program objectives should reflect this.

2. *Analysis.* Some authors recommend trying to analyze the motivations for specific acts of vandalism so that programs can eliminate causes rather than simply reduce effects. This may work well in small park districts or isolated regional parks used on a regular basis by local constituents. But for larger units, more dispersed use, and fewer oversights in operations, designers must focus on immediate behavior at the site and ways of mitigating the impact of that behavior.

Christiansen categorized acts of vandalism into eight categories:

1. breakage
2. surface graffiti
3. disfigurement
4. disassembly or removal
5. burn
6. blockage
7. vegetative damage or loss
8. miscellaneous[6]

Inventory or inspect the entire park or recreation area on a regular basis to document particular acts and their locations. You should also establish a system to report any incidents as soon as possible. Timing may be critical to minimize additional damage, e.g., graffiti on rocks should be removed as soon as possible. If possible, incident reports may help in analyzing target groups by category, location, and frequency. If particular groups of users can be isolated, then you can better tailor the actual program for a particular situation.

From a programmatic perspective, it would also be appropriate to categorize acts according to the intent of users — ignorance versus malicious intent. Those done out of ignorance may be correctable with a softer, low-profile approach — improved design, an informational program, etc. Others typically require a much more high-profile approach to oversee operations, apprehend offenders, and warn potential offenders of legal consequences. Even then management must continually remind itself that there are two generalized consequences of vandalism: increased costs and decreased benefits.

The final step in analysis is to set priorities according to need. Below is a list of general concerns:

a. Safety (any act which creates unsafe or potentially unsafe conditions).
b. Recreational opportunity (any act which affects user perception of the quality of the experience).
c. Increased costs of operation.
d. Other (such as socially offensive acts).

3. *Control Strategies.* The following are program strategies you can use to mitigate impact:

a. *Area Planning.* Proper location can help to reduce vandalism. Typically, extensive facilities in more secluded areas are vandalized to a greater degree and more frequently.[20] This is particularly true when casual (non-targeted) users are allowed or encouraged.
b. *Site design.* Proper design and use of more resistant materials can reduce the impact of certain types of vandalism. Even

architectural barriers can discourage certain behavior such as driving cars over ground vegetation.
c. *Surveillance.* The visible presence of uniformed personnel reduces the probability of destructive acts.
d. *Law enforcement.* Enforcement of regulations, apprehension and prosecution, and published results are also important.
e. *Information and education.* These programs are aimed at preventing acts committed through ignorance and at those users who are typically at the preconventional and conventional stages of moral decision-making.[8]
f. *Creative responses.* Many acts require creative responses, and analyzing these can help you respond to future problems. One example is using "hack" trees in campgrounds. Place sawn logs on the ground with signs that say "if you need to hack, do it here." Indiscriminate hacking essentially disappeared when this was done at a large park. Elsewhere an agency included representatives of four-wheel drive clubs on a planning team to eliminate indiscriminate four-wheeling. Up to that point, no control strategy had worked. Once the final strategy was agreed upon, the clubs not only abided by the agreement but also became on-the-ground enforcers of the rules.

A Final Thought. The five DO's in developing a park or recreation law enforcement program are as follows:

1. Do emphasize management by design. If we can alter the physical environment and/or informational programs to encourage or discourage certain behavior, we need less direct control through law enforcement.
2. Do emphasize the need to have the program requirements correspond to those of the general recreational opportunity.
3. Do maximize education and information efforts that increase visitor awareness and consequently the quality of use. If we are to improve user etiquette to protect prime park values, we must educate visitors about these values and how their behavior affects them.

Figure 15-3. Rescuing a Hiker from a Crevass, Mt. Rainier National Park (Photo by B.W. Twight)

4. Do delineate staff and other agencies' roles and responsibilities. These roles must be outlined and coordinated so that you can create an effective, total program.
5. Do maintain immediate response capability for both crime prevention and emergency treatment. You must be able to respond to any emergency on a twenty-four hour basis. This may only dictate a coordinating or liaison role for some management units, particularly smaller ones. Others may require full staffing on site.

SEARCH AND RESCUE

Search and rescue are two separate but coordinated operations. They may involve a single party or separate parties. Both operations require planning, team skills, and coordination. Setnicka (1980) divided search-and-rescue operations into four phases: locate, reach, stabilize, and evaluate. Depending on the situation, search involves the locate and reach phases, and stabilization may simply be reassurance for "found" person(s). This section primarily focuses on search operations because they are the essential first steps, are often a function of the land manager, and can often be accomplished with sufficient leadership and volunteer help. (See Figure 15-3.)

Many local searches involve little rescue. They are simply matters of finding people who have wandered away from campgrounds or other sites, and who are in no real danger other than from the psychological damage of being lost for a short period of time. However, searches for lost children can take several days, hundreds of personnel, aircraft, and dogs. Sometimes they have sad endings, too.

On the other hand, rescue operations often require very specialized skills such as mountain helicopter flying, mountaineering, scuba diving, etc. in conjunction with EMT or specialized first-aid training. In those cases where very specialized skills are needed, search-and-rescue operations are usually handled by the same team. At other times, a search team may comb an area only to locate the missing person down a rock slide or other hazardous area requiring special rescue. This does not alleviate the need for normal rescue skills among park personnel.

Preventive Programs. Many search-and-rescue efforts would not be necessary if resource managers and participants had assumed greater responsibility prior to the incident. Participants should become accountable for their own behavior — develop necessary skills, acquire proper clothing and equipment, check on weather patterns, and plan and organize specific trips sufficiently to accomodate the unusual and the unexpected. They should also notify a non-participant of their particular itinerary and expected return date in the event that something does happen. Managers can assist this process and avoid liability through information programs, but the responsibility is still the individual's.

Typically, planned trips are not a problem unless the unusual happens — bad weather, flooding, an accidental fall, or whatever. Often the problem occurs because of a spontaneous decision — a child wanders away from a campground, a mountain-goat hunter gets stuck on ledge, and so on.

Preventive programs include:

Information. If you can predict the types of use and users of an area, and have a good inventory of potential hazards, then you should be able to project potential hazards. Information programs devised to reach users prior to participation can officially warn them of risks and potential danger, and show how to properly prepare for a trip into the area. Visitors should understand that they must file a travel schedule with a friend so someone anticipates their return.

Design. Through planning and design, you can attract certain types of user groups, and encourage/discourage specific behavior. Transportation systems are a primary tool for directing use and encouraging given activities at particular nodes along the transportation ribbon. If there are some unique natural/cultural attractors along that ribbon, use concentrates there. Kinds of activity and users reflect kinds of associated facilities and services. If hazards occur at these points, design access and facilities to capture natural values yet minimize risks to users. Even wilderness trail planning should consider designs that encourage particular behavior, especially when risk is involved.

Regulation and Enforcement. Even with good design and information programs, you often need to establish regulations, particularly if there is high risk and a high proportion of novice users. It in unconscionable, however, to create a rule and never enforce it. Whatever technique you use — from the continuous presence of personnel to periodic patrols, it is important to generally enforce regulations first to protect visitors and second to preclude potential liability. Otherwise people begin taking regulatory warnings less than seriously, both encouraging visitors to take foolish chances and creating a legal indication of agency negligence.

Planning. Management, even if preventive programs work well, must still develop contingency plans for search-and-rescue operations. The role the individual agency plays depends on legal jurisdiction. Regardless of this role, you must devise a plan for search-and-rescue operations that explicitly states the responsibility of every party and how each should respond to a call for help. The plan should include:

Delineation of responsibilities. Is there a mutual agreement in effect? Who is to do what? When? How?

Communications. Communications are essential for any search and rescue. They start with teaching participants about conditions they might encounter and properly preparing them for such. This includes designating someone to notify authorities if they do not return. Once an agency is alerted, it must notify team members and other cooperating organizations, collect all possible information about the missing party, establish a plan of attack, and maintain communications with all team members.

Coordination. Coordination is essential so that voids and duplication of search efforts are minimized and response is as rapid as possible. Coordination is even more important when several agencies, volunteers, or related groups all participate in the search. For larger, more complex operations, a radio communications center and portable radio relay stations are essential to maintain contact and direct operations.

Manpower. Usually the plan specifies what manpower and mutual aid is locally available, along with how it will be used and under what conditions.

Equipment. The plan should indicate what equipment is available, who is responsible for its maintenance, where it is located, and whom to contact to get the equipment. For specialized equipment and manpower such as that used in mountain helicopter rescues, offer detailed instruction on when and how to use them in search and rescue.

Budget. Create a policy that delineates who pays for what. This is important so that all concerned can anticipate certain costs and budget for them. If the participants being rescued are expected to pay the costs or some portion thereof, then they should be reminded of this prior to their trip into the area. Incidentally, such a policy reduces calls for search and rescue considerably. Some people abused the system in the past because they had aching backs or "saddle sores." At all times, make rescues first and then submit bills after the fact.

Training. All potential search-and-rescue operations that involve equipment and tactics should be regularly practiced. Even real operations should be critiqued afterwards to determine if there are ways of improving future response.

Conduct of Operations. Initial response depends on the information received. If there is a call for rescue from a credible source, like one of the team members or other reliable source, and the location be pinpointed, then plan and execute a search and rescue operation. On the other hand, if you are notified of a lost or missing person without any indication of injury, then emphasize search operations to locate that individual first. Possibly no real rescue will be needed once the person is located.

What we traditionally envision in search and rescue are people lost in a general location and known or anticipated to be in trouble, such as a climbing party caught in a major storm. The actual search can be conducted in the air or on the ground. If the area to be searched is large, an initial aerial effort may turn up clues or discover the missing parties. Aerial searches require tremendous coordination and pilot discipline. If they check a few key areas in the initial search and find no clues, then you must organize a sustained aerial search. Such an effort generally requires pilots to fly some sort of grid pattern to ensure adequate coverage.

Make ground searches the initial and sustained method if the area is relatively small, the overstory vegetation is dense enough to minimize aerial viewing, or the weather is so bad as to preclude flying. Since weather may be adverse, a ground search must always be planned for. Ground efforts may not be very fruitful in large areas unless you find clues to isolate the likely location of the missing parties. Some well-trained ground crews may be used in conjunction with aerial searchers to uncover clues. Do not commit ground-search parties wholesale unless they have discovered sufficient clues to isolate the probable location. Use volunteers, the military, or other less-skilled groups only after the search area has been narrowed, if the lost party is in immediate danger such as hypothermia, and if deploying such people under the supervision of skilled personnel poses no danger to themselves.

It is important to distinguish between summer and winter search-and-rescue operations. All operations require skilled personnel, but winter efforts are extremely dangerous and require team members to have special survival skills. Without proper field equipment and prior training, winter operations can be disastrous.

Timing is important, but managers must weigh the information they receive against the manpower and equipment available. If the information is sketchy, or the probability of someone being in danger is not known, or the geographical area is very large, your best initial response is to gather as much information as possible, verify all possible leads, and probe all details. Under these circumstances, it is prudent to determine if someone is actually lost, in immediate danger, and within identifiable geographical boundaries. Unless you can determine this, any field operations are likely to be fruitless and expensive.

For example, a man was flown into a mountain area in Alaska to stake a homesite under a state land program. He had told his neighbor that he would then walk out to a nearby village and return in about a month. After this period of time had passed, his neighbor reported him missing. The agency decided to wait four or five days to see if he showed up. He didn't.

The potential search area covered several million acres. Agency managers sent out a couple of reconnaissance planes and instructed the pilots to fly two possible routes to the village from the homesite area, buzzing any trapper cabins or other structures along the way. The missing person turned up at one of the cabins, out of food, but no worse for his adventure than a fifteen-pound loss. The agency did the right thing to wait, and then to initially probe the area with reconnaissance aircraft.

Did they get lucky in finding this man? Not really. Early ice breakup on intervening streams had kept him from reaching the village, so he sought shelter in a cabin that was easily identifiable from the air. Most importantly, he notified his neighbor of his trip plans, making the search-and-rescue operation much easier. Even if he had not been located during initial reconnaissance, the sustained search would have been conducted from the air because of the size of the area and the difficulty in ground travel due to ice breakup.

Suspending an operation, although difficult, is an important decision. It usually rests on two factors — the probability that the person still lives and the clues uncovered during the search. If there are sufficient clues, — even though probability dictates that the person is already dead — then in all likelihood the search should continue until the body is recovered. You must also contend with the possibility that a body is not recoverable, as in an avalanche.

Throughout the entire ordeal, the agency should maintain contact with relatives and friends, and keep them informed. But you should also follow your own plan, using common sense about conditions without undue influence from the family. Public relations are

ever so important, but you should never forget your responsibility to those members of the search-and-rescue parties who endanger themselves in the process of helping others.

SELECTED READINGS

1. Allen, S. 1981. "No Rescue Wilderness — A Risky Proposition." *Journal of Forestry,* 79(3):98-100.

2. Bard, M., and R. Shellow. 1976. *Issues in Law Enforcement: Essays and Case Studies.* Englewood Cliffs, NJ: Reston Publishing Co.

3. Beckman, E. 1977. *Law Enforcement in a Democratic Society: An Introduction.* Chicago: Nelson-Hall Co.

4. Brockman, C.F., and L.C. Merriam, Jr. 1979. *Recreational Use of Wild Lands.* 3rd edition. New York: McGraw-Hill Book Co.

5. Campbell, F.L., J.C. Hendee, and R. Clark. 1968. "Law and Order in Public Parks." *Parks and Recreation* 3:28,51.

6. Christiansen, M.L. 1983. *Vandalism Control Management in Parks and Recreation.* State College, PA: Venture Publishing, Inc.

7. Davis, C. 1966. "Legal Problems and Liability in Outdoor Recreation." *Park Maintenance* 19(12).

8. Dustin, D. 1984. "To Feed or Not to Feed the Bears." *Parks and Recreation* 20(10):54-57.

9. Fazio, James R. and Douglas L. Gilbert. 1981. *Public Relations and Communications for Natural Resource Managers.* Dubuque, IA: Kendall-Hunt Publishing Co.

10. Frakt, A.N., and J.S. Rankin. 1982. *The Law of Parks and Recreation.* Medford, NJ: Brighton Publishing Company.

11. LaValla, R., and G. Fear. 1978. *Resource Guide for Search and Rescue Training Material.* Tacoma, Washington: Survival Education Association.

12. MacInnes, H. 1972. *International Mountain Rescue Handbook.* New York: Scribners.

13. McAvoy, L.H., and D.L. Dustin. 1985. "Regulating Risks in the Nation's Parks." *Trends,* 22(3):27-30.

14. National Park Service. 1975. "Law Enforcement Program." Grand Canyon National Park, Arizona: Horace M. Albright Training Academy.

15. National Recreation and Park Association, 1971. *Manual and Survey for Public Safety.* Management Aid Series No. 20.

16. National Recreation and Park Association. 1973. *Park Police.* Management Aid Series No. 32.

17. National Recreation and Park Association. 1975. *Litter Control.* Management Aid Series No. 53.

18. Poynter, M. 1980. *Search and Rescue: The Team and the Missions.* New York: Macmillan.

19. Setnicka, T.J. 1980. *Wilderness Search and Rescue.* Boston: Appalachian Mountain Club.

20. Sharpe, G.W., C.H. Odegaard, and W.F. Sharpe. 1983. *Park Management.* New York: John Wiley & Sons, Inc.

21. Smith, F.E. 1966. *The Politics of Conservation.* New York: Pantheon Co.

22. Snarr, R.W., and L.N. Craft. 1976. *Student Programmed Learning Guide and Introduction to Law Enforcement and Criminal Justice.* Springfield, IL: Charles C. Thomas, Publisher.

23. Wicks, R.J. 1974. *Applied Psychology for Law Enforcement and Correction Officers.* New York: McGraw-Hill Book Co.

PART IV.
SERVICE MANAGEMENT

Providing facilities and services to accommodate visitors is an essential role of management, particularly where visitors must travel long distances or simply require them to enjoy a given setting. Even when facilities are "extras," managers should ensure that these services and accommodations are accessible.

While you might think that environment alone creates satisfactory recreational opportunities, your programs affect how your clientele receive these experiences. If targeted clientele enjoy their activities, then you can judge your efforts successful. Satisfied visitors support good programs, not dissatisfying ones. Thus, in service management, it is important to monitor users' responses to particular programs so that you can adjust them over time to meet the needs of various groups.

At the same time, you must recognize that all services and accommodations need not be provided within a park or recreation area. In fact, if you can appropriately and conveniently offer them outside site boundaries, do so. This maximizes the potential of the private sector without undue regulations from the public sector, and minimizes the immediate impact on the environment that attracts people to the area.

Included in Part IV are chapters on concessions, maintenance, and hazards. Concession management focuses on planning, developing, and overseeing those facilities and services that are essential to the public's enjoyment of the environment. The chapter on maintenance is not a "how to" process but instead brings together important elements and procedures. Hazard management is included here because of the emphasis on providing necessary facilities and services to ensure a reasonably safe environment within the constraints of the activity offered.

CHAPTER SIXTEEN

HAZARD MANAGEMENT

Figure 16-1. Removing Rotten Tree Limbs In A Heavy Public Use Area (Photo by Gordon Wissinger)

Hazard management is the purposeful action taken by management to reduce the probability of injury, loss of life, or loss of property occurring to the participant from known or suspected, natural or manmade hazards within the recreational environment.

Some people refer to this as "risk management;" however, risk management is an entrepreneurial term that means minimizing the risk of loss to the firm. The role and responsibility of the public land manager, however, is to provide a given recreational opportunity. Part of that opportunity typically involves hazards, so management has a responsibility to deal with those hazards to reduce the probability of injury or loss of property. The course of action taken reflects many situational variables, such as the type of activity, anticipated participants, need to preserve the environment and where on the ROS the particular opportunity is located. Individual participants are still in charge of their own behavior, and if they conform to special management programs they should minimize risks to themselves. In sum, participants are in charge of themselves; managers provide hazard management programs to warn visitors or otherwise reduce unnecessary and undesirable dangers.

INTRODUCTION

Peril is part of today's lifestyle — the automobile, the hurried approach to life, the attractive nuisances, and the last-minute decisions. Life may seem more rushed, decisons more complex, and problem issues more numerous, but this does not mean we should merely accept associated hazards as part of modern life. On the contrary, they should be enumerated, evaluated, and managed. This task should be a primary goal in any activity, but particularly those associated with park and recreation settings.[5] When you participate in any leisure activity, you often lower your guard to potential jeopardy. Perhaps you do not understand or appreciate the possible hazards, or you feel that management has minimized the danger, or your attention is diverted by an enjoyable activity, or you accept the risk and are possibly attracted by it.

As managers of parks and recreation areas, we should feel some obligation to identify and effectively reduce known hazards. How far should we carry this obligation? Do you, as recreation manager, make your area completely free of danger? Do you selectively choose certain hazards for specific management action? If so, which ones? If complete removal is unwarranted or perhaps even impossible, how do you manage risk?

Hazard management requires the following four steps:

1. *Establishment of objectives.* Managing any hazard must measurably contribute to the recreational objectives for an area and the legitimate mission of the agency. Determine how you can do this.
2. *Identification of hazards.* Identify all known or potential hazards and locate them on a base map.
3. *Evaluation of hazards.* Evaluate all hazards within the framework of your area's specific recreational objectives and the degree to which they meet established standards.
4. *Development of management strategies.* Adopted strategies should reflect the

previous steps and be continually validated by positive feedback. Do they improve the quality of visitors' experiences? Positive feedback might include a decline in injury rates, tort claims, complaints, etc.

ESTABLISHMENT OF OBJECTIVES

Managers should determine where the anchor point or recreational opportunity of an area falls on the spectrum. Specific hazard management programs should be aligned with requirements for this opportunity. Consider expert opinion and public involvement when you develop your hazard management program. Develop specific program objectives that address risk reduction in a specific zone for specific identified hazards within the constraints of the ROS classification.

Management assumes greater responsibility for the safety of visitors at the more modern end of the ROS. Many primary natural attractors are also natural hazards. When management deliberately exposes visitors to these dangers through improved access, the hazard management program must be sophisticated enough to accommodate novices participating in low-risk activities in high-risk zones. At the other end of the ROS, visitors assume greater responsibility for their own behavior in the face of specific risks. Even then management has a responsibility to inform or enlighten participants of known hazards. It is in the intermediate portions of the spectrum that responsiblity and subsequent program objectives become hazy.

While this text does not pretend to provide legal advice, you should consider the legal implications of most program decisions.* Programs dealing with public safety issues such as hazard management are obviously more controversial and have greater legal implications.

Several interrelated legal concepts relate to program planning, including establishment of objectives. A *public trust doctrine* means that

* For a more formal discussion, see A.N. Frakt and J.S. Rankin, 1982.

real property — the natural resource base — is held and administered by a trustee for a third party. The particular legislative body imposes legal constraints to administer that resource. These constraints are typically very broadly defined, and leave much discretion to the individual agency. The *discretionary function* of governments exempts them from public liability for broad, policy-oriented decisions that primarily deal with resource allocation, e.g., designation of a four thousand acre area as a backcountry zone.

In order to help encourage this designation, you might put in an intensive trail system with large-capacity parking lots on the periphery of the zone to expose the visitors to the beautiful river gorge for which the area was originally preserved. (In Chapter Three, we discussed how this resource allocation created the Smith Gorge backcountry hiking opportunity). To fully develop and maintain your area, you must align *operational decisions* — like those dealing with the Smith Gorge hazards — with the selected anchor point, or recreational opportunity. These operational decisions are not exempt from public liability. The best defense against liability is to show *due care*; that is, to be aware of inherent risks and take appropriate action, within the limits of a particular opportunity, to prevent or at least decrease the dangers. In the case of Smith Gorge, participant risk could be appropriately reduced through proper trail design, construction of barriers at critical points, installation of warning signs, imposition of regulations to restrict use to certain locations, and enforcement of those regulations. If the gorge is twenty miles from the nearest road over a very primitive trail, the requirements of *due care* are obviously lessened.

This brings us to a final concept called *voluntary assumption of risk* (VAR). You cannot assume that participants engage in VAR just because they enter an area of their own free will. Instead, visitors must understand the perils, the danger that they face, and then voluntarily assume responsibility. This places greater emphasis on proper design of access systems and any associated facilities along with warning signs and other verbal communication.

IDENTIFICATION OF HAZARDS

Types of Hazards. Managers should be able to recognize various types of natural hazards since recognition is the first step in minimizing danger. The following is a general list:

1. *Natural — Land.*
   a. *Lightning.* One of the deadliest threats to recreationists is lightning, particularly on high, exposed sites. Lightning-strike patterns are predictable, so known lightning zones can be avoided.
   b. *Cliffs.* Cliffs and other places of abrupt relief like chasms and pits should be identified and avoided through proper road and trail location. Jeopardy can also be reduced through adequate site preparation, including such items as safety barriers.
   c. *Landslides and Falling Rocks.* Local areas of medium to high relief that have unstable soil or rock outcroppings should be avoided. You can usually identify these by early signs of erosion or sloughing. A knowledge of soil types, along with an understanding of geology, helps you to predict loose rock breakup and massive soil movement.
   d. *Snow and Ice Avalanches.* Areas of avalanche activity are generally known and identified easily by old avalanche paths. The environmental conditions under which avalanches occur are temporal and must be monitored to predict an event. If possible, avoid planning sites in avalanche areas. In places where diverse winter sports are offered, managers should monitor for avalanche conditions; ideally they can then curtail any activity in these areas during critical times. Unfortunately avalanches can occur in the most unlikely places, so consult a specialist.
   e. *Icefields, Snowfields, and Crevasses.* Icefields pose many hazards for recreationists. First are weather conditions. Whiteouts due to fog and snow are not unusual, and without

guiding landmarks travel is extremely hazardous because of sheer drop-offs and crevasses. Heavy snowfalls over short periods and low temperatures also add to this risk. Even mountain rescues are often difficult both because of the weather and not being able to locate the injured party.

   f. *Vegetation.* Overstory vegetation can be a hazard in developed sites due to environmental conditions such as heavy wind, shallow soils, and high soil moisture or due to rot or dieback caused by mechanical injury.

   g. *Wildlife.* Wild animals such as bears, moose, buffalo, and rabid coyotes present real danger to recreationists. Often user areas are deliberately located on the edge of prime wildlife habitats so that people can observe these animals.

   h. *Others.* Other land hazards such as volcanic action and dust storms may prove harmful to recreationists.

2. *Natural — Water.* Any body of water is a potential hazard to people depending on how well they are both physically and mentally prepared. Water hazards are probably more obvious but should be enumerated anyway:

   a. *Tidal Changes.* Abrupt tidal changes can prevent use. They may cause people to make irrational decisions that they would not think of under ordinary circumstances.

   b. *Ocean and Lake Currents.* Water currents may not appear on the surface but can still be very hazardous to users. A knowledge of local conditions is essential for understanding and locating water currents.

   c. *Water Obstacles.* Obstacles to normal movement over water, such as boulders, log jams, rapids, and waterfalls, create danger. Some people are qualified to handle these difficult situations; others are not. Certain obstacles are acceptable as part of a given recreational opportunity, but not for another.

   d. *Flooding.* Flooding creates hazards for users as well as nonusers; each may suffer if they happen to be in the flood zone. Although high water is usually predictable, many places support a large amount of recreational use, and managers are pressured to develop and encourage activities within the flood plain.

   e. *Others.* Other water hazards include harmful animal life and water pollution. Exact problems vary with local conditions.

3. *Manmade.* Manmade hazards are potentially the most difficult to manage because people often do not recognize their precariousness.

   a. *Buildings.* Poorly maintained or abandoned buildings, rotten bridges, and similar manmade objects are often focal points in a landscape and thus attractive nuisances.

   b. *Road Design.* This encourages or discourages speed levels, traffic bottlenecks, blind turns, and other problems. Roads are often overlooked, yet much recreation is auto-oriented.

   c. *Altered Landscapes.* Sometimes man creates natural risks through strip mining, wells, mine shafts, etc.

SURVEY TECHNIQUES

Make local hazard surveys to determine specific hazards and their potential impact. The following are some basic techniques:

Review Accident Records, Tort Claim Records, and Lawsuits. Past occurrences are the best predictors of the types and possible locations of future accidents. All agencies should maintain records of accidents. Other sources include mountaineering groups, law-enforcement offices, and land-management agencies.

Use Aerial Photography. Stereo pairs of large-scale aerial photos help you survey large areas for potential hazards. Thus you accomplish much of your work in the office with minimum cost and delay, provided recent photos are available. Fall photos are generally the best for this type of survey since they maximize detail (because the leaves have fallen) and depth perception (because of maximum contrast from shadows). You can transfer this information to a base map — preferably a medium-to-large-scale topographic map — and verify it with minimum field sampling. Plotting past accident records may also be helpful.

Inventory work of this nature is usually associated with area planning so that you can take all hazards into account when you allocate land for specific sites. While much of this work can be accomplished in the office, verify results in the field to check the accuracy of photo information. Also, data on water depth, velocity, obstacles, and seasonal changes are better obtained through field studies.

Conduct Intensive Field Studies. Intensive field studies on prospective sites can determine existing hazards and how management can cope with these in the future. For most auto-oriented sites, these are necessary. Many travelling visitors may not understand the potential perils in a casual stop at a developed site. Therefore managers should try to reduce these hazards during the site planning phase before visitor use begins. On dispersed-use areas, intensive field studies may not be necessary; the information needed to alert visitors to possible dangers can be provided by aerial photos.

For example, suppose a park manager is in charge of a site adjacent to a series of small bluffs overlooking a swift river. Along the base of the bluffs is a tilted ledge. Several drownings have occurred during previous seasons because people walking along this water-splashed mossy ledge have slipped and fallen into the river. Warning signs and complete physical barriers can probably solve the problem. Aerial photos can show the general risk of strolling near the swift river, and intensive development could be directed away from the water. Detailed site studies can indicate specific actions to reduce danger near or within the site.

Monitor Seasonal Use. To ensure the success of any hazard management program, monitor seasonal fluctuations. Certain dangers, such as increased water velocity and flooding, may not show up in measurements taken at only one point in time.

Reconstruct Past History. While conducting surveys of potential manmade hazards, you should attempt to reconstruct the history of man's activities in that particular area. This can help pinpoint potential problems left by previous developments. With a sufficiently detailed history, you can discover the exact locations of old mine shafts, covered wells, and building foundations.

EVALUATION OF HAZARDS

The following criteria should help you evaluate hazards:

Recreation Opportunity. As suggested throughout this chapter, the first and most important criterion is the experience you wish to provide and the alignment of the hazard management program with the overall opportunity. The Smith Gorge roadless area illustrates this point. To move the hazard management program from the existing anchor point, or activity area, towards the modern end of the ROS would certainly reduce the risk to participants. The problem is twofold. First, it escalates costs, which means that we have not sought the most efficient solution. Second, we may dramatically alter an opportunity, or the perception of an opportunity, or even give mixed signals which confuse potential users. Moving sites may also generate public criticism and legal or political opposition.

Transferring a program away from an anchor point towards the primitive end of the ROS does not meet the needs of the intended user population because you signal that risks are fewer than they really are. In the short run, you may save money. In the long run — after a major accident and lawsuit — you may overcompensate by moving too far in the other direction.

Type of Resource. The very nature of the resource may determine the direction that hazard management will take. As mentioned throughout the text, resources, particularly environmental attractors, are the essence of activities and as such should be carefully considered in your program. If a resource is unique and worthy of preservation, hazard reduction should manipulate users rather than environments. On the other hand, maximum modification of the landscape, such as sealing a cave or removing hazardous overstory vegetation, *may* be more appropriate. Also consider manmade developments and their historical significance and condition, like abandoned buildings, pits, and debris, and modify or remove these to reduce danger.

Type of Activity. Consider the activity that you encourage; technical rock climbing may be attractive because of associated risks. Skilled climbers understand and accept these perils; they also minimize them through proper instruction, good equipment, and recognition of individual limitations.

Other concentrated activities — picnicking — should be considered relatively hazard-free and thus planned and managed that way. Make a maximum effort to eliminate, reduce, or modify hazards in developed recreation sites. Intermediate activities, such as hiking and bicycling, may require some decrease in physical risks. You may simply tell participants about others.

Accessibility. Possibly the level of accessibility dictates the type of hazard management program. If an area is somewhat unaccessible, minimal information that stresses potential risks may be most appropriate. On the other hand, when a dangerous area is easily accessible so that people can enjoy its unique scenic beauty, maximum safety precautions may be necessary. The overlook at the Lower Falls of the Yellowstone River is an example of this kind of situation. We assume a greater responsibility with increasing accessibility.

Levels of Predictability. If the hazard is geographically and chronologically predictable, such as the stability of a bluff zone, then the manager must consider it in program planning. If certain circumstances occur on a predictable

basis, use this information and the location in formulating your hazard management plan. Natural disasters like floods, storms, and tornadoes, are becoming more predictable. Some are predictable on a cyclical basis; others on an immediate, emergency basis. You can make changes, including possible relocation of facilities, to reduce the effects of predictable hazards. Others require an emergency plan to reduce immediate effects. Unfortunately, if the circumstances are not highly predictable, managers often overlook the need to plan for emergency situations.

Maturity of Participants. Factors considered to this point relate to recreational activity or environmental effects that influence that activity. But you should also consider user reactions. Maturity means both emotional prudence — the capacity for rational decision-making in the face of risk — and perceptual acuity — how accurately particular hazards are interpreted. Emotional maturity is usually, but not always, associated with chronological age. Perceptual maturity is usually determined by previous learning experiences or previous exposure to potential hazards. We should also consider who the primary decision-maker is in a group of participants since decisions are generally made by group leaders.

People may be emotionally mature and still have had little experience with certain environs or recreational activities; therefore they may not understand the significance of the hazards they are facing. Many drownings are the result of rational decision-making by an individual who incorrectly perceived a dangerous situation as involving minimum risk. When a real hazard is seen as minimal or nonexistent, a much more intensive management program is required.

SYSTEMATIC REDUCTION OF HAZARDS

As defined in the beginning, hazard management is the purposeful action taken by management to reduce the probability of injury, loss of life, or loss of property due to known,

Figure 16-2. Recreation Site Design that Minimizes Risk to Visitors: Stairs to base of Upper Yellowstone Falls in the Grand Canyon of the Yellowstone River (Photo by B.W. Twight)

suspected, natural, or manmade hazards. Notice that a hazard-free recreational setting is not mentioned in our definition. This kind of setting would most likely be very sterile.

Once you have identified and evaluated hazards using the above criteria, you should classify or prioritize them for management action. Each fits into one of two categories — significant and routine. Each item can also be rated as modification or preservation. Modification means that it is acceptable to change the landscape or the facility to mitigate a dangerous condition. An example of this is adding a rustic handrail along a boardwalk surrounding a hot springs. Preservation means that modification is generally unacceptable; consequently any mitigating measures would involve manipulating visitors or at least warning them of the dangers involved.

Significant hazards receive priority in

program development. A modification or preservation rating indicates the direction that the program should follow. Routine programs take less effort; however, it may be possible to immediately implement a program to reduce some routine hazard without a great deal of analysis or cost.

After identifying and rating problems, managers must formulate specific programs. These offer some balance between maintaining a desirable landscape and facility and protecting visitors. An example of poor action is the previous case in which the superintendent failed to seal off an attractive water-splashed rock ledge along a river near a main parking area. Several drownings resulted from people accidentally slipping off the ledge into the water. Instead of tastefully sealing off the ledge and hopefully dropping the number of drownings to zero, he constructed a one-rail, three-foot-high fence. The following year, the number of drownings dropped from six to three.

The exact method of hazard reduction may be dictated by the resource — avalanche zones, unique natural areas, and so forth — or by visitors such as those who demand beachfront activities. But managers must deal with a larger problem — the realization that most hazards cannot and should not be removed; they can only be reduced. The following are common techniques for doing this:

1. *Area Planning.* Through the process of area planning, needs dictate specific site developments which are then given functional locations according to the experience opportunity being provided, the resource, and the existing transportation systems. The same process that determines the location of specific site developments should account for hazards. If necessary, they can be avoided by redirecting the access or location of facilities along the access.

2. *Site Planning.* Site planning reduces risks to users via carefully designed facilities that encourage particular behavior. For some major hazards, proper site design can minimize the risks and still be appropriate for the immediate landscape. In some cases, the safety factor may override the concern for aesthetics.

   In reality, you can use only two methods to reduce the hazards associated with a particular site, assuming that this is the only logical place to locate the site. The first is a physical barrier that directs people away from a hazard or restrains them. (See Figure 16-2.) The second is a psychological barrier that, theoretically discourages any visitors except skilled participants. For example, a manager is inviting disaster if he or she builds a road into an area reserved for technical rock climbing. This encourages participation by casual climbers who do not have the skill or the understanding of the risks involved.

3. *Hazard Removal.* Hazard removal is a tool for eliminating the risk to the participants. It is simply eradication — cutting dead trees, removing buildings, dynamiting mine shafts. This does not necessarily mean removal is only a last resort. It is simply another alternative for managers to use in particular situations.

4. *Information and Education.* You can devise programs that raise levels of skill, increase awareness of the risks involved, or warn and allow people to make their own choices. Each approach or combination of approaches may be sufficient. However, even if we reduce the risk, we should still attempt to remind people about potential hazards through an information program.

   Information programs are often the first step toward hazard management in sites that have already been developed. They may be stop-gap measures until more sophisticated programs such as trail relocation, close out of a facility, or establishment of permanent barriers can be worked out. Post information signs in conjunction with permanent measures to make people aware that certain dangers still exist. On dispersed-use areas, informational programs may be the best technique for managing associated hazards.

5. *Regulation.* Reducing potential risks by regulation is effective but expensive. Establishing a regulation means creating a concomitant program for its enforcement. This becomes an expensive procedure. One example of hazard reduction through regulation is the requirement that a raft meet certain design specifications, carry specific safety items like life preservers and extra oars, and fulfill certain on-water safety requirements. To enforce this regulation, qualified technicians must inspect rafts and boat patrols must ensure that users comply with on-water safety regulations and have all specified equipment on board.

   To reiterate a previous question, How far do you take this? We could perhaps regulate an activity to such a point that it is no longer satisfying to the using public. This type of regulating is mostly reserved for situations in which there is great potential for loss of life or property. Much depends on the activity, the danger to others, and general societal values. For example, in order to obtain a hunting license, a hunter safety course is now required in many states. To obtain a permit for technical mountain climbing, a statement of experience and qualification is now necessary in some climbing areas. The number of permit requirements like these are increasing. We should first check to see if we have done a thorough job of planning, hazard removal and education, before creating stringent regulations.

SELECTED READINGS

1. Bailey, R.G. 1971. "Landslide Hazard Related to Land Use in Teton National Forest, Northwest Wyoming." Ogden, Utah: US Forest Service, Intermountain Region.

2. Brown, P.J. 1975. "White Water Rivers: Social Input to Carrying Capacity Based Decisions." *White Water River Management Conference,* Moab, Utah.

3. Brown, P.J., B.L. Driver, and G.H. Stankey. 1976. "Human Behavioral Science and Recreation Management." XXI I.U.F.R.O., World Congress, Division VI, Oslo, Norway.

4. Burton, I., and K. Hewitt. 1971. *The Hazardousness of a Place: A Regional Ecology of Damaging Events.* Toronto: University of Toronto Press.

5. Burton, Ian; Robert W. Kates and Gilbert F. White. 1978. *The Environment as Hazard.* New York: Oxford University Press.

6. Campbell, F.L., J.C. Hendee, R. Clark. 1968. "Law and Order in the Public Parks." *Parks and Recreation* 3(12).

7. David, C. 1966. "Legal Problems and Liability in Outdoor Recreation." *Park Maintenance* 19(12).

8. Frakt, A.N., and J.S. Rankin. 1982. *The Law of Parks and Recreation.* Medford, New Jersey: Brighton Publishing Company.

9. Hendee, J.C., W.R. Catton, Jr., L.D. Marlow, and C.F. Brockman. 1968. *Wilderness Users in the Pacific Northwest — Their Characteristics, Values, and Management Preferences.* US Forest Service Research Paper PNW-61.

10. Jubenville, A. 1983. "Analysis of the Hazard Management Program at Otter Creek Park, Project Report." Park and Recreation Consultants, Alaska.

11. Kozlowski, J.C. (ed.). 1985. *Parks and Recreation Law Reports.* Alexandria, Virginia: National Recreation and Park Association.

12. McAvoy, L.H., and D.L. Dustin. 1985. "Regulating Risks in the Nation's Parks," *Trends* 77(3):27-30.

13. Paine, L.A. 1966. "Accident Caused by Hazardous Trees in California Recreation Sites," US Forest Service Research Note PSW-133.

14. Spurr, S.H. 1966. *Photogrammetry and Photo-Interpretation (2nd ed.)* New York: The Ronald Press Co.

15. Torres, K. 1977. *A Selected, Partially Annotated Bibliography of Recent Natural Hazards Publications.* Boulder, Colorado: University of Colorado, Natural Hazards Research and Applications Information Center.

16. Van Arsdel, E.P. 1969. "Detection of Hazard Trees in Recreation Areas by Remote Sensing." *Remote Sensing Conference for Recreation and Resource Administrators, Proceedings,* G.R. Harker (ed.). College Station, TX: Texas A&M University.

17. Wagener, W.W. 1963. "Judging Hazard from Native Trees in California Recreation Areas: A Guide for Professional Foresters." US Forest Research Paper PSW-11.

18. Wenger, K.F. (ed.) 1983. *Forestry Handbook.* 2nd Edition. New York: John Wiley & Sons, Inc.

19. White, G.F. (ed.) 1974. *Natural Hazards.* New York: Oxford University Press.

CHAPTER SEVENTEEN
MAINTENANCE MANAGEMENT

Figure 17-1. Maintenance of Facilities Is Important (Photo by Gordon Wissinger)

Maintenance management is closely related to site management. (See Chapter Seven.) However, managing a site means you design and develop the natural environment, its soils, vegetation, landscape, etc., whereas maintenance management means you exercise continual care to ensure that services provided on the site produce a continuing high-quality, safe visitor experience. This means that access developments like roads, trails, and bridges, facilities like outhouses, visitor centers, and tables, and utilities like solid-waste disposal, sewage disposal, and water supply, are continuously provided at a quality standard which meets visitor expectations, agency policy, and safety requirements for the site's location on the ROS.

For example, at a wilderness campsite maintenance management may only insure that no litter or garbage is present, that human waste is sanitarily covered, that potential drinking water is regularly tested for contamination and warning signs posted, and that trails and bridges meet both safety and aesthetic standards. On the other hand, at a highly developed automobile campground, maintenance management may arrange for the following: daily litter pickup throughout the grounds, garbage-can emptying after the dinner hour each evening (reducing the attraction for bears), restroom cleaning three times a day, a full-time tertiary treatment sewage disposal plant, continuous pumping, filtration and chlorination of water for a 200,000-gallon reservoir, the operation of diesel generators supplying electric power to the visitor-center, restrooms and ranger stations, scheduled annual painting of restrooms and triennial painting of other buildings, patching and sealing of asphalt roads and nature trails, and weekly shoveling of ashes from campsite fireplaces.

Regardless of the type of activity you provide, maintaining high-quality services is costly, and adequate funding has always been difficult to obtain. Constant care doesn't create capital-intensive developments that elected representatives can point to with pride at election time, either. Thus it has always been easier to obtain funds for constructing a big new visitor center than to obtain them for care over time.

However, by failing to demand a high standard of continuous care for grounds and facilities, which create quality experiences for visitors, a public agency may detract from user enjoyment of a scenic resource. Indeed, an outing can literally go down the drain for the family that has to use a mucky, stench-filled restroom or a garbage-strewn, filthy campsite. Lack of neatness and upkeep often counteracts any previous public support, lending credence to the old saying that "if you can't keep it up, don't put it in."

Maintenance management is therefore one of the more important programs in outdoor recreation. Because of this fact, fully half of the annual operating budget in some National Park Service areas goes to maintenance. Visitor protection, interpretation, and resource management share the remaining funds.

TWO FACTORS OF IMPORTANCE

Two factors are of primary importance in providing maintenance operations — standards, and cost estimates.

Standards are statements that identify the elements of each maintenance activity. They express in measurable terms results or conditions that exist when activities are managed satisfactorily — that is at a standard level. Standards should be prepared so they express a single level of acceptability, such as building maintenance in a manner that makes it possible to identify the manpower and funds needed to attain the stated standard. Activity standards should apply uniformly to all offices and areas in the recreation management agency. That way each member of the organization either knows or readily understands the approved quality level for the activity in question.

An example of maintenance standards for "Buildings, Utilities and Other Facilities," under the sub-category "Buildings, Floors," applies uniformly throughout the National Park Service as follows:

Buildings
Floors
    a. All are structurally sound with no signs of displacement or deflection.
    b. Coverings such as tile are free of objectionable deterioration, evidence of vandalism, excessive wear, etc.
    c. Coverings are clean and protected with acceptable materials.
    d. Floors are free of litter, dirt, markings, etc.

Standards such as these are outlined in your agency's administrative manual, the agency maintenance division's central office, or your local written standard operating procedure. If not, they should be developed and written into a local operating procedure for the guidance of all employees. For measurability, create standards with known and established engineering criteria such as from the Uniform National Building Code, the National Electrical Code, the National Fire Code, and various American Standard Safety Codes published by the American Society of Mechanical Engineers, the US Public Health Service, the American Public Health Association, etc.

Standards should *also* incorporate visitor feedback obtained from complaints and surveys. For example, ask random samples of visitors how satisfied they are with the level of restroom or other facility cleanliness. Also respond promptly to any complaint by increasing the quality level of maintenance to

UNITED STATES DEPARTMENT OF THE INTERIOR
NATIONAL PARK SERVICE

Form 10-577
(March 1970)

SAMPLE
H-3-2-5

JOB ORDER REQUEST

(See Instructions on Reverse)

JOB ORDER NO.

FY___

JOB DESCRIPTION			LOCATION		DISTRICT
Seal Coat			Route 3		Blue Sky

PROPOSED START DATE	TARGET COMP. DATE	NO. OF UNITS	UNIT OF MEASURE	EST. COST PER UNIT	ACT. COST PER UNIT
7/1	9/1	5.5	mile	$2,170	

STANDARD AND LEVEL PROPOSED

R & T General 1,2,4; Flexible Pavement 1, 2, 3, 4

STATEMENT OF WORK PROPOSED

Seal and chip 5.5 miles Route 3 between Rocky Campground and Valley Overlook.

POSITION, TITLE, GRADE AND SURNAME	EST. M/DAYS	DAILY RATE	EST. COSTS	ACT.M/DAYS:	ACTUAL COSTS
Engineering Equipment Operator	12	46.40	557		
Moter Vehicle Operator	31	42.00	1,302		
Laborer	13	32.80	426		
Road Foreman	2	52.40	105		

TYPE OF EQUIPMENT	EST. HRS/MIS	RATE	EST. COSTS	ACT. HRS/MIS.	ACTUAL COSTS
Truck, 3-ton	80/hr	4.00	320		
Roller, 12-ton	20/hr	6.00	120		
Oil Distributor	10/hr	12.00	120		
Spreader	20/hr	16.00	320		
Loader	15/hr	8.00	120		

ITEM	EST. COSTS	ACTUAL COSTS
Chips, 645 tons	6,450	
Asphalt, RC-800, 52 tons	2,080	

COST ACCOUNT	PERSONAL SERVICES	EQUIPMENT RENTAL	SUPPLIES AND MATERIALS.	OTHER	TOTAL
230	$2,390	$1,000	$8,530		$11,920

REQUESTED BY (Title & Signature) | CONCURRED BY (Title & Signature) | APPROVED BY (Title & Signature)

COMPLETED BY | DATE COMP. | INSPECTED BY | DATE INSPECTED

Figure 17-2. An Example of a Work Order for Action on a Maintenance Job.

Form 10-576
(March 1970)

UNITED STATES DEPARTMENT OF THE INTERIOR
NATIONAL PARK SERVICE

H2-6

OPERATING PROGRAM FY ___7X___

(See Instructions on Reverse)

AREA OR OFFICE									ACTIVITY	
Great National Park									Buildings and Utilities	

PRIOR. NO.	ACCT. NO.	STD. LEVEL	JOB DESCRIPTION	MAN-DAYS	EST. COSTS	SCHEDULE START	SCHEDULE COMP.	REMARKS
			Refuse contract	—	15000	7/1	6/30	
			Maintain signs — B & U	20	874	7/1	6/30	
			Paint comfort stations (3)	30	1240	3/5	4/27	
			Clean and operate maint. shops					
			Mountain park boundary					
			General maintenance on buildings	50	2459	7/1	6/30	
			Rehabilitate campsites					
			Paint maintenance shops (2)	50	1873	5/28	6/29	
			Paint VC-Admin. — Int.	30	1149	5/7	5/25	
			Paint VC-Admin. — Ext.	20	885	9/15	9/28	
			Operate & clean VC — Admin. Bldg. & mow lawn					
			Operate campground					
			Litter collection B & U	50	1525	7/1	6/30	
			General supervision	468	22410	7/1	6/30	
			SUB-TOTAL.....					XXXXXXXX

PREPARING OFFICIAL *(Title and Signature)*

APPROVED BY SUPERINTENDENT *(Signature)*

Figure 17-3. An Example of a Maintenance Operating Program Form that Summarizes a Series of Work Orders Involving a General Maintenance Activity Area.

prevent future complaints. Just a few unhappy articulate visitors can soon give your facility and agency a bad reputation, particularly if they write letters to congressmen, newspapers, travel magazines, or organized constituency groups.

Detailed manpower and fund estimates help provide the documentation necessary to obtain funding for maintenance at the quality standard set for your agency's services. The basic tool for estimating these manpower needs and the dollar costs for each maintenance job is the work order or job order request. (See Figure 17-2.) As shown below, work-order forms provide a way of planning proposed maintenance jobs in terms of schedules, standards, and various costs.

The maintenance operating program form in Figure 17-3 provides a way of aggregating and identifying all work orders prepared. The maintenance activity, priority, description, man days, costs, and scheduled start and finish dates are all summarized on this form.

Use the basic maintenance operating plan — the work order — to estimate actual job costs, detailed descriptions and standards for a proposed task. You can break down the work into number and type of personnel needed to do the job, number of estimated man days, and approximate salary cost per man day. Equipment needed for the job and materials and supplies necessary to complete it are also estimated here in terms of time and cost.

Once the job is completed, enter *actual* costs on the form. This gives you a measure of your ability to accurately estimate. File copies of these completed work orders (or computerized records) are valuable development tools and supporting documentation for future operating plans and budget requests.

Use a maintenance operating program form that summarizes all work orders by type of activity to plan actual yearly work schedules. Then you can schedule work which can be done in the winter to provide year-round employment for key maintenance personnel. The total cost of all work orders is aggregated with this program plan, then compared with the actual budget available. When the budget is less than the summary cost for all maintenance

work, use the priority number and standard level you have entered on this form to eliminate less important jobs or reduce their standard level. That way you can bring the cost of programmed work into balance with the funds available.

The number of man days estimated for each job and scheduled dates for work tell managers how many people are required to get the job done and when they need to be hired. These latter estimates also help determine when you should contract work out because of insufficient agency personnel. Operating program estimates, when multiplied by an inflation factor, also give you a basis for making both preliminary and final budget-request estimates for the three-year federal budget cycle or any alternative cycle at other governmental levels. Additionally, operating program forms provide recreation managers with documentation that justifies each year's budget request up the agency chain of command. Summaries can be used by the agency head to document agency requests to congressional appropriations committees.

A further requirement for manpower and funding estimates, as well as the final budget, is to have some extra dollars available somewhere to handle any maintenance emergencies. You can often obtain these at the regional or main-office level if the director or regional director has an appropriated contingency fund. At the field level, handle emergencies by postponing the completion of one or more lower-priority *funded* work orders until nearly the end of the fiscal year. Should an emergency occur prior to that time, such as culvert washout or the wrecking of a critically needed vehicle, sufficient funds can then be reprogrammed locally and those lower-priority jobs postponed until the next fiscal year. It is therefore important to have *some* non-critical budgeted work orders so that funds are available for an emergency.

MANAGING A MAINTENANCE OPERATION

You can best carry out these tasks by planning, budgeting, and programming.

Plans must identify *what* services and facilities are to be maintained, each service or facility's useful life (how long it is to be maintained before replacement), and what schedule of maintenance is necessary to ensure a high standard of operation until that useful life is finished. For example, the interiors of heavily used public restrooms may require repainting once every year for high-quality surfaces that resist moisture, stains, cleansers, disinfectants, and vandalism. Other facilities such as water chlorinators may require chlorine replacement and filter cleaning every two weeks during the operating season. Trail grading and light-bulb replacement may be necessary only once a season. Each task, however, requires a plan for manpower, equipment, and supplies. Perform periodic inspections and keep a written record of these on file to insure that you schedule planned maintenance often enough to keep each facility up to your standards.

It is obvious that planning such activities requires a thorough knowledge of equipment and facilities, of the work to be done, of the tools needed, and of necessary materials and supplies.

You can generally learn how to plan and estimate maintenance work through extensive experience with the particular jobs to be done. If recreation managers do not have that type of experience, they can acquire the information by hiring a maintenance supervisor who does or by using written records and manuals that document the learning of others. This is where files of prior work orders, showing the actual costs of jobs in previous years, become invaluable sources of information. You can better estimate the cost of operating a particular facility by multiplying the costs incurred in earlier years by the yearly changes in the consumer price index or other inflation factor. Old work order records are even more useful if you enter the data from them into a computer file. Then you can make various comparisons and develop spread sheets of summary statistics easily. Some agencies also provide in-service courses for maintenance management problems like these. For example, National Park Service courses at its Mather Training Center, Harpers

Ferry, West Virginia, are sometimes open to personnel from other agencies.

Budget requests with inflation corrected estimates for the next and following fiscal years can also be developed from prior years' work orders and summarized operating programs. You can project minimum amounts of the necessary "person" power, along with supplies and equipment, from such data. Then you can use it as a basis for planning, purchasing, and maintaining necessary inventories of such items as toilet paper and spare parts, for hiring seasonal personnel, and in leasing pickup trucks for the summer ahead. All of these actions, however, depend on your records of operating costs from the existing operation or similar operations.

Programming maintenance operations is necessary to carry out maintenance plans and get high-priority work done efficiently and in time to ensure a high-quality recreation experience for most visitors. Several components are necessary for effective and efficient operation of a maintenance program. According to John A. Rutter, longtime manager of various US National Parks, you should first create a basic schedule of routine operating and maintenance requirements. *This is a schedule of what must be done.* Second, you should have a complete inventory of maintenance, rehabilitation, and operating deficiencies. *This is a statement and schedule of what additionally needs to be done.* Third, you should do a cost analysis of the routine maintenance operating requirements. *This is the cost of what must be done.* Fourth, you need the stack of work orders compiled for other-than-routine requirements. Finally, you should make a spread sheet showing the distribution of operating funds for the current fiscal year according to the broad categories of potential expenditures, personal services, equipment rental, supplies and materials, etc.

Former Superintendent Rutter's programming guidelines are worth repeating here, particularly for less-experienced managers. They go as follows:

1. Programming must be realistic in cost and scope.

2. No work should be performed outside the programs except in the case of unforseen emergencies.

3. Costs must be determined for routine operations in order to plan for special operational projects.

4. Program planning *must* reflect input from all levels of operation and supervision.

5. Program planning *must* reflect input from the appropriate unit manager.

6. Program planning should be initiated at the lowest possible effective supervisory level. Job supervisors and foremen must participate in planning their activities and determining job costs, as much as possible. (Cost consciousness and job planning are supervisory musts.)

7. Programming should be done as far ahead as *practical* in the most usable increments — quarterly, seasonally, yearly.

8. All work must be covered by a work order, and no work, except in emergencies, should be performed without a work order.

9. After an emergency, a work order must be made out to cover the time and cost involved.

After the work orders and costs have been summarized, the next step in programming is placing all jobs in sequence. Maintenance managers should determine the sequence for each job by surveying needs or priorities and determining if the job is required or not. After needs and priorities are identified, you must plan the work as follows:

1. Survey the extent of job. Be sure you end up with a completed, usable unit.

2. Prepare a site plan if appropriate.

3. Prepare a sketch of the work to be done with sufficient detail to fully portray the finished product, if that's appropriate.

4. Secure plan approval as necessary from your
   a. landscape architect,
   b. agency engineer,
   c. forest or park superintendent or district manager.

5. Prepare a detailed work order for the job.

6. Enter the work order in the work program in the order of its appropriate priority.

7. Review work orders for the following:
   a. approval by the appropriate foreman.
   b. a checklist of materials needed.

8. Order and secure materials needed far enough ahead of time so they are available when work is scheduled. A critical path analysis helps for larger jobs.

9. Make sure *all* purchase orders are signed or countersigned by the division head responsible for the funds involved.

10. Check the availability of the equipment required.

11. Check manpower requirements and availability.

Now the maintenance program is ready for the year's work, so you are ready to execute it. The responsibility for getting the job done rests with the job foreman. The foreman has, or has been provided with, the skills, material, equipment, standards, and work orders necessary to do the job. In carrying out maintenance work, remember the following important factors:

1. The responsibility for execution *must* be placed at the job level.

2. Standards set by the agency or the area superintendent are acceptable minimums only. You should gladly accept a better job at the same or less cost.

3. Each employee responsible for performing a job or series of jobs should be encouraged to use maximum initiative and ingenuity to accomplish his or her work for better production at less cost.

4. If sacrifices must be made, it is best to accept less work of better quality. Each dollar invested in a project must be well invested, as you cannot afford to redo a job or waste effort.

5. A planning process *must* be completed before starting any regular maintenance job.

6. All material should be on hand, all equipment arrangements made, and all manpower requirements met. Figure out what you are going to do, get what you need to do the job, and then do it. Do the job on your terms — not the terms of expediency.

7. Supervision and inspection must come from established sources and through established channels.
8. Changes or modifications should be accepted only if they come through proper administrative channels. The right hand *must* know what the left hand is doing.
9. *Don't over-man a job.* If anything under-man it. We all work better and accomplish more under a little pressure. The job foreman should be held directly responsible for efficient use of equipment and full use of manpower to complete a thoroughly satisfactory job.[1]

MAINTENANCE OF EQUIPMENT AND PHYSICAL FACILITIES

Earlier in the chapter, we discussed the work order and the work program as ways of planning, budgeting, and managing maintenance work. Three important items on the work-order form shown in Figure 17-2 are estimated costs for wages, equipment operation, and materials and supplies. As fees for personnel, supervision, and materials and supplies are generally paid from funds appropriated for maintaining particular facilities, it should be obvious that such labor and materials costs are proportionally distributed or prorated over each job by type of expense. It is not as obvious how equipment costs are handled.

It should be noted here that equipment costs are also prorated for each job under "equipment rental" on the work-order form. This means that hourly or mileage costs for each job are charged on the basis of operating rates set for equipment. Since equipment is often very costly, such items as dump trucks, backhoes, and power saws are considered to be "rented" for each maintenance job. The rate is set according to the established useful life of the particular piece of equipment and is generally paid into a local "revolving fund" or account. At the end of the useful life of the truck or tractor, this account contains sufficient money to purchase a new piece of equipment.

Useful life generally ends at the number of

miles or operating hours when the annual cost of repair begins to exceed the prorated annual cost of a new purchase. Public agencies that use proration methods of "renting" their equipment to each maintenance or other job, and accumulate proceeds into a "revolving" equipment replacement fund, generally have new or relatively modern equipment to work with. Those that don't use such methods are easily identified by their archaic, run-down, inefficient gear, excessive repair costs, slow rate of job completion, and low morale among maintenance employees. Similar revolving funds or "clearing accounts" are sometimes used to accumulate funds and prorate maintenance costs for other types of facilities — like employee housing where the agency is authorized to retain employee rental payments for maintenance.

Maintenance for facilities other than equipment generally involves care and upkeep-to-standard of buildings, utilities, communications and electrical systems, garbage and trash disposal systems, grounds, camp and picnic sites, and sewer and water systems.

Other facilities that must be maintained are signs, roads, trails, and their appurtenances. Roads and trails include pavement, right-of-way grounds, bridges, culverts and snow fences, grading and drainage, and snow and ice control. Except for housing and large equipment, as mentioned above, maintenance for each of these facilities is generally funded by annual appropriations according to priority. Priorities are generally set highest for "must be done" items — those critical to public safety and the overall existence of the recreation operation.

Also of highest priority are the facilities which the public sees and uses most often. These attract and maintain public support for the agency. The only time that public-use facilities don't receive top priority is when a top-level agency decision dictates that the public become aware of an agency's need for additional funds. At such times you may find severely run-down and perhaps closed facilities, along with employees who explain to unhappy visitors that the facility is run down and/or closed because of lack of funds. It is risky for agency heads to try to obtain public support in this manner. Elected officials may feel that such actions do not indicate loyal support of their cost-cutting or retrenchment policies.

Finally, a word about signs. It is particularly important to keep them in good condition because they communicate directly to the public. Signs can be regulatory, interpretive, and informational, as you have seen earlier in the text. Agencies post them in all the various segments of the recreational activity provided. Therefore they not only have to be functional and visible, but aesthetically pleasing and *cared for* to effectively communicate. This generally means that signs not only be uniform and eye-catching, but also well-painted or otherwise finished, damage resistant or easily replaced, mounted solidly, and checked regularly for damage or necessary replacement. Signs which command respect are those that are well cared for — not "jack-legged" or home-made. Extra signs of the type most often damaged or stolen should generally be kept on hand for quick replacement during the busy season.

The importance of maintenance is probably best illustrated by the fact that many agency personnel often seem preoccupied with second-guessing the maintenance operation. Everyone has his or her own maintenance program. Everyone knows how to improve the maintenance operation. The management problem is how to make this interest helpful and productive.

While maintenance is often a separate function, performed by special maintenance-division employees, it *is* in everybody's interest to fully cooperate with these efforts. Maintenance standards for facilities seen and used by the visiting public must be the highest practicable, so please remember these principles:

1. Clean, neat, well-organized facilities receive good respectful use.
2. Junky, poorly maintained facilities are abused and poorly used.
3. Once inside a park or recreation area, visitors probably have more contact with maintenance employees than with any other group. Hence these employees should be neat, polite and informed with answers to common questions.
4. Visitors are very responsive to maintenance activities since they usually involve personal convenience or personal participation.
5. An otherwise completely satisfying park experience can be destroyed by poor maintenance or a poorly indoctrinated maintenance employee.
6. There should be no "jackleg" or "homemade" solutions, particularly signs. *Appearances do count.*
7. Be careful to follow your agency's established standards for design, materials, techniques, and procedures.[1]

You should have very definite ideas as to what end product you want from your maintenance program.

Remember that its aim is to produce a quality experience for visitors active in the particular segment of the recreation opportunity spectrum that you are providing at that site.

SELECTED READINGS

1. Rutter, J.A. 1966. "The Superintendent's Viewpoints." Mount Rainier National Park Operating Procedure, mimeographed.

2. Sharpe, G.W., C.H. Odegaard and W.F. Sharpe. 1983. *Park Management.* New York: John Wiley.

3. Sternloff, R.E. and R. Warren. 1977. *Park and Recreation Maintenance Management.* Boston: Holbrook Press.

4. USDI — National Park Service. 1976. Management System and Maintenance Programming Course. National Capital Region. (Materials for the mid-level managers course on the relationships between basic resources, park mission, and planning, programming, and standards for all maintenance activities are offered each year by the NCP Maintenance Division.)

CHAPTER EIGHTEEN
CONCESSION MANAGEMENT

Figure 18-1. A Major Park Concession Area Is Often Necessary to Provide Visitor Services, Old Faithful Inn, Yellowstone National Park (Photo by B.W. Twight)

The objective of concessions management, as we view it, is to see that the park visitor's needs for food, lodging, transportation and other services are identified and provided at reasonable rates and at acceptable quality.

Our role as concessions managers is, I believe, to use the tools of management — policies, plans, contracts, standards, evaluations, etc. — to achieve the objective. Social change, however, continually presses us to restate policies, redesign facilities, and redefine standards, etc. Concomitantly, technological change gives us new opportunities to feed, house and move more visitors with diverse needs and aspirations better and faster and more efficiently. We believe that the concessions manager — whether he comes from the public or the private sector — will play a larger and more vital role in the planning, development and management of parks than he has in the past.[7]

Concession management refers to planning, developing, and supervising visitor services that enhance the quality of the experience. Managers must first decide what services are needed and where they should be located. This is critical — to decide what is needed and where.

Too often we assume that any service the

public may wish to have should be provided. However, we need to evaluate each amenity by a set of criteria so that we, as park and recreation area managers, can determine whether or not we should provide it. To evaluate a service, the guiding terms here are *necessary* and *desirable*. Each service should be necessary to the enjoyment of the particular outdoor recreational opportunity we wish to promote. Necessary, in this case, refers to something that is absolutely required for a particular activity — overnight accommodations, food service, a winter sports site, etc. Next, any service must meet the test of desirability. Should you locate it within park boundaries or outside of them?

For example, in a major national park it may be necessary to offer overnight accommodations and food service so visitors can enjoy their stay. You might deem these services necessary because the normal travel distance to the park and the length of stay are fairly long. However, with the large numbers of visitors, any major development could detract from the total opportunity because of resource impact, visual intrusions, or significant changes in the intended recreational opportunity. Therefore, although some services are necessary, they may not be desirable within a particular management unit. In this case, the solution may be to encourage the private sector to develop these ammenities outside the park so you can maintain its ecological and visual integrity. After all, as shown in Chapter Three, these represent the essence of the opportunity.

PROVISIONING FOR CONCESSIONS

In the United States, development, although controlled, is often diffused throughout parks. Some countries have used the enclave concept to develop visitor service. They do this by establishing enclaves in places where intensive development can handle the visitor needs. Then other portions of the parks can be maintained with fewer disruptions. Banff National Park in western Canada is a good example of how concessions are

encouraged within the town site. Three primary considerations in provisioning for concessions are area planning, type of ownership or operation, and specific leases.

Area Planning. Ideally we should try to cluster visitor services where they are most needed, but in an area that is environmentally sound. By clustering, we can often provide more services in a more economical way, with a minimum effect on space and the total environment. Clustering has been used in some national and state parks; it will probably be used increasingly as the rise in recreational participation places more demands on the limited parkscape.

The first step in this process, of course, is to determine normal travel patterns and activity participation for a particular park and then locate and develop those facilities that are *necessary* and *desirable* to facilitate or enhance travel and activities.

The second step is to make the facility easily accessible and visually harmonious with the landscape. Some areas may be properly located but difficult to reach from the main road — consequently, they are not efficiently used. In most park units, managers understand that the development must blend with the landscape. Yet there may also be considerable pressure from concessionaires, particularly larger, more powerful companies, to deviate from this requirement. Remember that it is important to maintain the integrity of the visual environment for visitor enjoyment and possibly the protection of the resource base.

The third step is cooperation with the private sector in the area planning process. This is essential if we are to offer a wide spectrum of services, or even all services, to satisfy the interests of all visitors. Sometimes we ignore certain legitimate needs. We cannot continue in this manner. If we are to do a reasonable job of providing amenities and meeting the criteria of *necessary* and *desirable*, we must recognize the role of the private sector outside the park and cooperate with it through the area planning process. The latter approach can also help to build support for the park among nearby communities, particularly those whose business activities may be hurt by its establishment.

Type of Ownership/Operation. After we have determined what is needed and where it is needed within the park, we must determine who develops and operates the concession. *Government Ownership and Operation.* This means that the administering governmental agency develops and operates the concession service. Generally, this is undesirable because managers may have difficulty in establishing and enforcing regulations themselves. Then the pressure for tourist development may become so great that we forget the basic planning criteria of *necessary* and *desirable*.

For instance in a county park system the local park district developed and operated a short-order restaurant adjacent to a beach. In the first year, the restaurant netted nearly eight thousand dollars, which was used for park operations. Because of this success and the scarcity of appropriations for park operations, the park district decided to add other short-order restaurants near the remaining beaches. As a result, maintenance of the beaches themselves suffered. This decision illustrates what can happen in concession development when you ignore the original goals for an area and do not evaluate specific service needs and alternatives to meet those needs. *Government Ownership and Private Operation.* This is a reasonable alternative in which there is a large investment in development with a marginal return. In other words, an agency develops the facility and then leases it for operation to a private concessionaire — sometimes the only way to get the needed services if you do not choose to have an agency provide them. In this case, the agency should thoroughly evaluate the need for a concession since a large investment is required to develop a facility that may serve only a small number of visitors. There must be some criteria for determining the limit beyond which no facilities are provided. *Private Ownership and Private Operations.* This has generally been the most desirable way to develop a service since it involves no government investment and less government

control. First, agency managers go through the area planning process to determine what is needed within their own boundaries. Then they develop and distribute the concession prospectus to all potentially interested private investors. This prospectus should show what is needed, and where it is needed, and what constraints there are on operation.

Next managers must allow the private sector to respond with specific proposals on facility development and services to be offered. These proposals are evaluated according to whether they meet the service needs of visitors as well as protect the environment. The individual selected is then offered a concession lease based on the original proposal or a modified version of it. It is the responsibility of managers to create the provisions of the lease. *Quasi-Public Corporation.* Sometimes certain services are needed, but the private sector is not interested in providing them. In this case, if agency operation is not desirable, establishing a quasi-public corporation to handle the operation is the only solution. That way, the agency does have to regulate itself but can still provide necessary concession services.

You should make sure an actual demand exists for these amenities. The real question is how those corporations are going to be subsidized. With public monies? Special tax exemptions?

The Concession Lease. The concession lease is a legal document that defines the basic relationship between concessionaire and agency. It is an explicit statement about the services to be offered, the administration of the operation, any special considerations such as pricing and advertising, and the monitoring of the operation.

Everything that you expect of concessionaires and the way you evaluate their services must be a part of the lease contract. This protects both parties and leaves little doubt as to roles and performance standards. For a small operation in a single park, the contract may be very short with a minimum of requirements; on the other hand, for a large,

Figure 18-2. Many Glacier Hotel, Glacier National Park, A Major Concession Operation
(Photo by Glacier National Park Company)

diverse operation you need a very detailed and complex contract. No matter what the operation, you must recognize the lease contract as the vehicle that establishes the quantity and quality of amenities in any park or recreation area. (See Figure 18-2.)

Unfortunately many concessions have been allowed to grow within park and recreation areas without management direction. Perhaps while they are small they are of little concern; however, they later reach a point where they create problems and seem "unmanageable." A detailed concession lease minimizes uncontrolled growth and theoretically maintains only *necessary* and *desirable* services at specified levels. *The lease is the management control mechanism.*

CONCESSION VARIABLES

The following are variables that you should consider when dealing with concessions.

Competition. It is important to examine competition. Should we encourage it as a means of regulating prices and service quality? In America, where capitalism is encouraged, the answer for park concessions is not clear. In general managers should adhere to the "necessary and desirable" principle, supporting only specific services that are deemed appropriate and controlling costs through *regulated* monopolies.

Our primary concern is providing necessary services at a reasonable price so that park visitors can enjoy the parkscape. For pure competition to exist, there must be sufficient business for two or more companies "to operate at something approximating lowest possible cost."[14] If there is insufficient supply, costs are high. This drives prices up, or one or more operations goes out of business, perhaps leaving a building to weather and become a blight on the landscape. Since the amount of available open space is already limited, it seems prudent to minimize the space needed for services and try to maximize the actual activity space for recreational use. Thus regulated monopolies are usually encouraged to meet identified service needs, minimize spatial requirements, protect important park features, and keep prices down and the quality of service up.

Many regulated monopolies already exist; they are not unique concept to park and recreation areas. Concessions, unlike other monopolies, are often faced with real competition from areas immediately adjacent to parks. This may cause real problems since the concessionaire is not allowed to adjust his business quickly enough to match the competition.

Sometimes we even regulate a concessionaire out of business. While you could argue that he or she should not have been there in the first place, we attract and encourage such development. Typically we adjust the lease to keep the concessionaire going. Perhaps we should ask why we should try to develop a service inside our park if there is a great deal of competition from the outside.

There are no simple answers, and obviously conditions change. For example, during the early development of our national parks, maximum overnight accommodations were in demand because of the time involved in traveling to the parks. Large hotel complexes were built to accommodate urban visitors, particularly those from the eastern states where political support was important to the development of the original National Park system.

With the increased mobility of the modern traveler and more general support for parks. these services no longer have to be provided within parks. In addition, developments have sprung up on the outskirts that meet changing behavioral patterns and demands. It is not surprising to see more long-range plans for moving concessions outside parks where they can compete within the private sector. This requires, as suggested earlier, maximum coordination between the public and private sectors. However, removing historic hotels from parks like Yellowstone, Glacier, Yosemite, and Grand Canyon may never be politically feasible or desirable.

Economy of Scale. Scale of operation is important to efficient management and the economic soundness of concession operation. Consider scale of economy in initial planning so that you can attract potential concessionaires, particularly those you prefer to have operating within the park.

The small-family operation may be the most desirable, but because of the seasonal nature of the business and other factors, this type of venture may be doomed to economic failure. How do you balance economy with both visitor needs and protection of park values? The answer is simple: you just do it. You have to make certain value judgments based on present conditions, then adjust things later as the conditions change. Possibly systems analysis or simulation modeling can help determine where services should be located and what effect they will have on concession and park management. This can give you more objective input into decision-making. Ideally you should attempt to foresee effects on visitor use patterns and associated developments. Otherwise, concessions must be as flexible as possible — to expand or contract as conditions dictate.

Managers should also consider clustering concession services in order to increase efficiency and make a concession attractive to private developers. Campgrounds are good examples. Most campgrounds on public lands are small and scattered over large areas; this often makes them uneconomical in terms of concession management. If they are clustered at desirable locations, they may be operated economically and become more attractive to entrepreneurs.

The problem that we must solve is one of the trade-offs. Are campgrounds properly located to provide necessary overnight accommodations? What have we done to convert small scattered camps into a single large, centrally located one? What are the acceptable trade-offs? Remember that changing campground size or development level can alter the opportunity and create social succession — the displacement of one type of clientele in favor of another.

Conditions of Lease. Consider the following factors when you develop a concession lease:

Roles and Responsibility. The roles and responsibilities of each party entering into the lease, as indicated previously, must be explicitly stated in the lease agreement. Nothing should be implied. Any loopholes or misunderstandings over the wording of the contract can lead to strained relationships and ultimately a decline in the very service the agency wishes to offer the public. It is only fair to both parties to clearly outline roles and responsibilities — both morally in terms of service management and legally to protect all involved.

Location and Level of Development. The location and level of development should be completely agreed upon by both parties. The agency makes the basic decision, possibly negotiating between the parties in considering changes. That way the location and level of development (with negotiated changes) both become parts of the lease.

Included in this process is a phasing-in schedule to make everyone aware of the actual timing of each stage of the development. Some provision should also be made for extending deadlines, if necessary, and each party should have some flexibility in future commitments. Therefore you must allow for future expansion. You can provide for this in the lease with nothing more than a statement of management philosophy — clustering developments or adding to existing ones — if future conditions may demand it.

Utilities and Energy Conservation. Energy conservation is extremely important from both an economic and a philosophical standpoint. If we are to promote conservation as well as protect many unique natural features, every phase of this operation should foster these ideals. The type of utility needed and its long-term effects must be considered in regard to scarcity of energy resources. Possibly we should consider an alternative power source, like solar collectors, and use parks and open spaces as demonstrations that man and nature can live in harmony. We suspect that in times of critical energy shortage, many park and recreational facilities will be denied energy resources needed to operate.

Maintenance, Sewage Treatment, and Refuse.
Caring for the concession area and buildings is essential to protect both the capital investment and the overall aesthetic appearance of the park. We also need to concern ourselves with sewage treatment and solid waste disposal to preserve the environmental setting and the well-being of visitors. Ideally we utilize regional sewer and water systems to minimize maintenance of on-site treatment facilities and reduce treatment costs. In solid waste disposal, a properly developed sanitary landfill is essential. This usually means cooperating with the local government to use existing facilities. Whatever the course, specify the requirements and roles of each party in the lease.

Quality of Service. Quality of service is a must if the visitors' needs are to be satisfied, but quality *per se* is a nebulous term. Since the concession lease initiates service, state the standard of quality you expect in that service in realistic, measurable terms. Included should be agency criteria as well as federal, state, and local requirements established by law. Sometimes a provision is even included in the statement of quality that makes low-cost services available to low-income visitors.

Franchise or Lease Fee. The annual fee paid to the government for the right to operate a concession may be a flat rate or a percentage of gross receipts. The choice of fixed versus fluctuating is a matter of management preference. For some managers, these charges are basically designed to cover lease supervision. Others feel they are a means of obtaining additional monies for other programs. Still others use them as a way of evaluating demand for a service.

The fixed rate is usually used for small operations in which a full accounting of receipts would not be necessary. For larger concessions, the percentage-of-gross-receipts method requires a complete accounting and shows changes in participation from year to year adjusted for yearly increases in cost of service. However, a more modern method is the "division of profits."[14] This simply means that you determine a "break even" point for the business and assess a percentage for gross revenues above that point. That way you provide service first, then assess excess profits.

The concessioner also covers expenses and gets a reasonable return on his or her investment, making up for unprofitable years and getting rewarded for efficient management.

Division of profits ensures a reasonable profit, in the long run, to better stabilize business. In the past, concessionaires did not receive a break during lean years and were possibly charged an excess profit fee during good years. They could not win either way. *Length of Lease, Guaranteed Renewal, and Exclusive Rights.* The length of the lease should be commensurate with the investment by the concessionaire; this makes the investment more financially attractive. The ordinary length equals the expected life of the facilities — i.e., the number of years over which they will depreciate. Typically, this is a maximum of thirty years, but it can be as few as one to five with little investment needed. The agency should set contact length at the minimum necessary to attract a desirable lease, yet maintain flexibility to allow for future changes.

Concession contracts with guaranteed renewal clauses are controversial. Many people feel that the agency should handle all contract options. On the other hand, people are reluctant to invest their money and effort in a concession when there is no guarantee that they will continue to operate after the lease expires. This does not mean that the old contract is automatically renewed if you have a guaranteed renewal. First the concessioner has to meet the terms of the original lease; then, under the guaranteed renewal clause, he or she has first option on the new lease. Provisions for facilities, maintenance, services, and so forth may change in the negotiated contract because of changes in service needs, legal requirements, and management philosophy. Yet this guaranteed renewal clause may be the best way to attract and keep good concessionaires.

Under ordinary circumstances, use patterns, management philosophy, or service needs do not change sufficiently to alter the new lease; consequently, a renewal clause is a logical way to continue the concession. You should not use lease renewal simply as an administrative prerogative to get rid of "bad" concessionaires.

If the lease contract is well written and the provisions properly monitored, administrators should be able to release undesirable concessionaires because they did not fulfill their contract obligations. They should not have to wait until lease-renewal time. Furthermore, experience has shown that many long-term concessionaires have great respect for their park or recreation area and for management's philosophy. Consequently, they support and protect many of the public values associated with that particular landscape.[9]

Exclusive right guarantees current concessionaires that they will recieve the first option on future concession additions and expansions. This is usually done in the interest of reducing competition and increasing economy of operation, like incorporating a new service into existing facilities. The new concession service is simply an "add on" to the original concession contract without the need for a formal contract bidding process. Also, managers do not have to worry about whether or not the new service will be large enough to attract a new investor. *Season of Operation.* The length of seasonal operation or the annual negotiated dates of operation should be stated in the lease so that the agency has reasonable control over the period of service availability. In this way, early- or late-season visitors can at least expect minimal services; otherwise, they may only be offered during peak season to maximize profits. A change in local conditions, such as year-round public schools, may also dictate a different operating season for concessions in a local or regional park. Changing winter recreational use patterns have caused changes in season length for many concessions. *Architectural Styles and Building Materials.* Controls on architectural styles and building materials ensure reasonable harmony between the natural landscape and the existing development. A pleasant manmade environment provides visitors with a more desirable opportunity by emphasizing the prime park values, including open space, while subordinating man-induced changes. This can be done effectively even in a relatively developed parkscapes.

The types of materials used also may affect the visual harmony of the development. Native timber and stone are very attractive yet expensive in construction and long-term maintenance. If you want to use those materials, perhaps you can adjust lease provisions to compensate the concessionaire for increased costs in development and maintenance.

Possessory Interest. Possessory interest means the right of ownership to buildings and related real property if they are located on public lands. Possessory interest in developed or acquired facilities must be stated in the lease in the event that the lease is legally terminated or not renewed. Even if a facility is located on public land, the concessionaire usually is given possessory rights if his or her money went into developing or acquiring it. This usually means that he or she is justly compensated for such a facility at the termination of the lease. Just compensation can mean "book value" (original cost less depreciation) or "present market value" based on an appraisal. The method to be used should be so stated.

Insurance and Bonding. The concessionaire should be required to carry a reasonable amount of insurance for fire, public liability, employee liability, and other business risks. Bonding should also be required to guarantee construction of proposed facilities and the "faithful performance of other obligations under the contract."[12]

Politics. Concession operations within our parks and recreation areas have come under a great deal of political scrutiny. Some politicians feel we are being too lenient with concessionaires; others feel we are too harshly controlling them. Often there is only a fine line between the two.

A concessionaire should not be continually looking over his or her shoulder, waiting for the "axe to fall." The park manager should take a positive approach to concession operations by planning, developing, and supervising as needed. Requirements should be explicitly stated in the lease, for example, to reduce the impact on normal park operations from external and internal politics. While pressure groups and individual politicians obviously influence the operation of an agency, such influence can be regulated within the constraints of the lease.

MANAGEMENT CONSIDERATIONS

The following is a summary of those considerations through which managers can exercise rightful control over concessions:

Planning. A basic service philosophy must be adopted before you can conceivably develop a concession management program. This should be the overall guiding doctrine in determining service needs and consolidating those needs into specific concession operations. We are all affected by our beliefs and attitudes when we develop management programs; this is especially true in controversial areas like concession management. Consequently it is important to outline a basic service philosophy, then compare it to agency management guidelines and the normal behavior of visitors. If trade-offs are to be made in providing concession services, what are you, as the manager, willing to sacrifice?

Area and Site Planning. As indicated in the beginning of this chapter, area planning that incorporates the basic service philosophy can determine specific visitor needs (including concessions), allocate space, and select proper locations for needed facilities. This is the most important step; if these facilities are improperly located or not developed to meet the needs of visitors, they will not be used adequately. Then, no matter what subsequent decisions are made, many visitor needs may go unmet or park values may be sacrificed. Without planning, certain services can increase or decrease without regard to overall needs.

Good site planning blends development that both fits the landscape and makes it functional. We remember a well-located camp store that was not well utilized, primarily because of difficult access from the main road and a poorly designed parking lot that often created safety hazards to pedestrians and motorists alike.

Prospectus. In this document we make service needs known, describe how they are to be handled, and encourage the private sector to provide these services on public lands. The prospectus responds to the concession questions of what, where, when, and how, and should include:

   a. Needed service facilities, their locations, and details of their operations
   b. All provisions discussed under Conditions of Lease, at least in summary form
   c. Statutes and regulations under which the concessions will operate
   d. A description of the area, including location, transportation systems, climate, existing use patterns, projected demand, and other data pertinent to the particular project
   e. Submission of offer (All submission requirements, including time schedule should be stated)
   f. The criteria by which the applicants will be judged

Special criteria are usually used in selecting the successful concession applicant — i.e., how appropriate is the proposed development, how well can the service be provided, and how financially stable will the operation be? Competitive bidding for the lease fee that concessionaires are willing to pay is important but generally not a prime criterion. Thus it is a good practice to require a background resume and a complete financial statement from each applicant.

Assessing Environmental Impacts. After you select a proposal that best meets your criteria, you should assess the total project in terms of its environmental effects. Develop mitigating measures to alleviate these problems, or modify or relocate the project to reduce environmental impact. A plausible approach to this is presented in Chapter Six.

Supervising. Once the project has been given final approval, concession management for privately owned or operated services is a matter of supervision. This starts with the groundbreaking and includes:

1. Monitoring construction to ensure that facilities meet the specifications set forth in the plan,
2. Monitoring services to ensure that they meet specified minimum requirements,
3. Monitoring potential environmental effects to adjust programs if problems arise,
4. Monitoring site maintenance to ensure the adequate protection and appearance of facilities.
5. Monitoring concession users and other agency clientele to ensure that they feel the concession provides quality services which enhance the visitors' experiences.

SELECTED READINGS

1. Bissonette, J.F., and D.G. Wright. 1966. "Vending Machines — A Survey of and Manual for Park and Recreation Department." Wheeling, WV: National Recreation and Park Association.

2. Buchinger, M. 1968. "Concessions and Service Arrangements in Various Parts of the World." *Canadian National Parks: Today and Tomorrow.* Nelson, J.G., and R.C. Scace (eds.) The National and Provincial Parks Association of Canada and the University of Calgary.

3. Cahn, R. 1969. "Will Success Spoil the National Parks?" *Christian Science Monitor.*

4. Chamberlain, C.J. 1970. "A Profitable Concession." Parks and Recreation 5(3):29.

5. Darling, F.F., and N.D. Eichhorn. 1969. "Man and Nature in the National Parks: Reflections on Policy." *National Parks Magazine* 4:13.

6. Everhart, W.C. 1983. *The National Park Service.* Boulder, CO: Westview Press.

7. Flynn, T.F., Jr. 1968. "The Management of Concessions in National Parks in the United States." *Canadian National Parks: Today and Tomorrow.* Nelson, J.G., and R.C. Scace (eds.). The National and Provincial Parks Association of Canada and the University of Calgary.

8. Hileman, R. 1957. "Concessions vs. Direct Operation." *Parks and Recreation* 4:151.

9. Ise, J. 1963. *Our National Park Policy: A Critical History.* Baltimore: The Johns Hopkins Press.

10. McKim, W. 1968. "Townsite Administration and Management in Canadian National Parks." *Canadian National Parks: Today and Tomorow.* The National and Provincial Parks Association and the University of Calgary.

11. Memmel, B.G. 1963. "A Manual on Concession Contracts for Park and Recreation Executives." Wheeling, WV: American Institute of Park Executives.

12. National Park Service. 1960. *Concession Management Handbook.* Washington, DC: US Government Printing Office.

13. Oehlmann, H. 1965. "A Concessionaire Talks Back." *American Forests* 6(7):13.

14. Rubini, F.F. 1969. "Fees and Charges, Leases and Contracts, Other than Food." *Proceedings, 19th Annual Great Lakes Park Training Institute.* Angola, Ind., p. 83.

15. Rubini, F.F., and V. Brackett. 1970. "Specifications and Contracts with the Concessionaire." *Proceedings, 20th Annual Great Lakes Park Training Conference.* Angola, IN, p. 136.

16. Runte, A. 1979. *National Parks: The American Experience.* Lincoln: University of Nebraska Press.

17. Sax, J.L. 1980. *Mountains Without Handrails.* Ann Arbor: The University of Michigan Press.

18. Shankland, R. 1970. *Steve Mather of the National Parks.* 3rd edition. New York: Knopf.

19. Stanford Research Institute. 1976. "The Concession System in National Parks: Background, Services Performed, Public Attitude Toward, and Future Consideration." Stanford University Research Report. Stanford, CA

20. US Congress. 1965. "National Park Service Concession Policies (P.L. 89-249)."

OTHER BOOKS FROM VENTURE PUBLISHING

Leisure In Your Life: An Exploration, Revised Edition, by Geoffrey Godbey

Planning Parks For People, by John Hultsman, Richard L. Cottrell and Wendy Zales-Hultsman

Recreation Economic Decisions: Comparing Benefits and Costs, by Richard G. Walsh

Leadership Administration of Outdoor Pursuits, by Phyllis Ford and James Blanchard

Acquiring Parks and Recreation Facilities Through Mandatory Dedication: A Comprehensive Guide, by Ronald A. Kaiser and James D. Mertes

Recreation and Leisure: Issues In An Era of Change, Revised Edition, edited by Thomas L. Goodale and Peter A. Witt

Private and Commercial Recreation, edited by Arlin Epperson

Sport and Recreation: An Economic Analysis, by Chris Gratton and Peter Taylor (Distributed for E. and F.N. Spon, Ltd.)

Park Ranger Handbook, by J.W. Shiner

Playing, Living, Learning — A Worldwide Perspective on Children's Opportunities to Play, by Cor Westland and Jane Knight

Evaluation of Therapeutic Recreation Through Quality Assurance, edited by Bob Riley

Recreation and Leisure: An Introductory Handbook, edited by Alan Graefe and Stanley Parker

The Leisure Diagnostic Battery-Users Manual and Sample Forms, by Peter Witt and Gary Ellis

Doing More With Less In The Delivery of Recreation and Park Services — A Book of Case Studies, by John Crompton

Behavior Modification In Therapeutic Recreation: An Introductory Learning Manual, by John Dattilo and William D. Murphy

International Directory of Academic Institutions in Leisure, Recreation and Related Fields (Distributed for WLRA)

Being At Leisure-Playing At Life: A guide to Health and Joyful Living, by Bruno Hans Geba

Venture Publishing, Inc.
1640 Oxford Circle
State College, PA 16803
814-234-4561